SEIZE AND HOLD

SEIZE AND HOLD

Master Strokes on the Battlefield

BRYAN PERRETT

'The enemy must not know where I intend to give battle. For if he does not know where I intend to give battle, he must prepare in a great many places. And when he prepares in a great many places, those I have to fight in any one place will be few.'
— Sun Tsu, *The Art of War* (*c.* 500 BC)

'The two factors that produce surprise are secrecy and speed.'
— Major-General Karl von Clausewitz, *On War* (1832)

'Most opponents are at their best if they are allowed to dictate a battle; they are not so good when they are thrown off balance by manoeuvre and are forced to react to your own movements and thrusts. ' — Field Marshal Viscount Montgomery, *A History of Warfare* (1968)

ARMS AND
ARMOUR

Arms and Armour Press
A Cassell Imprint
Villiers House, 41-47 Strand, London WC2N 5JE.

Distributed in the USA by Sterling Publishing Co. Inc.,
387 Park Avenue South, New York, NY 10016-8810.

Distributed in Australia by Capricorn Link (Australia)
Pty. Ltd, 2/13 Carrington Road, Castle Hill, NSW
2154..

British Library Cataloguing-in-Publication Data: a cat-
alogue record for this book is available from the British
Library

ISBN 1-85409-187-5

Cartography by Rod Dymott

Jacket illustration: *The Snipe Action* by Terence
Cuneo, reproduced by courtesy of the artist and the
Royal Greenjackets Museum.

Designed and edited by DAG Publications Ltd.
Designed by David Gibbons;
edited by Michael Boxall; printed and bound
in Great Britain by
Hartnolls Limited, Bodmin, Cornwall

Contents

Acknowledgements

I should like to express my sincere appreciation and thanks to the following for their generous assistance: Major T. L. Craze, Archivist, The Royal Green Jackets Museum; David Fletcher of the Tank Museum, Bovington, Dorset; the Goethe Institute, London; Captain Takuo Isobe, formerly of the 215th Infantry Regiment, Imperial Japanese Army; Major A. W. Kersting, Curator of the Household Cavalry Museum; Oberstleutnant Joh. Kindler, Militargeschichtliches Forschungsamt, German Army; Mr Larry McDermott, Hon. Secretary 106th (Lancashire Yeomanry) Regiment RHA Old Comrades Association; Oberstleutnant Paprotka of the Wehrgeschichtliches Museum, Rastatt; Major A. E. Saunders of the Northamptonshire Yeomanry Association; Lieutenant Colonel A. W. Scott Elliot of the Argyll & Sutherland Highlanders; and Mr Andrzej Suchcitz, Keeper of Archives, the Sikorski Museum, London.

Bryan Perrett
August 1993

Introduction

S*eize and Hold* is a term often used in armoured car operations to describe the capture of a bridge or other feature along an intended axis of advance, but it might equally be used in connection with the coup de main. The coup is a cousin of the raid but tends to be more permanent in its results and can be defined as the sudden acquisition of a bridge, railway junction, communications centre or other feature, the loss of which can result in the destruction of the enemy army, compel its withdrawal, or foil its offensive intentions.

Two types of coup exist, the first involving prior recognition of the opportunity by the higher command, who then create the tactical conditions in which the decisive action can take place; the second involving recognition by troops already engaged that the opportunity exists, who then take the decisive action on their own initiative. The requirements of the coup are speed, surprise and sufficient firepower to secure the objective and hold it against all comers until the participants are relieved by friendly troops.

Perhaps the first recognisable example of the coup in the recorded history of warfare was the Trojan Horse. Thereafter, cities, fortresses and castles continued to be captured by similar stratagems. The battlefield coup, however, was rare and seldom decisive, because for many centuries armies were small, lived off the country they passed through, and were virtually self-contained. Even when they began to grow, only cavalry possessed the mobility to deliver so telling a stroke yet, lacking the firepower to maintain itself, it was clearly more suited to the raid than to the coup. In due course this limited ability was itself challenged by the superior mobility conferred on the defenders by railways, who were able to move troops into the threatened area before the raiders could get there.

An example of this can be found in the Russo-Japanese War of 1904–05. The intention of General Kuropatkin, the Russian commander-in-chief, was to employ a 7,500-strong force of cavalry, accompanied by six batteries of horse artillery, to destroy the facilities of the port of

Yingkau, where the enemy had established a supply depot, and thereby delay the arrival of the Japanese Third Army at the front. Everyone thought that the idea was a good one but it was typical of the climate of bungling mismanagement that characterised the last decades of Imperial Russia that they should tell everyone else, with the result that the Japanese learned of Kuropatkin's intentions from the St Petersburg newspapers.

It took two months to mount the operation, which was then conducted at walking pace because the lack of natural forage meant that the column was accompanied by 1,500 pack animals. Whatever chance of success may have remained was swiftly eliminated by further incompetence. Sensibly, a detachment was detailed to cut the Yingkau branch line and so prevent the Japanese reinforcing the port's small garrison. The detachment commander dawdled and eventually completed his task - after the reinforcement train had passed. The Russian squadrons were making their final approach to Yingkau station when they were overtaken by the train, the occupants of which experienced no difficulty in beating off subsequent attacks on the town. Having been thus foiled in its intentions, the expedition was forced to retire whence it had come, violating neutral Chinese territory on the way.

Possibly the example is extreme, but it makes the point. It was not until the internal combustion engine had been thoroughly developed that strokes of this nature could be delivered with the necessary mobility, speed, stamina and firepower. The object of this study, therefore, is to trace the evolution of the battlefield coup in the 20th Century.

Ironically, the widespread use of the internal combustion engine coincided with the era of static trench warfare that characterised much of World War 1. There were, however, some fronts where movement remained possible and it was during the 1916 campaign in Romania that the first recognisable coup involving mechanised forces took place. Here a small motorised battlegroup, operating deep within enemy lines, was used to eliminate a Romanian division blocking the critical Danube supply route. Despite its obvious importance, the operation is rarely mentioned in accounts of the campaign and its details might have been lost forever had they not appeared in the history of the regiment concerned, which was itself disbanded in 1918. They attracted sufficient interest for the American Army's Infantry School at Fort Benning to produce a paper on the subject between the wars, and were also included by Captain C. R. Kutz of the US Armored Corps in his book *War on Wheels*, published in 1940, but have seldom been referred to since.

As mountain warfare is subject to its own rules, it might be thought that the achievements of Lieutenant Erwin Rommel's detachment of the Württemberg Mountain Battalion during the Battle of Caporetto in 1917 are not strictly germain to the subject. Nevertheless, since they resulted in the capture of numerous vital features, as well as thousands of Italian prisoners and scores of guns, they must be regarded as battlefield coups in their own right. Furthermore, they revealed for the first time the same drive, energy, aggression, leadership and impatience with authority that the future field marshal was to display when commanding armoured formations in France and the Western Desert.

The shape of things to come was demonstrated in the Russo-Polish War of 1920. Outnumbered but more flexible in outlook, the Poles mounted deep-penetration motorised operations to strike at the Soviet Twelfth Army's communication and command centres at Zytomierz and Kowel, with the result that the Bolshevik front collapsed.

During the 1940 campaign in Western Europe a major factor in the Wehrmacht's early elimination of Holland and Belgium was a series of airborne and air-landing operations which added a third dimension to the concept of the coup. Of these, the use of gliders to land troops on top of the allegedly impregnable defences of Fort Eben Emael is probably the best remembered, although others showed equal imagination and daring.

Early the following year the first phase of the war in the Western Desert was brought to a dramatic conclusion when Lieutenant-General Richard O'Connor directed the 7th Armoured Division, reduced to a fraction of its established strength by two months of continuous campaigning, to drive across the base of the Benghazi Bulge and intercept the withdrawal of the Italian Tenth Army from Benghazi itself. The trap was sprung at Beda Fomm and, unable to break out, the Italians surrendered after three days of fighting.

The Japanese invasions of Malaya, Burma and the Philippines provide numerous instances of the tactical coup. Of these, the breaking of the Slim River Line, involving the use of tanks and lorried infantry to fillet the road-bound British defence in depth, was probably the most important. After this disaster, in which much irreplaceable equipment was lost, British chances of holding the Malayan peninsula declined sharply.

The story of 'Dickie's Bridge' is an excellent example of a coup achieved by the initiative of the troops on the spot. The circumstances in which the coup took place were created in Operation 'Bluecoat', during the closing stages of the Normandy campaign. A probing armoured car troop of the Household Cavalry secured an undamaged bridge several miles behind German lines. As luck would have it the bridge lay on the boundary between two German armies, each of which believed the other was responsible for guarding it. Reinforcements were quickly rushed across and the subsequent exploitation marked the formation of the northern arm of the Falaise Pocket, in which the German armies in Normandy were destroyed.

In 1945, after forcing the Japanese to concentrate their strength along the Irrawaddy near Mandalay, General William Slim used part of his IV Corps to seize and hold Meiktila, their communications centre for the entire front. When the Irrawaddy Line collapsed through lack of supplies, the entire Japanese Burma Area Army disintegrated. The Meiktila operation was described by the Japanese themselves as the master stroke of the entire campaign.

No study of the coup de main would be complete unless it included an account of the capture of the Rhine bridge at Remagen by the US 9th Armored Division, giving the Allies their first bridgehead on the eastern bank of the Rhine. As a direct result of this Hitler dismissed his able Commander-in-Chief West, Field Marshal Gerd von Rundstedt, and the latter's successor was forced to commit reserves that were desperately needed elsewhere.

During the Korean War, General Douglas MacArthur's thoughts on the port of Inchon ran parallel to those of Slim on Meiktila. Inland lay Seoul, the capital of South Korea and hub of the country's communications network; if Seoul could be captured, the North Korean Army, grouped around the UN troops in the embattled Pusan Perimeter, would be isolated. Though technically difficult, the landings achieved complete surprise and the shattered remnants of the communist army were pursued deep into their own country.

It was the evolution of the helicopter in all its forms that refined the coup's potential in the third dimension. Recognition of this led to the US Army forming the 1st Cavalry Division (Airmobile), which reached Vietnam in 1965. In the autumn of that year one of its brigades balked a major North Vietnamese offensive into the Central Highlands region when it landed unexpectedly in the Ia Drang valley, inflicting such severe casualties that the communists withdrew across the border into Cambodia and were compelled to re-think their strategy. In addition to its immediate results, the battle is important in that it demonstrated that the coup, hitherto used to best effect against armies on the defensive, was equally appropriate when employed against an attacker.

The subsequent history of the coup, which has been summarised in my Postscript, tends to confirm that what was once regarded as an unusual event, hailed for its original thinking, has now become an essential feature in the planning of battles.

CHAPTER 1

Opening the Iron Gate

'The difficulty of all the small countries of south-eastern Europe was that their territorial did not correspond to their racial boundaries. The Turkish wars had dislocated the natural frontiers of races, and each state saw numbers of her own 'nationals' under an alien and frequently oppressive rule.'

These words might well seem appropriate in the 1990s, when areas of the Balkan peninsula are once again torn by ethnic and religious civil strife, yet they have been extracted from John Buchan's *History of the Great War*, published in 1922, and were written in the context of Romania's reasons for declaring war on the Central Powers in August 1916. It is indeed a sad reflection that in the intervening 80 years, which have been further complicated by a second global conflict and the imposition of Communist rule for four decades, attitudes have changed so little.

'The "unredeemed" areas of Romania,' continued Buchan, 'were Transylvania and Bessarabia, notably the former. Under the Dual Monarchy [of Austria-Hungary], in the Bukhovina, in the Banat of Temesvar, and above all in Transylvania, lived some four millions of Romanian blood.' It was the idea of incorporating these areas within a Greater Romania that was the driving force of politics in Bucharest, where the course of the war was watched in keen anticipation of the collapse of the Austro-Hungarian Empire, an event which alone would enable Romania to take possession of the territories she coveted.

By the late summer of 1916 it seemed as though the moment had come and must be seized before it passed, for everywhere the Central Powers were apparently in trouble. The mighty German Army was bleeding to death in the Verdun Salient and along the Somme. On the Italian Front the Austrians had been thrown firmly onto the defensive. The Turks had again been defeated by the Russians in the Caucasus and by the British in Sinai, and although they had succeeded in capturing Kut-el-Amara in distant Mesopotamia, this had no impact on the fighting in Europe. Closer to hand, however, events of supreme importance were taking place, for on 4 June the Russian South West Front, commanded by General Alexei Brusilov, had launched a brilliant offensive which routed the Austrians and forced them back into the Carpathian mountains. Had it not been for prompt German assistance it is possible that Austria-Hungary could well have been knocked out of the war by the year's end. Less immediately apparent was the fact that the Imperial Russian Army had incurred in excess of half a million casualties in the process, and that these, added to the horrendous losses sustained in the previous two years, would prove to be a major contributory factor in provoking the revolution which, in March 1917, would sweep away the Tsarist regime. For the moment, however, what mattered most to the Romanian government was that it was the Austro-Hungarian Empire which was tottering on the brink of disintegration. Romania had, in fact, been mobilising in secret for some time, and on 27 August she formally declared war on Austria-Hungary and Germany.

Altogether, Romania was able to mobilise a 560,000-strong field army which included 23 infantry divisions, two cavalry divisions and several independent brigades, producing a total of 366 infantry battalions, 104 cavalry squadrons and 377 artillery batteries. Superficially impressive though this might be, the army as a whole suffered from a number of serious deficiencies. Machine guns, for example, were issued on the scale of one or two per infantry battalion, contrasting unfavourably with the heavy weapons possessed by a German battalion, which included 12 machine guns, the same number of automatic rifles and four howitzers. Again, while 233 of the artillery batteries were equipped with modern weapons of German or French origin, and ammunition for these had been stockpiled, it was beyond the capacity of Romania's industry to make good any expenditure.

In terms of quality the Romanian Army was regarded with some suspicion. Its officer corps in particular was looked upon as decadent, devious and lacking integrity. One story, probably apocryphal, certainly malicious, but undoubtedly based on observation of unhealthy attitudes, had it that in an attempt to tighten discipline after mobilisation an order was issued prohibiting the use of make-up by officers below field rank! The verdict of a Royal Naval Air Service armoured car unit, hastily posted from the Caucasus to the Dobruja, was that their new allies were more suited to operetta than real warfare. Even more telling was the self-critical comment of the Russian military attaché in Bucharest, Colonel Tatarinov, who observed that the Romanians seemed to have inherited some of the less positive qualities of their composite descent,

namely Slavonic lethargy and Latin garrulity. Such generalisations, however, should not be allowed to obscure the fact that there were some
good officers to be found. Nevertheless, the army as a whole was
untrained, inexperienced and unready for the shock of modern warfare.
Its real strength lay in its rank-and-file, consisting in the main of hardy,
patient, peasant soldiers who, once they had become accustomed to the
battlefield, settled down and even in adversity fought with a dogged
courage that impressed their opponents.

Romania's position was therefore that of a small, weak, isolated
country surrounded by the Austro-Hungarian Empire to the north and
west, by her ancient enemy Bulgaria to the south and by the Black Sea
to the east. In such circumstances it might well be considered foolish to
even contemplate going to war, yet her political leaders and general staff
believed that Austria-Hungary was about to collapse and planned a brief
campaign which was intended only to secure the disputed territories to
the north. There was no consultation with the Entente Powers as to how
Romania could assist in achieving joint strategic objectives, for the simple reason that her mind was set on exploiting a purely local situation
for her own advantage.

The result was disastrous. Two Romanian armies crossed the
Transylvanian Alps and penetrated Austro-Hungarian territory, enjoying
a brief honeymoon period as they were welcomed by the population,
while a third remained on the defensive to watch the Bulgarian frontier.
The Central Powers, however, quickly re-deployed their resources so
that in the north the Romanians suddenly found themselves confronted
by the German Ninth Army, commanded by General Erich von Falkenhayn, while across the Danube to the south was an army group, consisting of the Bulgarian Third Army, supplemented by German and Turkish
formations, under the command of General August von Mackensen.

Falkenhayn had served in China during the Boxer Rebellion and
had succeeded von Moltke the Younger as Germany's Chief of General
Staff in September 1914. He had only recently vacated that post, partly
because of the failure of his attritional strategy at Verdun, and because
of the antipathy of Hindenburg and Ludendorff, whose star was now in
the ascendant. Mackensen had served throughout the war on the Eastern Front, where he had commanded various German armies and
achieved a major breakthrough at Gorlice-Tarnow. In late 1915, as the
commander of a combined Central Powers army group, he had overrun
Serbia. In one respect Mackensen was extremely fortunate in that his
own undoubted abilities were reinforced by those of his Chief-of-Staff,
General Hans von Seeckt, the future architect of the Reichsheer.

Romania was therefore faced with two of Germany's best commanders whose immediate reaction was to take full advantage of the country's isolation. In the south, Mackensen ordered the Bulgarian Third Army to penetrate the Dobruja, an area lying between the Danube Delta and the Black Sea, which it did to such effect that the sorely tried Russians were forced to commit large numbers of their own troops to stabilise the situation. In the north Falkenhayn mounted a counter-offensive at the earliest possible moment. By the end of October the Romanian First and Second Armies, shaken by the superior fire-power available to the enemy's battle-hardened formations, had been thrown back into the Transylvanian Alps, where they rallied.

Falkenhayn, determined to penetrate the Romanian heartland and drive east on Bucharest, maintained the pressure. He was at first held at the eastern passes but at the second attempt managed to force the Vulkan Pass at the western end of the line and advanced down the Jiu and Gilort valleys, inflicting a serious defeat on the Romanian First Army at Targul Jiu between 15 and 17 November. His plan was that the troops involved in this action, consisting of four infantry divisions and a cavalry corps of two divisions, known collectively as Group Kuhne, should then debouche from the hills onto the Wallachian plain and wheel east towards the Aluta with the twin objects of breaking through the new defence line the Romanians were attempting to establish along the river, and outflanking the enemy's positions covering the Red Tower Pass.

Group Kuhne's cavalry corps, commanded by Lieutenant-General Count von Schmettow, consisted of the 6th and 7th Cavalry Divisions with a total strength of 48 squadrons and six artillery batteries, covered the right flank of the operation, spread across a wide area. In its ranks were to be found many names familiar to students of German history, and of the Army in particular. For example, a Count von Schmettow had commanded a cuirassier regiment in the famous Death Ride of von Bredow's 12th Cavalry Brigade at Vionville in 1870; in the 3rd Lancers alone, a regiment which, in a curious contradiction of the spirit of the times still retained the honorific title Emperor Alexander II of Russia's, the officers of the Machine Gun Squadron included Lieutenants Udo and Joachim von Alvensleben, kinsmen of a corps commander at the same battle; and serving on the regiment's staff was an attached hussar officer, Captain Ewald von Kleist, a scion of an old Prussian military family who, in World War 2, was to become a field marshal and the commander of an army group.

Schmettow's command was also remarkable in that it was the first German cavalry formation to receive direct support from an armoured car unit, the recently raised 1st Armoured Motor Machine Gun Battalion, equipped with five cars, which had been transferred to Romania from the Western Front. The cars themselves, built by the Daimler, Ehrhardt and Bussing organisations, were armed with three machine guns, but their great size and weight of approximately 10 tons detracted from their manoeuvrability and speed. Again, unlike the British, French and Belgians, the Germans had not yet learned to exploit the full potential of armoured car warfare and, given the nature of their cars, it seems improbable that their role was anything more than to provide mobile fire-support bases for the operations of the forward cavalry squadrons.

The defeated Romanians, outnumbered and outgunned locally, were unable to offer serious resistance to the advancing cavalrymen and it soon became clear that they were falling back eastwards towards the Aluta. By 19 November Filiasu was firmly in German hands and Schmettow's divisions continued their march south-eastwards down the Jiu valley towards Crajova, leaving the town in the hands of Major-General Schmidt von Knobelsdorff's 41st Infantry Division.

The capture of Filiasu opened up new strategic possibilities, for it was the point where the main Budapest-Bucharest railway line, running roughly from west to east, threw off a branch line to the north.

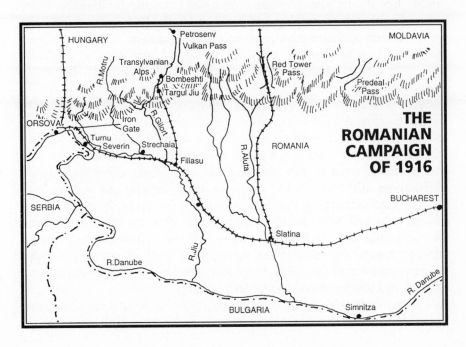

15

This ran up the Gilort valley through Targul Jiu to Bombeshti but stopped short of the Vulkan Pass. On the Hungarian side of the pass was another branch line, but at the time no railway ran through the pass itself and even had the two systems been connected they would have been incapable of supporting the Ninth Army during its advance on the Romanian capital.

For Falkenhayn, therefore, the obvious answer was to use the main line, but here a problem arose. Some 50 miles west of Filiasu the railway passed through the area known as the Iron Gate where the Danube flowed into the Wallachian plain through a valley in the hills to the west. A few miles beyond, the frontiers of Romania, Serbia and Hungary met at Orsova, which was held by the Romanian 1st Division under the command of Colonel Anastasiu. This formation had held off an Austrian brigade for several weeks, and although it had been isolated by the German advance from the Vulkan Pass, it would still have to be dealt with before the railway could be opened. This was more easily said than done, as its rear was protected by the town of Turnu Severin, which was in turn surrounded by small forts, to the east of the Iron Gate. With the advance of Group Kuhne reaching a critical stage, Falkenhayn was reluctant to divert one of its major formations for the task, but at length decided that Turnu Severin would be captured by a motorised battlegroup using speed and surprise to counter the enemy's superior numbers. Once the town had been secured, the rear of Anastasiu's division would be exposed and its only alternatives would be to retreat or surrender.

For its day the decision was bold and unconventional, and it provides a milestone in the development of mechanised warfare. By now, all armies employed motorised transport to carry at least a proportion of their supplies, and in some instances motor vehicles had been used for the rapid movement of troops for tactical purposes. In August 1914, for example, the Rifle regiments of the German cavalry divisions leading the advance through Belgium had been briefly issued with a limited number of touring cars to enable them to keep up. Better known is the use of Paris taxicabs to transport infantry to the front the following month, although the importance of the movement has become elevated into something of a legend; in the event only 1,200 of the capital's 10,000 taxis were involved, and they transported two regiments of the 7th Division a distance of 32 miles while the rest of the division travelled by train. What made Falkenhayn's operation so very different was that it involved a motorised force of all arms which was to be sent into battle with the intention of securing a specific objective.

The 41st Division at Filiasu was obviously the best placed of Group Kuhne's formations to mount the operation. Knobelsdorff received orders to make the necessary troops available early on 20 November and in his selection of units he did his utmost to provide a balance which he hoped would ensure the success of a mission some might be inclined to regard as a fool's errand. The bulk of the force consisted of one infantry battalion, 1/148th Infantry Regiment, with four rifle companies and 12 machine guns. The provision of supporting artillery required some thought, as horse-drawn guns would be unable to keep pace over the long distance to be covered. Knobelsdorff therefore ordered the under-employed 1/79th Anti-Aircraft Regiment to detach two of its lorry-mounted 77mm BAKs (Ballonabwehrkanone or Anti-Balloon Guns) for use in the ground role, plus half the unit's ammunition lorries. Further attachments included an officer's patrol (about 20 men) from the 10th Dragoons, presumably for forward reconnaissance, and a signals detachment. Altogether, the force numbered about 500 men who, with the exception of the BAK crews and the dragoons, would be transported in two-and-a-half ton lorries provided by part of 41st Division Transport Column. It might, perhaps, be wondered why none of Group Kuhne's armoured cars were attached; the answer is almost certainly that since they were operating under Schmettow's command, and therefore outside Knobelsdorff's jurisdiction, it would have taken a direct order from Falkenhayn or Kuhne to effect the transfer and in any event, being so few in numbers, the probablility is that they were fully committed elsewhere.

The officer selected to command the force was a Captain Picht, of whom the records tell us very little. He was commissioned in 1895 but was not promoted to captain until 1911, over three years after he had first become eligible for the rank. He had then been given command of 1/148th Infantry Regiment's No 4 Company and evidently remained with the regiment since, advancing only to the extent that he was now commanding its 1st Battalion. This does not suggest a brilliant career, nor do his superiors appear to have regarded his abilities as being outstanding. Possibly they saw the 40 year-old captain as dull, competent in a run-of-the-mill sort of way, but indecisive, inclined to err on the side of caution, and probably not the ideal choice for this kind of task. Such traits were clearly apparent at the start of his mission, but Picht was to surprise everyone.

The column left Filiasu during the afternoon of 20 December. It made a slow start because the road bridge across the Jiu had been demolished and, while the railway bridge had been left intact, it was necessary for the men to manhandle their lorries one at a time along the track. Once across, the column closed up and moved slowly and steadily westwards. The troops had been briefed as to their mission, but since the method of its execution was new to them all they were a little uneasy at being projected so far into the unknown, particularly when one of Schmettow's cavalry patrols, guarding Group Kuhne's outer flanks, told them that it was madness to consider proceeding further. However, by evening the column had reached the village of Butoesti on the Motru, where it formed a defensive leaguer for the night, having covered 20 miles without the sight of an enemy.

In the morning the column continued along the Motru valley and reached Strechaia. Here a bakery was plundered of its hot rolls and, as there was still no sign of the enemy, the atmosphere became more optimistic. At the next village, Prunisor, Picht halted and ordered his signallers to tap into the telephone line. The first message to be intercepted was from the leader of a Romanian cavalry patrol to the commandant at Turnu Severin, and confirmed that the patrol had just left Prunisor, which he reported as being clear of the enemy. This was certainly encouraging, but other eyes had clearly been watching the Germans' progress as the next transmission, the sender and recipient of which remained unknown, reported the approach of 'an enemy cavalry division reinforced by infantry, artillery and armoured cars'. As Schmettow's divisions were now far away to the east, the report could only

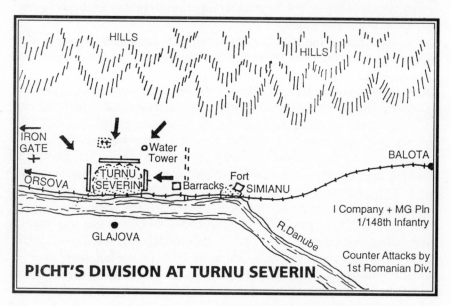

PICHT'S DIVISION AT TURNU SEVERIN

refer to Picht's command, although its composition and strength had been wildly exaggerated.

The column had covered approximately two-thirds of the distance to Turnu Severin and was within striking distance of its objective. Picht can hardly be said to have cracked the whip thus far and now, worried by the enemy's possible reaction, he decided to remain where he was until the situation became clear. At length another call was picked up, this time from the commandant to one of his outlying forts, on the routine matter of bedding straw. Evidently, the earlier report had either been ignored or passed to higher authority for evaluation. Picht decided to move on. Almost immediately Lieutenant Schonfeld's No 2 Company, in the lead, found itself the target of a number of civilians firing large diameter gravel from their shotguns. The situation was quickly brought under control and, as the German Army as a whole had always detested this kind of warfare, the participants in the ambush were given short shrift; as the regimental history puts it, 'The light of their life was blown out behind a house.'

Because of these delays the column did not proceed much further before leaguering for the night. On the morning of 22 November it continued to make slow progress and does not appear to have reached Balota until some time in the afternoon. At the station the signallers again tapped into the telephone system and learned that the enemy had belatedly reacted to the previous day's report and was sending two regular and three home guard infantry companies, together with two guns, back from Orsova to Simianu.

A glance at the map told Picht that an immediate response was required and from this point his actions became firm and decisive. Simianu village lay six miles east of Turnu Severin, within a defile where the hills closed in on the Danube from the north, and some distance to the east was a fort containing two casemated guns covering the river and the Bulgarian shore opposite. At all costs, therefore, Picht had to secure the fort, village and defile before the Romanian reinforcements should arrive.

Under cover of the winter twilight, thickened by gathering mist, the column advanced to a point from which an assault could be mounted on the fort. The infantry left their lorries, deployed without being observed, and moved forward. The design of the fort was essentially that of a coast defence battery in that its defences were only formidable where they faced the river, but were weak on the landward side. It was in the latter area that the Germans broke in, sweeping through the interior from east to west with barely a shot being fired in return by the startled defenders. The garrison, consisting of two officers and 130 men, promptly surrendered and were disarmed.

Picht reformed his column and pressed on into the village, from which the distant lights of Turnu Severin could be seen upstream. As there was no sign of the Romanian reinforcements, he deployed his men among the houses to await their arrival. He had, in fact, won the race by a narrow margin, for shortly after a lorry approached the forward company's position and, failing to stop, was fired on. Firing quickly became general and then the Germans charged with the bayonet. Most of the Romanians fled into the darkness, leaving behind two machine guns and a further 65 prisoners. Across the river the Bulgarians, wondering what the uproar was about, snapped on a searchlight to illuminate the scene. Picht's men, elated by their success, gave him three cheers, but there was no time for celebration and he bundled them back aboard their lorries and set off on the last leg of the journey, with the prisoners jogging along behind the convoy under escort.

His principal concern was that the fugitives had raised the alarm in Turnu Severin, but he probably reached the town before they did. By 2000 he had arrived in the central market square to find it deserted. While his signallers reported the situation by radio, he immediately deployed his command into defensive positions. Fortunately, the town itself was compact and this enabled him to allocate one company and a machine gun platoon to each of its western, northern and eastern sides, reinforcing the more vulnerable western and northern sectors with his self-propelled anti-aircraft guns; in the south the town fronted the Danube, a mile wide at this point, and as no threat existed from this direction he was able to retain his fourth company as a reserve in the market square.

Picht's 500 men were now dispersed among a potentially hostile civil population of 24,000. Obviously the situation would have to be handled with care, for although the civilians expressed relief that the new arrivals were Prussians and not Bulgarians, their dreaded hereditary enemies, their attitude could not be taken for granted. One of Picht's first acts, therefore, was to break into the Town Hall and obtain the addresses of the council and other officials, who were rounded up and held hostage for the good behaviour of their citizens. Finally, when the gaol was opened a number of Austrian prisoners were released, issued with captured Romanian weapons and added to the reserve.

On the northern sector, Lieutenant Bellin, having seen his company securely dug in, retired to a house behind to snatch a few hours' rest. Shortly after first light he was awoken from a heavy sleep by the sound of the windows shattering and bullets thudding into the plaster over his head. Outside, he could hear his machine guns hammering away and, after the briefest of toilets, he ran out to join his men. Some 900 yards distant he could see a Romanian column which was attempting to by-pass the town on its way east. This was quickly dispersed by the German fire, leaving two ox-drawn heavy guns standing in the open, but shortly after the Romanians commenced a series of attacks against the town which were to last all day.

The arrival of Picht's force in Turnu Severin had produced precisely the result Falkenhayn intended. Colonel Anastasiu had recognised that his position at Orsova was no longer tenable and had decided to withdraw his division through the Iron Gate in the forlorn hope that he would be able to rejoin the Romanian First Army. That would be difficult enough to achieve on its own, but the German presence in his rear made it even more so and he would therefore have to contain or, better still, eliminate it.

Four Romanian battalions were involved in the first day's heavy fighting, mounting piecemeal attacks all round the perimeter, all of which were beaten off. The most dangerous of these developed around the churchyard to the north, a water tower to the north-east and a barracks to the east of the German line. The water tower was especially troublesome to the defenders as the Romanians had mounted machine guns on it and their fire enfiladed the company positions to the north and east of the town, one company losing no less than six platoon commanders in quick succession. Many of the townspeople, keen to watch the battle, turned out to lean over fences and sit on walls until several were hit and the rest stampeded into their cellars. One, however, was made of sterner stuff. He suddenly appeared on a white horse from among the houses, galloping hard for the Romanian lines, and escaped the hail of rifle fire directed at him by the Germans. This was most unfortunate, as it meant that Anastasiu would be informed as to the true size of the force confronting him.

When attacks were not actually in progress the German machine guns directed long range fire at the enemy columns which were now by-passing the town at a respectful distance. To counter this the Romanians brought up their artillery, against which only the two anti-aircraft guns could make any sort of effective reply. However, much of the enemy's fire was wasted, since it was directed at the buildings on the edge of the town and the Germans had entrenched themselves in front of these. Meanwhile, the signals section in the market place broadcast continuous requests for reinforcements and ammunition without knowing whether these were being heard. Towards evening two Bulgarian machine gun detachments arrived by boat, commanded by a Lieutenant Milschow who had evidently decided to make the dangerous crossing of the river on his own initiative.

Darkness brought an end to the fighting but the morning of 24 November saw renewed Romanian attempts to capture the town, pressed home with the utmost courage and determination. These rose to a climax at about 1300, when assault columns closed in all round the perimeter. Fighting raged throughout the afternoon until Picht had committed all his reserves. One of the anti-aircraft guns was wrecked by a direct hit. When the ammunition supply began to fail the riflemen collected what cartridges they could from the pouches of their dead and wounded comrades. Worst of all, the water-cooled machine guns, the very backbone of the defence, began to boil from continuous use, but not a man could be spared to bring up fresh supplies of water. The clouds of steam disclosed the position of the guns so that, one after another, they were knocked out. Only one machine gun, its fire controlled by the wounded Lieutenant von Bohlendorf, remained in action on the northern sector; so worn had its barrel become, and so expanded by excessive heat, that it merely spat out its rounds to a distance of 100 yards.

It had begun to look very much as though Picht's command would be overwhelmed when, at about 1700, the pressure suddenly eased on the eastern sector. Then, two lorries loaded with ammunition roared into the town from the direction of Simianu, followed by growing numbers of grinning Bavarian infantrymen. Group Kuhne had picked up the signals detachment's calls for help and, reacting to the obvious need for speed and mobility, had ordered the 11th Bavarian Division to despatch a cyclist brigade under Colonel von Quadt to Picht's assistance.

The Romanians, recognising the radically altered situation, discontinued their attacks and disappeared during the night. Much of the next day was spent clearing the battlefield. Here and there, a mute tableau showed what had taken place. Two paces from a German machine gun crew, killed beside their weapon, was a dead Romanian, and some way behind him, lying in the ranks in which they had been cut down, were the bodies of his comrades. Altogether, nearly 600 men had been killed in the battle for Turnu Severin, the majority of whom were Romanians. The wounded were taken to the town's hospital where they received attention from the regimental surgeons. Captured equipment included seven locomotives and 300 railway wagons. On 26 November,

Colonel von Scivo's Austrian brigade reached the town, having followed up the Romanian withdrawal from Orsova. The Iron Gate was now open.

In the meantime, the Romanian First Army had been brought to the point of collapse. To the south, Mackensen had decided to transfer the emphasis of his army group from the Dobruja to the central sector and on 23 November had secured a bridgehead on the north bank of the Danube at Simnitza, effectively turning the left flank of the line the Romanians were attempting to form along the Aluta. With the opening of the Iron Gate it became possible to tow barges laden with bridging material down the river, so that the bridgehead was quickly expanded and Mackensen was able to tie in his left flank with Falkenhayn's right. On Ninth Army's front Group Kuhne had closed up to the Aluta and, while Schmettow's cavalry had been unable to prevent demolition of the railway bridge at Slatina it was able to secure another bridge intact nearby. To the north the Predeal Pass was penetrated and the defence of the Red Tower Pass was crumbling. On 27 November the Romanians abandoned the Aluta line and began withdrawing steadily eastwards. They did not attempt to defend Bucharest, which fell on 6 December. By January they had been pushed back into all that remained of their territory, a portion of Moldavia, and, with Russian assistance, continued to hold out there. The 1916 campaign had cost Romania over 300,000 casualties, of whom half were prisoners, and huge quantities of equipment; the Central Powers sustained approximately 60,000 battle casualties plus a comparable number of sick, but gained unlimited access to Romanian supplies of wheat and oil.

It was against the background of these events that the Detachment Picht continued its career. Hardly had it recovered its breath after the fighting at Turnu Severin than it was designated as the advance guard of Scivo's Austrian brigade, which had been detailed to pursue Anastasiu's division as it continued its retreat to the south-east. Anastasiu never abandoned hope that he would eventually break through to his own people and kept one step ahead of his pursuers although there were frequent skirmishes between his rearguards and Picht's men. His exploits were to make him a national hero but by 6 December he had been penned into a triangle formed by the confluence of the Aluta with the Danube and his position had become hopeless. At a village called Isbiceni an officer with a flag of truce indicated Anastasiu's willingness to surrender to German troops and despite his surprise that these consisted solely of a now seriously depleted battalion commanded by a captain, he accepted the situation. The remnant of the 1st Romanian Division, consisting of 91 officers and 3,600 men, then laid down its arms, including seven guns, four machine guns and 80 lorries.

Detachment Picht rejoined its parent division on 21 December and was welcomed by Knobelsdorff with a Divisional Order of the Day in which he summarised its achievements, including the seizure and defence of Turnu Severin with inadequate resources, the pursuit of the enemy until his capitulation, the capture of 137 officers, 6,500 men, 14 guns, 20 machine guns and much rolling stock, the protection of the Ninth and Danube Armies' rear, and the opening of the railway from Orsova. He concluded by expressing pride that the detachment commander and his troops were serving under his command. In the light of this, therefore, it seems probable that a reference elsewhere in the order to Picht's circumspect (umsichtigen) leadership is not so much a deliberate attempt to damn him with faint praise but rather an unspoken comment that Turnu Severin could have been seized somewhat earlier than was the case.

Picht's rewards included promotion to major, in which rank he retired when the war ended in 1918. Subsequently, the exploits of his small motorised battlegroup have received less attention than they deserve; indeed they are often omitted altogether in general studies of the Romanian campaign, perhaps because of their peripheral nature. Yet Detachment Picht undoubtedly broke new ground and achieved a coup which was almost certainly beyond the reach of conventional troops. In the light of this, therefore, it can be regarded as the grandfather of all mechanized battlegroups, and in particular of the ad hoc groupings so successfully employed by the German Army in World War 2, especially on the Eastern Front.

CHAPTER 2

Young Mister Rommel

For most of World War 1 the most important problem facing senior commanders on all the main battle fronts was how to achieve a clean breakthrough and exploit it before the enemy could close the gap in his front. At the root of the problem was the fact that, for the moment, the combination of massed artillery, machine guns, entrenchments and barbed wire gave those who were defending a pronounced advantage over those who were attacking. Even when the attackers gained some ground, invariably at heavy cost, their advance would always have to traverse shell-torn ground intersected with trenches and strewn with barbed wire entanglements which made it extremely difficult for the horse-drawn artillery of the period to cross the battlefield; whereas the defenders were able to move up their reserves at far greater speed through country which had not been devastated by war. It was a race which the defenders would always win and the inevitable result was attritional deadlock. To a considerable extent these difficulties were exacerbated by the custom of commanders committing their reserves against the strongest sectors of the enemy front, thereby adding to the price of such successes as were achieved.

Both sides tried hard to find a solution to the deadlock. Artillery preparation became heavier and heavier but the results merely aggravated the situation. The Germans tried using poison gas but found it was a two-edged weapon. British and French faith in the tank was not fully justified until the closing months of the war. In the meantime, the Germans had adopted a fresh tactical approach which, had it been introduced earlier, might have altered the course of the war.

This was first demonstrated on the Eastern Front during the summer of 1917. The Tsar had gone but Lenin had yet to come and the Russian Army, though now of little value in offensive operations, was still holding its lines and would fight if attacked. On the Baltic sector General Klembovsky's Twelfth Army was defending the port of Riga and retained a bridgehead on the west bank of the River Dvina. Opposite was General Oskar von Hutier's Eighth Army, which had been given the task of capturing Riga as the preliminary step in a planned German advance on St Petersburg.

Klembovsky was aware of German intentions and believed that Hutier would eliminate the bridgehead before attempting to cross the river. He therefore concentrated his best troops within the bridgehead and left the rest of the river line to be defended by less reliable formations. Hutier, however, had changed the rules. Instead of attacking the bridgehead, where he knew the Russians were strongest, he would force a crossing of the Dvina on a less heavily defended sector upstream, then wheel north to the coast, thereby placing Riga and the greater part of the Twelfth Army inside a trap. Tactically, too, he made a number of innovations. His infantry was to move as quickly as possible, avoiding centres of resistance, and infiltrate their way through successive Russian defence lines while waves of ground attack aircraft strafed the enemy's trenches with machine gun fire. Gas was also to be used, but instead of being released from canisters which depended on favourable wind direction it was, for the first time, to be fired in newly issued shells right onto the objective. The preparatory bombardment and support programme to be fired by the guns was to last for five hours, a mere fraction of the time normally considered necessary on the Western Front, and was carefully tailored by Colonel Bruchmuller, the Eighth Army's senior artilleryman, to fit the requirements of each phase of the operation, using gas to choke the defenders, smoke to blind them and high explosive to smash up their positions.

When the attack went in on 1 September the Russians, already stunned and disorganised by the bombardment, were completely unnerved by the speed with which the German assault troops penetrated their rear areas, by-passing such positions as were still holding out, and they began to shred away to the east in a blind panic. The very success of the German plan almost prevented Hutier from reaping the rewards of his victory, for he had prepared a strict timetable and local commanders tended to halt their troops on captured objectives until it was time for the next phase to begin, rather than pressing on northwards towards the coast. Before the trap could be closed, therefore, Klembovsky interpreted Hutier's intentions correctly and was able to withdraw most of his army from Riga along the coast road. Even so, the capture of the port was regarded as one of the German Army's most significant coups of the war and Hutier was rewarded with a personal visit from the Kaiser. One of the most remarkable aspects of the battle was that in terms of killed and wounded the casualties incurred by both sides were negligible by the standards of the time, although 9,000 Russians were taken prisoner.

The new tactics were employed again the following month on the Isonzo Front in Italy. Here, the Italian Army had mounted no less than eleven major offensives since June 1915 in the hope that it would defeat the Austrians and break through to the port of Trieste, yet, despite Herculean efforts, it had only been able to advance a few miles. By September 1917 such heavy casualties had been incurred that the morale of troops and civilians alike was seriously affected. There had already been violent rioting in Turin, a munitions manufacturing centre always regarded as a hotbed of radical activity, and the heavy-handed reaction of the government had included drafting many previously exempt munitions workers into the Army. Resentful and obviously unreliable as they were, these men would have been best employed on lines of communication duties but, by a singular error of judgement, they were sent as replacements to the Caporetto sector of the Isonzo Front.

The Isonzo battles had also accelerated the continuing decline in Austria-Hungary's military potential so that, once again, she was compelled to request German assistance to avoid collapse. This was forthcoming and it was decided to employ General Otto von Below's newly formed Austro-German Fourteenth Army in a counter-offensive which was intended to knock Italy out of the war. This would take place on the Caporetto sector, where the mountainous terrain favoured the sort of tactics employed by Hutier at Riga, and the detailed planning was undertaken by Germany's leading expert in mountain warfare, General Konrad Krafft von Dellmensingen. General Luigi Cadorna, the Italian Chief of General Staff, was aware of the developing threat and had given orders that General Capello's Second Army, deployed around Caporetto, should prepare its defence in depth. Unfortunately for the Italians, Capello had been absent on sick leave and little or nothing was done prior to his return to comply with these instructions.

Serving in Below's army was a Lieutenant Erwin Rommel who in the coming battle was to demonstrate the same ruthless drive that in later life would earn him his field marshal's baton. Rommel was a native of Württemberg, a small south German state lying between Baden and Bavaria. Contrary to his father's wishes, he had chosen a military career, being accepted as an officer cadet by the 124th Infantry Regiment (6th Württemberg) in July 1910 and commissioned some eighteen months later. His regiment was not one of the most fashionable in the Imperial Army's Prussian-dominated pecking order and there were few 'vons' to be found in its mess. This troubled him not at all and, throughout his career, he was content to be with, rather than of, those of his contempo-

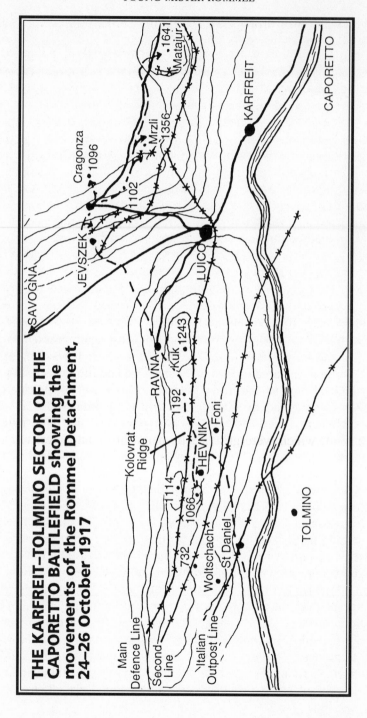

THE KARFREIT–TOLMINO SECTOR OF THE CAPORETTO BATTLEFIELD showing the movements of the Rommel Detachment, 24–26 October 1917

raries who had been brought up in the old German military Establishment.

He fought with his regiment in Belgium and France during the early battles of 1914, being awarded the Iron Cross Second Class, but received a serious leg wound in September. Rejoining in January 1915 he was given command of a company and took part in further fighting on the Argonne sector and in the Vosges mountains. In September he was promoted to first lieutenant and transferred to the Württemberg Mountain Battalion, then in the process of forming at Munsingen. This unit, consisting of six rifle companies and six machine gun platoons, was trained in all aspects of mountain warfare and the intention was that it would be allocated to army commanders for employment in circumstances where its specialist skills were required. The battalion was commanded by Major Sprösser, whom Rommel described as a martinet, yet despite this the relationship between officers and men was more relaxed than was usual in the German Army.

The Württemberg Mountain Battalion fought its first actions in the High Vosges on the Western Front. In August 1916 it was transferred to Romania and on the conclusion of that campaign returned to the Vosges in May 1917. The following August it again crossed Europe to the Carpathian sector of the Eastern Front where it was engaged in heavy fighting in the area of Mount Cosna. The battalion was withdrawn for rest and refitting to Carinthia, where the firepower of the rifle companies was augmented by the issue of the Bergmann MG 15nA light machine gun, an air-cooled weapon weighting 28.5 lbs. The machine gun platoons, which were grouped by pairs into companies, remained equipped with the Maxim MG 08 medium machine gun which, together with its sledge mounting, weighed no less than 137 lbs.

The severe demands of mountain warfare on strength and stamina do not appear to have affected Rommel despite his being a little below average height and of comparatively slight build; indeed, he wrote of his time with the battalion as being one of the happiest periods in his career. He seemed to be one of those individuals who obtain complete release in action, drawing immense strength from a vast reserve of nervous energy. Always in the forefront of the battle, he drove his troops beyond what they believed to be their physical limits, but drove himself harder still. He was able to focus intense concentration on any tactical problem, read his opponents' collective mind, reach his decisions with astonishing speed, then, gathering whatever troops were to hand, he would turn his thoughts into action. If he appeared to take risks, they were finely calculated, produced results and kept his casualties to a minimum. Such a combination of drive, cunning and aggression would be described as a highly developed killer instinct had it not been tempered by humanity. Rommel's duty as a professional soldier was to defeat the enemy, but he preferred to do so by creating the conditions that would compel his surrender rather than by inflicting heavy casualties. In this respect he was a natural practitioner of Hutier's tactics of applying the indirect approach.

In October the Württemberg Mountain Battalion, reinforced by a mountain howitzer battery, joined Below's Fourteenth Army in the Isonzo valley and was attached to Major General von Tutschek's Alpine Corps, which also contained the Bavarian Infantry Life Guards and the 1st Rifle Regiment, in the region of Tolmino. Sprösser divided his command into detachments, one of which, consisting of three rifle companies and a machine gun company, was placed under Rommel's command. If, perhaps, this seems a surprisingly large force to be commanded by even a senior subaltern, it has to be remembered that the German Army's refusal to modify the lengthy process of entry into the regular commissioned ranks had resulted in a shortage of officers only partially remedied by granting reserve commissions, the holders of which held subordinate appointments, and by increasing the responsibilities of senior NCOs. Again, the experience of the previous two years had left Sprösser in no doubt as to Rommel's qualities of leadership.

The objective of the Alpine Corps was to secure the crest of the mountains dominating the west bank of the Isonzo. On the right, the Life Guards, with the Württemberg Mountain Battalion protecting their right flank, were to capture Monte Hevnik, Hill 1114, Kolovrat Ridge and Monte Kuk, and establish themselves along the line of the mountain track leading from Luico, a small town at the head of a pass, to Monte Mrzli and Monte Matajur. On the left the 1st Rifle Regiment was to secure the village of Woltschach followed by Hill 732, then assist in the capture of Hill 1114 from the south-west. The range was protected by three defence lines, the lowest consisting of outposts, with the strongest defences along the crest. The entire position was one of immense strength and in normal circumstances could have been expected to hold out indefinitely.

In its assembly area the Württemberg Mountain Battalion was subjected to harassing fire from the Italian artillery, to which the German guns replied only with ranging shots for their preparatory bombardment. This commenced at 0200 on 24 October when 1,845 German and Austrian artillery weapons, including 492 heavy mortars, suddenly opened fire along a 25-mile front, using a high proportion of gas shells.

The continuous banging of the guns and the bursting of shells opposite echoed and re-echoed across the valley to create the impression of a mountain thunderstorm, heightened by torrential rain which the enemy searchlights on the heights tried in vain to pierce. As the gas did its deadly work the reply of the Italian guns became progressively weaker.

From 0745 some guns switched to smoke rounds, blanketing the first objectives beneath a grey pall while lowering rain clouds closed in on the summits above. At 0800 the Life Guards move off from their start line. On their right the Württembergers closed in on the hamlet of St Daniel, the shaken defenders of which staggered out to surrender, and were then directed up a footpath to Foni, with the Rommel Detachment leading. The enemy's first line of defence had been overrun without the slightest difficulty.

Rommel's men climbed through dripping woodland for over a mile. Suddenly the point platoon came under machine gun fire from a well-wired position and five of its men were wounded. Rommel decided to leave the point where it was while he outflanked the position with the rest of the detachment, using a narrow ravine to the left. As this climbed straight up the hillside some hard scrambling was required. Dislodged rocks bounded downhill through those below, one of them catching Rommel so painful a crack on the foot that he required the assistance of two men for the next half hour. At length the ravine emerged at the edge of the tree line. Ahead, some 60 yards distant, lay another Italian position, apparently connected to that covering the Foni track. A path, camouflaged to view from across the valley, ran through the position and disappeared into the woods downhill to the left. There was little sign of the enemy, who were clearly unaware of the Germans' presence and sheltering from the rain in their dugouts. Rommel decided to send a patrol along the path to capture those troops in its immediate vicinity, preferably by stealth; in the event of a violent enemy reaction, the rest of the Rommel Detachment, now deployed along the edge of the trees, would mount an immediate assault. The patrol, consisting of Lance Corporal Kiefner and eight men, boldly walked along the path as though they were Italians returning from the forward position, silently captured a dugout containing 17 men and a machine gun, and sent back a man to report. Rommel then led his companies, followed by the regiment's similarly constituted Schiellein Detachment, which had just joined him, through the gap. This was then extended for 50 yards on either side of the path, producing several dozen startled prisoners, without a shot being fired.

Under the old tactical system the Germans would have continued to roll up the enemy line to right and left, but the day's orders had emphasised the need for continued penetration. Realising that he had just broken through the Italians' intermediate defence line, Rommel therefore led off up the extremely steep slope, now covered with scrub, his men taking advantage of every fold in the ground to make their way uphill unseen. The pace of the advance was governed by the medium machine gunners, each of whom, even with the weapons dismantled, was carrying a tremendous weight. Numerous positions were captured from the rear, including an entrenched medium artillery battery and a battery of 210mm heavy guns, both having been abandoned when their crews were gassed during preliminary bombardment. Sometimes, to avoid capture, Italians would abandon their weapons and bolt downhill towards the trees; in such circumstances, the Germans did not open fire as to have done so would simply have alerted the enemy higher up the hill. 'The further we penetrated into the hostile zone of defence,' noted Rommel, 'the less prepared were the garrisons for our arrival, and the easier the fighting.' This knowledge, an essential element in the Blitzkrieg technique, was something he would repeatedly use as an armoured battlegroup commander during World War 2.

By 1100 Rommel had reached the ridge running eastwards from Monte Hevnik and was in contact with the Life Guards on his left. The latter chose to rest while the German artillery completed its bombardment of the peak itself but Rommel, wishing to obtain the maximum benefit, climbed the northern slope with his companies and, when the shelling ceased at noon, occupied the summit without meeting resistance, taking several prisoners in the process. The rain had now ceased and as visibility improved his presence was spotted by Italian observers on Hill 1114 who promptly brought their own artillery the bear. Moving his detachment off this exposed position, which became the responsibility of the Life Guards, he proceeded to clean up enemy gun positions between Hevnik and Foni, chalking the captured weapons with the unit's symbol. By now his detachment had taken 17 guns, of which a dozen were of large calibre, although the enemy's rations, including a cooked meal, were of more immediate interest to his famished troopers.

On the left of the Alpine Corps the 1st Rifle Regiment was still held up at the enemy's second defence line but at 1600 the Life Guards received permission to resume the advance. Their next objective was Hill 1114, which they approached by way of the intervening Hill 1066, with their right flank protected by the Rommel and Schiellein Detachments. The leading company came under fire as soon as they reached Hill 1066 and a fire fight developed. The Italians, manning a series of well wired trench lines terraced up the slopes of Hill 1114 and a lower adjacent feature, were offering the most determined resistance this far encountered. Rommel ordered one of his companies to clear some out-lying positions on the right, which it succeeded in doing without loss, simultaneously adding seven officers and 150 men to the bag of prisoners taken, but he concurred with the opinion of the Life Guard officers that Hill 1114, as yet untouched by gunfire, could only be taken with artillery support.

Little further progress had been made by the time darkness descended. Rommel established his own headquarters in a former artillery observation post and at 1900 was summoned to that of the Life Guards' 3rd Battalion, located in a dugout 100 yards distant. There he was met by the Guards' commanding officer, Major Count Bothmer, who was in a none too civil frame of mind. The Count clearly felt that the Württembergers' capture of Monte Hevnik had up-staged his Guardsmen, and the chalking of so many captured guns cannot have helped. He told Rommel that he was taking his detachment under command. Rommel tartly replied that he took his orders from Major Sprösser, whose seniority, he believed, exceeded that of the Count. Bothmer then not only forbade the Württembergers to take any part in the capture of Hill 1114 the following day, but also insisted that they should follow the subsequent advance of the Life Guards as a second line. Rommel, by now extremely angry, commented that he would report the conversation to his own commander, and was dismissed.

At 2100 Lieutenant Autenreith, the Württemberg Mountain Battalion's quartermaster, reached Rommel's command post and informed him that the battalion's third striking force, the Wahrenberger Detachment, had captured Foni as dusk was falling. Rommel told him that, thanks to difficulties with the neighbours, his own detachment was immobilised. He asked Autenreith to report the situation to Sprösser and request that the latter should come forward. He then turned in for the night but, unable to sleep, strove to form a plan for the following morning which would not interfere with the Life Guards' operations on Hill 1114 yet would produce a breakthrough into the enemy's rear areas. At length he decided that a hitherto unassailed area of Kolovrat Ridge, some 1,100 yards east of Hill 1114, offered the best possibilities.

Sprösser, followed by the Wahrenberger Detachment, reached Hill 1066 at 0500 on 25 October. He accepted Rommel's plan but declined to make more than one machine gun and two rifle companies available. Presently, Count Bothmer arrived with the news that during the night one of his companies had secured the summit of Hill 1114,

although the Italians held the surrounding positions and were expected
to counter-attack very shortly. Rommel comments dryly that Sprösser
reached an 'understanding' with the Count; whatever its nature, he was
not to be troubled again by the Life Guards' commander.

Rommel's detachment left Hill 1066 at first light, just as the Italians were starting their counter-attack on Hill 1114. Painfully working
their way across the slope, using bushes, contours and latterly the beds
of mountain streams for concealment, they reached a deep re-entrant
below the summit of Kolovrat Ridge. A sleeping Italian outpost containing some forty men and two machine guns was surprised and overrun
without a shot being fired or any alarm given. Rommel deduced that the
outpost was one of several intended to guard against an attack from the
Isonzo valley; apparently no consideration had been given to a German
approach from Hill 1066 to the west, and now his men had arrived
unseen within striking distance of the main enemy position, the outer
wiring stakes of which were visible above the lip of the re-entrant. While
a small patrol under Lieutenant Streicher crept upwards to reconnoitre
the defences and cut gaps, Rommel concentrated his companies for the
attack and then spoke to Sprösser over the field telephone line his signallers had reeled out behind the detachment, requesting speedy reinforcement in the event of success. No sooner had he replaced the instru-
ment than a runner from Streicher arrived with the news that the patrol
had not only penetrated the enemy wire but also surprised the gunners
of an Italian battery at their ablutions and captured them and their guns
before they could react. Rommel launched his attack immediately and,
gaining the summit of the ridge, his troopers began winkling the unsuspecting enemy infantry out of their dugouts. Soon no fewer than 1,000
prisoners had been assembled.

The question now was how best to exploit the breakthrough.
Rommel decided to use his 2nd Rifle Company, commanded by Lieutenant Ludwig, to consolidate the far end of the ridge while he led the
3rd Rifle and 1st Machine Gun Companies down a camouflaged mountain track leading westwards into the Luico valley. These moves had
hardly begun before his own companies came under heavy if ineffective
fire from Hill 1192, lying between Kolovrat Ridge and Monte Kuk, while
an outbreak of sustained firing, punctuated by the explosion of
grenades, indicated that Ludwig was being counter-attacked from the
same direction. Hurriedly retracing his steps, Rommel reached a point
from which he could see that Ludwig's 80 riflemen and six light
machine gun teams were pinned down in some trenches from which
retreat was barred by wire entanglements. They were just holding their

own against a full battalion which was closing in from three sides, but the enemy were now within 50 yards of the position and were obviously on the point of launching an assault which would swamp the isolated company.

Panting from their run back up the track, the 3rd Rifle Company joined Rommel, who quickly ordered an attack against the enemy's flank and rear, covered from the right by the fire of two labouring medium machine gun teams who had also returned to the crest of the ridge. The attack was mounted at the critical moment when the Italians were commencing their own assault. Taken aback by this unexpected onslaught from the rear, they halted and turned about to meet it. Ludwig's company promptly swarmed out of their trenches to assail them from behind. Now apparently surrounded themselves, the Italians began throwing down their arms. However, as the Germans closed in, the Italian officers opened fire with their pistols and the needless casualties thus caused so infuriated the Germans that Rommel had to intervene personally to save their lives. The engagement had cost him two men killed - one of whom was Lance Corporal Kiefner, who had distinguished himself the previous day - and several wounded. Against this, by 0915 the Kolovrat Ridge position had been penetrated, the garrison of Hill 1192 had been eliminated, and the 1,500 prisoners taken since dawn were being shepherded down to the Isonzo by a handful of riflemen.

From the peak of Hill 1192, now coming under distant artillery and machine gun fire, Rommel could see across most of the battlefield. In the Luico valley the enemy were moving up reserves and seemed to be committing most of them to Hill 1114 where fighting was still in progress. On the adjacent Monte Kuk, which appeared to be heavily entrenched and held in strength, some two battalions of infantry were advancing downhill in skirmish lines towards the connecting saddle, as though on the point of mounting a counter-attack. This Rommel felt ill-prepared to meet and although he had been informed that Sprösser was already on his way to join him with the rest of the battalion, he was nonetheless relieved when the Italians halted and began to dig in.

As the enemy seemed to be more concerned with his own defence than ejecting the Germans, yet was having serious difficulty cutting new trenches in the rocky terrain, Rommel decided that as soon as reinforcements arrived he would mount an attack himself. Temporarily out of touch with Sprösser, he spoke to Alpine Corps HQ through the field switchboard which had been established on Hill 1066 and obtained approval plus the promise of support from the corps' heavy artillery batteries between 1115 and 1145. He then established a fire base on Hill 1192 to shoot in the attack, using the whole of the 1st Machine Gun Company and the 2nd Rifle Company's six light machine guns.

Sprösser arrived at 1030 and, apart from diverting one rifle company to clear the Kolovrat Ridge back in the direction of Hill 1114, agreed with his dispositions. The artillery preparation commenced promptly at 1115, the heavy shells creating deadly showers of stone splinters and dangerous rock slides among the enemy. Two assault teams, one from 2nd Rifle Company on the right and one from 3rd Rifle Company on the left, began probing their way forward onto the saddle, Rommel's stated intention being to commit the rest of the battalion in support of whichever made most progress. Both quickly came to grips and the Italians facing the 3rd Rifle Company team began to surrender.

At this moment Rommel changed the rules. The 1st Rifle Regiment, having finally broken through the enemy's intermediate defence line, was now attacking Hill 1114 in its turn and the Life Guards were following the route taken by the Württemberg Mountain Battalion. Instead of attacking the summit of Monte Kuk, the defenders of which were fully engaged in a machine gun duel with his fire base on Hill 1192, he decided to proceed with the previously-abandoned exploitation into the enemy's rear areas and, gathering 3rd and 4th Rifle and 2nd and 3rd Machine Gun Companies, he set off from the saddle at a run down the camouflaged track which wound round the southern shoulder of the mountain. The gruelling pace soon told on the medium machine gunners, panting for breath under their heavy burdens, but they kept moving. Once behind the shoulder the running column encountered gaping groups of Italian infantry and pack trains climbing the track, all of whom were disarmed and thumbed to rear before they could react. Rommel's first objective was a mountain hamlet named Ravna, a small collection of houses and barns lying on the south-western slopes of Monte Kuk, and from this the small garrison fled without firing a shot as soon as his troopers rushed the first buildings.

It was now midday and he paused briefly. Below lay the Luico valley along which traffic was flowing in both directions; to the right was Luico village, lying between Monte Kuk and Monte Mrzli at the head of a pass down which the road descended to the Isonzo; from this direction came the sound of heavy fighting, which he interpreted correctly as being the German 12th Division attempting to secure the pass. There were now three possible courses of action open to him. He could assault the now-encircled Monte Kuk from the rear, but rejected this believing that it would fall to the rest of the battalion and the Life

Guards; as indeed it did, some two hours later. Or he could attack Luico and open the pass for the 12th Division, an alternative in which surprise would offer an excellent chance of success; this, too, he rejected, as it could not guarantee the elimination of the considerable enemy forces in the Luico area. Instead, he decided to block the Luico valley road and then cut the Luico-Matajur road by capturing Monte Cragonza beyond, thereby placing the Italians within a trap.

Turning off the Ravna-Luico track, he resumed his breakneck gallop downhill, passing through woodland and then across Alpine meadows to reach the valley road a mile and a half from the village. As only 150 of the fittest men from the 4th Rifle and 3rd Machine Gun Companies had managed to keep up with him he sent back an officer to chase up the rest and advise Sprösser of developments. He then cut the telephone lines connecting the Italians in Luico with their rear HQ, deployed his men in ambush positions on either side of the valley, and established a roadblock at a hairpin bend. During the next hour the Württembergers enjoyed themselves immensely, snapping up horse-drawn transport from both directions, directing the captured drivers into a previously designated parking area, and feeding themselves from the wagons' contents, all without the need to open fire. A car approaching from the south-west was shot up, contrary to Rommel's orders; it contained several staff officers who, because of the break in telephone communications, had come forward themselves to ascertain the situation in Luico.

It seemed as though the Italians had decided to abandon the village, as a long column of infantry appeared from that direction, marching unconcernedly along towards the road block. Rommel sent Unteroffizier Stahl, suitably equipped with a white arm band, to meet them with a surrender demand. He was promptly seized by the indignant Italian officers, who ordered their men to deploy and open fire. During the ensuing fire fight, which lasted some 20 minutes, Stahl managed to escape, and the Italian attempts to break through were foiled by the superior positioning of the German machine guns on the surrounding slopes. At length the Italians, belonging to the 4th Bersaglieri Brigade, threw down their weapons and walked forward with their hands raised. Altogether the number of prisoners taken in the valley, including 150 or so transport drivers, amounted to over 2,000; to compensate Stahl for the manhandling he had received, Rommel ordered him to march the prisoners back to Ravna and gave him a few riflemen as escort.

Shortly before 1530 sounds of fighting were heard in Luico itself. Rommel drove there in the captured car to find that the remainder of the battalion and the Life Guards' 2nd Battalion had attacked down the track from Ravna and were now driving the Italians through the village and along the Matajur road. Sprösser agreed that the Rommel Detachment should capture Monte Cragonza by the direct route from the roadblock and allocated the 2nd, 3rd and 4th Rifle Companies, the 1st, 2nd and 3rd Machine Gun Companies and the Signals Company for the task, retaining the rest of the battalion to press the enemy's rear-guard.

Rommel wasted no time in getting his weary troops moving. The first part of the way required hard climbing and scrambling straight up the side of the valley. At length a footpath was reached but night had long since fallen before the column was within striking distance of its first objective, the village of Jevszek. A full moon was shedding a brilliant light and, because the movements and voices of Italian troops were clearly audible from time to time, progress was slow and cautious. At length the point arrived at a meadow beyond which was wire fronting an enemy position. This blocked the intended route to the village and Rommel, well aware that his men were utterly exhausted, doubted whether an attack would succeed. Keeping his pack animals tethered downhill, where their sounds and movements would not alert the Italians, he allowed his men to rest in a re-entrant and sent out patrols to reconnoitre the route forward.

Lieutenant Aldinger's patrol returned at 2230. It had found a way up to Jevszek and reported that it was wired in but unoccupied, although there was plenty of enemy activity in the area. As soon as the moon had set Rommel prodded his detachment in motion again. As it approached the village it was fired on, fortunately without loss, but did not betray its presence by responding. The Italians, it seemed, were merely nervous, for more apparently motiveless shooting, punctuated by grenade explosions, occurred at intervals during the night.

By approximately 0200 the Württembergers were in possession of Jevszek, the well disposed Slovenian inhabitants of which provided them with hot coffee and dried fruit in their homes. Rommel again allowed his troopers to rest while, with the aid of his map, he pieced together the overall situation. The summit of Monte Cragonza, some 900 feet above the village and approximately 1,000 yards to the west, was almost certainly held in strength, as was an intermediate trench line just up-slope of the houses. Jevszek itself evidently formed part of a lay-back line covering the Luico valley although, for some reason, its designated garrison had not yet moved into position. He detailed Lieutenant Leuze to take out a patrol to discover whether the trench line extended south of the village and, if it did not, to reconnoitre the area between it and the enemy positions on Monte Cragonza. Leuze decided to carry out his mission alone, returning at 0430 with a prisoner; the trenches, he reported, ended opposite the southern end of the village, and the slopes between them and the upper defences were clear.zzz

Rommel therefore decided to lead the 2nd and 4th Rifle Companies and the 1st and 2nd Machine Gun Companies round the flank of the Italians' forward position and storm the summit while the 3rd Rifle and 3rd Machine Gun Companies, under the command of Lieutenant Grau, engaged the trench line itself from Jevszek. Although it was still dark when the assault force filed silently out of the village at 0500 the sun soon began to illuminate the surrounding peaks, creating in Rommel an uneasy feeling that he had delayed the move too long. He had just positioned the 2nd Machine Gun Company to cover the left flank of the attack and was hurrying towards the centre of the line when the Italians on the summit opened fire. Caught on the open slope, the attack was halted before it got moving. In the ensuing fire fight the Württembergers were at a disadvantage and their losses began to mount.

Drastic action was needed at once. Extracting several light machine gun teams from the 2nd and 4th Rifle Companies Rommel ran downhill to a position directly overlooking the enemy trenches above Jevszek, the occupants of which were fully occupied in their own fire fight with Grau's men in the village. Rommel shouted for them to surrender. Those closest to him promptly did so, recognising that their trenches offered no protection at all to an attack from the rear. Then, to his surprise, those manning the neighbouring trenches as far north as the Luico-Matajur road did likewise. Suddenly, he found himself having to disarm and find guards for an entire Italian regiment of 37 officers and 1,000 men who, he believed, had misinterpreted the sound of heavy fighting on the upper slopes and were now under the impression that they were surrounded.

Even more important was the release of Grau's companies, which were committed to the fight for Monte Cragonza as quickly as possible. This now became a straightforward frontal assault in which no subtlety was possible. Each trench and machine gun post had to be taken by hard fighting. The 2nd Rifle Company lost Lieutenants Ludwig and Aldinger, both seriously wounded, but went on under the command of Sergeant Hügel to capture the summit at 0715. While the assault was in progress Rommel had reached a loop in the Luico-Matajur road and found a convoy of ammunition wagons and 14 field guns, lacking teams and apparently abandoned by their crews; his otherwise detailed account of the battle contains no mention of these weapons having played any part in the defence of the feature.

Rommel had now achieved what he set out to do, but he still had the bit between his teeth and was determined to eliminate the threat to his right flank posed by the large numbers of enemy troops on Monte Mrzli and Monte Matajur. As a first step he directed Sergeant Hügel to take the much reduced 2nd Rifle Company along the ridge towards the former. By 0830 the intervening Hill 1102 had been secured, although further progress was blocked by intense machine gun fire. Rommel estimated that a minimum of one rifle and two machine gun companies would be required for the capture of Monte Mrzli, but assembling these was easier said than done, as his detachment had become widely dispersed and intermixed during the assault. Moreover, the situation on the battlefield had suddenly become very confused. The sounds of renewed firing from below indicated that Sprösser and the rest of the battalion were pushing the Italian rearguard up the Luico-Matajur road and were approaching Jevszek. Large numbers of enemy troops were attempting to retreat over Monte Cragonza, with the result that scattered fighting was taking place across the slopes of the mountain. Rommel himself was almost captured when, rounding a bend, he suddenly found himself confronted by a squad of Bersaglieri. Pursued by bullets, he escaped first by running downhill through scrub, then climbing Hill 1102 to rejoin Hügel.

Not until 1000 was he able to assemble a sufficiently strong force, drawn from all his companies, to attempt an assault on Monte Mrzli. Without any real hope that results would follow, he got his signallers to flash a request for support to the German artillery in the Isonzo valley; to his complete astonishment, shells began bursting in the hostile positions. Leaving his machine gunners on Hill 1102 to keep the enemy's heads down, he advanced in dead ground below the ridge road and had soon turned the flank of the trench line. Most of the Italians fled around the eastern shoulder of the hill and the remainder surrendered without the need for a fight.

Calling up the machine gun company, Rommel decided to continue his march along the ridge road. In the distance he could see a very large body of men completely inactive in the saddle between the two summits of the Mrzli, simply watching his advance. The road wound eastward round a wooded spur and, leaving the companies to proceed along this, he climbed through the trees with a few companions. Emerging some 300 yards from the Italians, he could see that they were engaged in some sort of noisy, animated debate with their officers. He walked steadily forward, waving his handkerchief and calling on them to surrender. For a moment there was silence then, when he was within 100 yards, the mass surged forward, sweeping aside the officers, and hoisted him on their shoulders with shouts of "Evviva Germania!' One officer who attempted to restore order was immediately shot dead by his men.

Rommel had captured the 1st Regiment of the Salerno Brigade, consisting of 43 officers and 1,500 men. Leaving one officer and three of his troopers to disarm the Italians, separate them from their officers, and march them to Luico, he proceeded with his column along the road to Monte Matajur, the last remaining and highest peak on the ridge. A prisoner had obligingly warned him that it was held by the 2nd Regiment of the Salerno Brigade, whose reputation was second to none in the Italian service, and that trouble could be expected. This was apparently confirmed when, as soon as the Württembergers' column appeared, heavy and accurate machine gun fire forced the troopers to take cover off the road. Rommel had only six medium machine guns and about 100 riflemen at his immediate disposal but he decided to mount an attack taking advantage of the broken country to his left, which provided a covered approach to the exposed flank of the objective. It was a risk, but no greater than others that had been taken, and he doubted whether the enemy garrison would really stand up to a determined assault by his own men.

He was positioning his machine guns when a runner arrived from Sprösser with orders to withdraw. Sprösser had reached Mount Cragonza where the long lines of prisoners filing down the road to Luico had created the impression that Rommel had broken the last resistance on the ridge. He had therefore withdrawn the rearmost elements of the Rommel Detachment, reorganised the battalion and was preparing to exploit westwards in the direction of Cividale. As Sprösser was evidently unaware of the situation on Monte Matajur, Rommel decided that he would complete this item of unfinished business and follow on.

Under precise and effective supporting fire from the machine guns, the attack was pressed home, driving the Italians from one position after another. Resistance suddenly collapsed and was followed by the usual mass surrenders, after which another 1,200 disarmed men were sent doubling down the road. At 1140 Rommel fired the coded flare signal which indicated that Monte Matajur was in German hands.

Some of the Salerno Brigade's officers were reduced to tears of rage and frustration when they saw the size of Rommel's command.

Their own men had been prepared to meet frontal attacks from the Isonzo valley, but the discovery that they were in danger of being cut off had proved to much for them; those on Monte Mrzli had mutinied, and those on Monte Matajur, now completely alone, were not inclined to pursue what they believed to be a hopeless struggle. Rommel was too experienced a soldier to believe that the troops he had encountered were representative of the Italian Army. The Alpini on Monte Nero, to the north of Caporetto, were still holding out days after the Alpine Corps had broken through at Tolmino, dying almost to a man in defence of the feature; and, some weeks later, Italian troops were to give the Württemberg Mountain Battalion one of the hardest fights in its history, earning Rommel's sincere respect. Nevertheless, as he gave his men a hour's rest before moving off, he was able to survey the entire battlefield and contemplate what his detachment had achieved, which was nothing short of astonishing.

In the 52 hours since the offensive began the Rommel Detachment had climbed 8,000 feet, descended 3,000 feet, and in the process had isolated, defeated or destroyed major elements from five Italian regiments. It had captured 150 officers, 9,000 men, 81 guns and numerous transport vehicles. Its own casualties amounted to six killed, including one officer mortally wounded, and 30 wounded, including one officer. For this Rommel received Imperial Germany's highest decoration, the Pour le Mérite, and promotion to captain, a rank which he was to hold for the next 15 years because of the post-war reduction of the German Army.

Capello's Second Army was shattered at Caporetto. Its staff reduced to the common lot of fugitives, it streamed back to the Tagliamento, where Cadorna hoped to make a stand, but the pursuit was as rapid as it was ruthless and crossings of the river were secured before the Italians could reorganise. On the more open country of the coastal sector the Third Army, commanded by the Duke of Aosta, was able to withdraw in better order. Here, the cause of the disaster was understood and, as one cavalry colonel put it to his officers: "The canaille have betrayed our country's honour - now we, the gentlemen of Italy, will save it!' In such a spirit regiments like the Novarra Lancers and the Genoa Dragoons launched a series of self-sacrificial charges each of which bought a little time. At length, partly because the Italians were holding a much shorter line, partly because British and French divisions were arriving from the Western Front, and partly because the Austro-German Fourteenth Army was equally exhausted and had outrun its supplies, a new front was stabilised along the line of the Piave, some

70 miles behind the Isonzo. The catastrophe had cost the Italians over 300,000 casualties and 2,500 guns; Cadorna was dismissed.

The emphasis of the war returned to the Western Front. In November the British Tank Corps tore a huge hole in the German line near Cambrai and, for the first time since 1914, church bells pealed out to celebrate a real victory gained at reasonable cost. Only days later, the Germans counter-attacked and recovered much of the captured ground. An official enquiry failed to find a rational explanation for the reverse, largely because those who could provide one were either dead or on their way to prisoner of war camps. Yet the truth was very simple; the Germans were using the same tactics they had employed at Riga and Caporetto.

At last Ludendorff had a winning tactical formula at his disposal and he decided to use it during the series of offensives he mounted in the spring of 1918. These were led by specially trained Storm Troop battalions, composed of picked men but, while the gains made were the best since the earliest weeks of the war, they were not decisive. A clean breakthrough was never achieved and when the Allies, now reinforced by American troops, counter-attacked with tanks in the autumn, the end for Germany was in sight.

The Württemberg Mountain Battalion was employed in the Storm Troop role during these battles, sustaining heavy losses throughout, as did every such unit. Rommel, now serving as staff officer with a higher formation HQ, watched its progress with great sadness. Of the men who had broken through at Kolovrat Ridge, blocked the Luico valley, taken Monte Cragonza and escorted prisoners by the thousand off the Matajur massif he comments, 'Only a few of them were destined to see their native land again.'

CHAPTER 3

Polish Eagle and Russian Bear

As a sovereign state, Poland had vanished from the map of Europe in the 1770s, her territory absorbed within the new boundaries of her more powerful neighbours. Throughout the 19th century, therefore, the dream of a free and independent Poland was a constant theme running through Polish political thought, and nowhere was this more apparent than in Warsaw and the central region of the country which was ruled by Russia. The Poles, western in outlook, shared neither a common cultural heritage, nor their religion, nor even an alphabet with their Russian masters, and they would willingly have shaken off the shackles of Russian rule had they been able to do so.

Prominent among those inspired by the Polish dream was Joseph Pilsudski, born in 1867, the second son of an old, impoverished but fiercely patriotic Polish-Lithuanian family. Attracted by socialist revolutionary theories, he was expelled from Kharkov University in 1885 for political activity and two years later was banished to Siberia for five years on being accused of plotting the death of the Tsar, a charge of which he was innocent. He returned on completion of his sentence even more determined to work, and if necessary fight, for Polish independence. In 1900 he was arrested and imprisoned again by the Russian authorities but managed to escape and fled to Krakow in Austrian Poland, where a less repressive regime existed. To his disappointment, the 1905 Revolution in Russia was not accompanied by a popular rising in Poland, although he was personally involved in numerous acts of sabotage and subversion. When the Revolution failed he began to study military science in all its aspects. He formed the opinion that a conflict between Russia on the one hand, and Germany and Austria-Hungary on the other, was inevitable and, with the approval of the Austrian authorities, he began to organise clandestine Polish military units which would take the field against Russia when the moment arrived.

When war broke out in 1914 Pilsudski correctly predicted that the Central Powers would defeat Russia and that, in turn, they would be defeated by Great Britain and France, supported by the United States. There were, of course, Poles fighting on both sides in the conflict. Those in the Polish heartland had no alternative other than to fight for the Tsar, while others formed units which served with the French Army. Pilsudski's Polish Legions, however, served with such distinction in the Austro-Hungarian Army that once the Russians had been driven out of central Poland the Central Powers declared the country independent under their joint protectorate in the hope that many more Polish recruits would be drawn to their cause. Pilsudski had no objection to leading a larger army but insisted that this belonged to a sovereign Polish state, rejecting the idea that Polish units should swear a binding oath of loyalty to their German and Austrian comrades in arms. In July 1917, with Russia racked by revolution and no longer posing a serious threat, the Germans, suddenly lukewarm to Polish aspirations, arrested Pilsudski and imprisoned him. Following the defeat of the Central Powers he was released in November 1918 and returned to Warsaw a national hero, being appointed Head of State and Commander-in-Chief by the Council of Regents.

The sudden collapse of the German, Austro-Hungarian and Russian Empires had left a power vacuum in Eastern Europe and in this contending ethnic and political groups each sought to impose their will, by force if necessary. In March 1917 the short-lived Provisional Government in Russia had recognised the independence of a Poland consisting of all areas with a Polish majority population, but the Provisional Government had been swept away by a Bolshevik coup that October and Russia was in the throes of a bloody civil war between those who supported democracy, the Whites, and the Bolshevik Reds, who wished to impose what they described as 'the dictatorship of the proletariat'.

With Russia preoccupied, Pilsudski set about establishing the boundaries of the infant Polish republic, which were expanded eastwards. This inevitably provoked a response from the Soviet government and a state of undeclared war existed between the two countries for much of the year. Alarmed, the Western Allies set Poland's provisional eastern boundary as being the river Bug, later known as the Curzon Line, only to be ignored when Pilsudski declared that nothing short of the country's historical frontier of 1772 would suffice.

By the end of 1919 it was apparent that the Bolsheviks were winning the civil war in Russia. Their better organisation, clear aims, central direction and ability to operate on interior lines enabled them to defeat one White army after another until, in the spring of 1920, they were able to devote their attention to the Polish incursion, with the further aim of spreading Bolshevism to central and western Europe once the Poles had been crushed. Two army groups were directed westward, Mikhail Tukhachevsky's West Front with four armies and one cavalry corps north of the Pripet Marshes, and Yegerov's South West Front with two infantry armies and one cavalry army under Semyon Budyenny to the south.

The Poles had most to fear from the 28 year-old Tukhachevsky, arguably the best of the Red commanders. Born into an aristocratic family, he entered the Imperial Guard as an ensign in 1914 and was taken prisoner the following year. A strange, demonic yet brilliant personality, he enjoyed destruction for its own sake and became a natural and enthusiastic Bolshevik. His nostalgia for the days when Mongols and Tartars had swept out of Asia, leaving utter devastation in their wake, led him to describe his own armies as hordes. The description, as Major-General J. F. C. Fuller has commented, was apt, for they consisted of nothing more than a horde of peasants who, after years of fighting during World War 1 and the civil war, wanted only to return to their homes and would have done so willingly had it not been for the merciless discipline imposed by a comparatively small handful of politically motivated fanatics. For all their dogma, hard experience had convinced the Bolsheviks that even a horde functions better if it is properly led and to fill this yawning chasm in their new order they had been forced to commission thousands of former Tsarist officers, holding their families hostage as a guarantee of loyalty and subjecting their every decision to the approval of the Party's permanently attached commissars. It was natural that in such circumstances of enforced motivation and stifled initiative that the officer's primary concern should be survival rather than vigorous action.

Other areas in which the Soviet armies resembled hordes rather than conventional armies were their technical and logistic services. During the civil war the Western Powers had supplied the Whites with large quantities of technical equipment, including aircraft and tanks. A great deal of this had been captured by the Reds, who were unable to make much operational use of it for the very good reason that, with so low a proportion of the population having received any sort of technical education, they were unable to maintain it in working order. It was a deficiency which acutely embarrassed the Bolshevik hierarchy and one which they attempted to explain away with the patently absurd comment that in a revolutionary struggle it was the massed rifles of the proletariat alone which guaranteed victory.

It was, however, in the field of logistics that the Soviet armies were most deficient. Supplying a modern army with all its needs is a complex process involving a highly trained staff and a well-developed transportation infrastructure. It was a sphere in which the old Imperial Russian Army can hardly be said to have excelled, yet compared with the Bolsheviks' performance it was the very model of efficiency. The administrative tail of the Soviet armies consisted simply of thousands of commandeered peasant carts which were used to haul ammunition; as for the rest, the troops had to make their own arrangements. As the Bolshevik horde advanced, therefore, it ate its way through the country it passed, then moved on or starved, as had that of the Mongols so admired by Tukhachevsky. In so doing it unconsciously devastated its own rear areas so that any check it sustained was bound to have serious and immediate consequences.

The Polish Army against which the Bolsheviks were advancing was very different in style and character. In November 1918 it consisted of a mere 24 infantry battalions, three cavalry squadrons and five artillery batteries. By January 1919 Pilsudski had increased this to 100 battalions, 70 squadrons and 80 batteries and a year later he had an army of approximately 110,000 men, organised in 21 infantry divisions and seven cavalry brigades with supporting artillery. The price paid was that the quality of the original cadre of experienced, battle-hardened soldiers who had served on various fronts in World War 1 was inevitably diluted by so rapid an expansion, although the troops were motivated and led by their natural officer corps. Against this, Poland was short of weapons of every kind and once hostilities against the Bolsheviks commenced the latter's sympathisers in the West tried by every means in their power, including dock strikes, to ensure that these deficiencies were not remedied.

To add to Pilsudski's difficulties, Poland had been combed repeatedly for remounts during World War 1 and there was a shortage of cavalry horses, a problem which was partially solved by mounting operations against the enemy's nerve centres with small motorised battlegroups, and it is to the study of two such operations that this chapter is devoted.

When it became clear that the Soviet government intended launching a full-scale invasion of Poland, Pilsudski decided to mount a pre-emptive strike of his own, designed to secure Kiev and establish an independent Ukrainian republic which would serve as a buffer state and fight as Poland's ally. Despite the fact that he had the support of a force of anti-Bolshevik Ukrainians, the plan was too ambitious for the resources at his disposal although during its initial stages all went according to plan.

The weight of the blow was to be directed at the Soviet Twelfth Army, which received its supplies through the two important railway and road junctions of Husiatyn and Zytomierz. These lay some forty miles behind the front; however, Pilsudski calculated that by capturing them he would render the Twelfth Army's position untenable and compel its prompt withdrawal. A cavalry brigade was detailed to secure Husiatyn and Zytomierz became the objective of a composite motorised force.

The latter, commanded by a Colonel Biernacki, consisted of a troop of Model T Ford light armoured cars, the 1st Legion Infantry Regiment, an engineer company, a motorised artillery battery and a troop of cavalry. About half of the 40 transport vehicles available were Fiat half-tracks and the remainder were heavy Packards with solid tyres. The artillery, believed to have been French 75mm field guns, was towed by four-wheel-drive Daimler lorries. The order of march decided upon by Biernacki was a vanguard of two armoured cars and two infantry companies with 15 machine guns, then the main body with the engineer company, six infantry companies and the artillery battery, and a rearguard consisting of one armoured car and the cavalry troop; there was

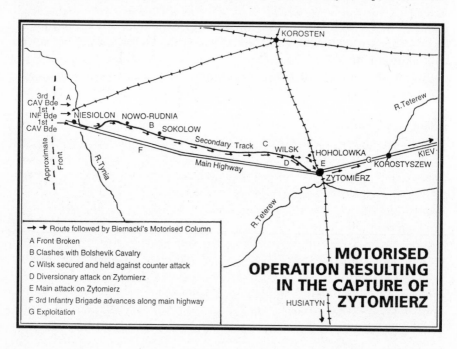

→ → Route followed by Biernacki's Motorised Column
A Front Broken
B Clashes with Bolshevik Cavalry
C Wilsk secured and held against counter attack
D Diversionary attack on Zytomierz
E Main attack on Zytomierz
F 3rd Infantry Brigade advances along main highway
G Exploitation

MOTORISED OPERATION RESULTING IN THE CAPTURE OF ZYTOMIERZ

insufficient transport for the whole of 1st Legion Infantry and the regiment's 3rd Battalion was to follow the column by forced march.

At 0430 on 25 April 5th Legion Infantry attacked the forward Soviet cavalry outposts at Niesiolon, capturing three machine guns and a field gun, simultaneously frustrating attempts by the Bolsheviks to burn the timber bridge over the river Tynia. Biernacki's column passed through the gap at 0615 but, instead of continuing along the paved highway to Zytomierz, which the enemy would expect it to use, it turned north for a mile or two before taking a parallel secondary road to the east, amounting to nothing more than a sandy track. Soon the marching battalion, making the best pace possible, had been left far to the rear.

The operation was being supported by attacks on either flank and Bolsheviks could be seen retreating eastwards in some haste. Some of the bridges along the route were found to be damaged, so that progress was halted from time to time while the engineers effected repairs. It was clear, however, that the enemy's demolition parties had been hasty and far from thorough in their work. At 0640, near the village of Nowo-Rudnia, the advance was briefly opposed by a cavalry squadron which scattered and fled after being raked by the machine guns of the leading armoured cars.

East of the village the track deteriorated and soon the column was in trouble as it laboured along through deepening sand. The root of Biernacki's problem was that the various types of vehicle were not operationally compatible. The Fiat half-tracks coped without the slightest difficulty, which is hardly surprising as the half-track owed its development to a French engineer named Adolphe Kegresse, a former manager of the Tsar's garage in St Petersburg, whose purpose had been to keep the Imperial limousines moving in snow; in fact, the device worked just as well in mud and sand. The light armoured cars also kept moving, as to a lesser extent did the Daimler gun tractors because of their four-wheel-drive, but the heavy Packards bogged down and had to be heaved out by their passangers. As a result of this a gap opened in the centre of the column.

At 0730 the advance guard had a further brief exchange of fire with Bolshevik cavalry at Sokolow, possibly survivors of the squadron which had been routed at Nowo-Rudnia, but after this there was no further contact with the enemy for several hours. Throughout the rest of the morning and much of the afternoon the advance continued at a slow but sustained pace which enabled the Packards to catch up. At about 1500 the advance guard approached Wilsk, a village just seven miles short of Zytomierz. This was held by the 1st Regiment of the Soviet 58th Infantry Division and a cavalry squadron, but neither had bothered to set up outposts and the Poles achieved complete surprise. While his infantry tumbled out of their vehicles Biernacki sent in his armoured cars. These reached the centre of the village without a shot being fired at them, then proceeded to beat up the place in fine style and chase the panic-stricken fugitives some way down the road to Zytomierz.

Rallied, the Bolsheviks attempted to recapture the village twice and were repulsed on both occasions. This was the first serious opposition Biernacki had encountered and, conscious not only of the small size of his own force but also that those in Zytomierz had been fully alerted, he sent back his transport vehicles with orders to bring up reinforcements. Fighting was still in progress when they returned at dusk with the 5th Legion Infantry's 3rd Battalion, but after dark the enemy melted away.

This was the most critical phase of the entire operation. Biernacki's orders required him to capture Zytomierz that day if possible, or early the following morning at the latest. He could allow his men no rest and at midnight they moved off again. The 3/5th Legion Infantry and the artillery battery were to continue along the secondary road and mount a holding attack against the town from the west. Simultaneously, 1 and 2/1st Legion Infantry and the armoured cars were to strike across country to the village of Hoholowka and launch the real attack on Zytomierz from the north. To coincide with this the transports were sent back once more, this time to bring forward part of the 1st Legion Infantry Division's 3rd Brigade, which was fighting its way eastwards along the main highway.

Elements of the Soviet 58th and 17th Cavalry Divisions were already converging on Zytomierz as they withdrew, so that clashes between these and Biernacki's detachments were frequent throughout the remaining hours of darkness and after first light. Nevertheless, by 0800 the Poles were fighting their way into the town and by 0900 had secured its bridge over the Teterew river. On several occasions during the street fighting the armoured cars found themselves duelling with two Renault FT tanks which the Bolsheviks had brought up. These were almost certainly the version mounting a single machine gun, as that armed with a 37mm gun would have quickly put an end to the proceedings. In the event, neither side was able to do the other much damage and both tanks were captured later; although no reason for this has been given, it seems probable that they were abandoned by their crews because of fuel shortage.

At 1000 the transports rolled in with part of the 3rd Brigade aboard and within an hour the whole of Zytomierz was in Polish hands. About 1,000 Bolsheviks had been captured, together with 10 guns, two tanks, numerous machine guns and a large quantity of equipment. General Rydz-Smigly, the sector commander, arrived and at 1500 despatched the 6th Legion Infantry, spearheaded by the armoured cars and two companies in the Fiat half-tracks, to harry the retreating enemy. After a column of the latter's horse-drawn carts had been overtaken and captured, the spearhead force headed at speed for Korostyszew where, after a brief fight, it drove out the Bolshevik rearguard and secured a further bridgehead over the Teterew at the point where its course swung north to join the Dniepr.

In 36 hours the Polish motorised force had advanced more that 50 miles, fought two engagements, captured an important railway junction, forced two Soviet divisions to withdraw and produced excellent results with its exploitation in the direction of Kiev, achievements which were all the more remarkable given its improvised nature and the incompatibility of the vehicles from which it had been formed. Biernacki's use of the transport element to bring up fresh troops as they were required is particularly interesting.

The success at Zytomierz had been matched elsewhere by the capture of Husiatyn so that the whole of the Soviet South-West Front was unhinged and compelled to withdraw. Kiev was captured on 7 May but unfortunately for Pilsudski he had overestimated Ukrainian enthusiasm for his further plans and underestimated the capacity of the Bolsheviks to react. On 15 May both Soviet Fronts launched a counter-offensive during which Zytomierz was re-captured by Budyenny's First Cavalry Army and in consequence all the gains made in the Ukraine had to be abandoned. To the north of the Pripet Marshes, Tukhachevsky's West Front steadily pushed back its opponents until by the end of July it seemed that Warsaw itself would fall.

Observers of the fighting, more used to the static conditions which had prevailed on the Western Front for much of World War 1, were startled to find themselves reporting a war of movement. There were, in fact, only 200,000 Bolsheviks opposing some 150,000 Poles across a vast operational area in which the wide spaces between major formations were held only by cavalry screens and, because of this and the fact that neither side possessed firepower comparable to that of Western armies, the war was one of manoeuvre rather than pitched battles.

Nevertheless, to the Western Allies it appeared that Pilsudski had seriously miscalculated and Poland was on the verge of being overrun.

Well aware that the ultimate goal of Bolshevism was world revolution, they were seriously alarmed by the implications of a Polish defeat which would, they believed, further de-stabilise eastern and central Europe to the extent that unrest, fomented by Bolshevik sympathisers, would inevitably spread westwards to undermine the established order. Such was the alarm generated by Tukhachevsky's apparently invincible advance that an Allied Mission, with General Maxime Weygand, formerly Chief-of-Staff to Marshal Foch, and Major-General Sir Percy de B. Radcliffe as its senior military members, was despatched to Warsaw in July. The Mission arrived to find that Pilsudski had resorted to a levée en masse so the strength of his army had now risen to 370,000 men of which only a fraction of the 185,000 already in the line could be described as adequately trained and equipped by any standards. What Pilsudski desperately needed at that moment was weapons, munitions and instructors rather than the advice which was all the Mission had to offer.

The situation, in fact, was serious but not critical. The Bolshevik horde, now operating far from its bases, was beginning to out-run its supplies and its overall strength had dropped to below 150,000. Nor was the morale of its troops good, for instead of being welcomed by crowds of oppressed workers and peasants eager to embrace the cause, as they had been promised, they encountered only hostility and were forced to fight their way forward, meeting stiffening resistance the further they advanced. In contrast, the closer the Poles retreated towards their own bases, the stronger they became, enabling Pilsudski to plan a counter-offensive.

Unlike Tukhachevsky, who controlled West Front from his HQ 300 miles distant in Minsk, Pilsudski could generally be found in the forward areas. As the Bolsheviks approached Warsaw, he became aware that West Front's open left flank was protected only by a screening force known as the Mozyr Group. He decided to form a 20,000-strong Strike Force consisting, at Weygand's suggestion, of good quality troops drawn from the southern sector of the front; these included the 1st and 3rd Legion Divisions and two cavalry brigades, all of which had distinguished themselves during the early operations in the Ukraine, under the command of General Rydz-Smigly. When the moment came the Strike Force, supported by the Polish Third and Fourth Armies, was to break through the Mozyr Group and advance northwards across the rear of West Front; simultaneously the First and Second Armies, defending Warsaw, and General Wladyslaw Sikorski's Fifth Army to the north, would go over to the offensive, effectively placing the Soviet armies within a double-envelopment.

The plan came close to being fatally compromised when the Bolsheviks found a full set of operational orders on the body of a Polish officer. Tukhachevsky regarded them as a deliberate plant and, supremely confident, continued his advance, intending to encircle Warsaw from the north. On 13 August an attack by the Soviet Sixteenth Army penetrated to within 15 miles of the capital, causing a temporary panic. The garrison commander threw in his reserve formations, spearheaded by tanks, and recovered the lost ground after heavy fighting. To relieve the pressure Sikorski attacked early, leading his advance with cavalry, tanks, armoured cars and two armoured trains, pushing back the Soviet Fourth Army. If West Front had functioned along conventional lines its cavalry corps, led by Ghai Khan, would at once have fallen on Sikorski's open left flank. However, as Radcliffe recalled, this formation was 'very unenterprising and badly commanded'. It was, in fact, operating well behind schedule and was still some 40 miles distant; nor was Ghai inclined to march to the assistance of Fourth Army, whose commander he disliked.

On 15 August Pilsudski struck. His Strike Force smashed through the Mozyr Group and penetrated deep into the enemy's deserted rear areas, covering 45 miles in 36 hours. During the next 10 days West Front collapsed like a house of cards. The Soviet Sixteenth Army, simultaneously under pressure from the west, was bundled across the rear of the neighbouring Third, whose own retreat became disorderly as it was forced into the area of the Fifteenth, which in turn affected the withdrawal of the already embattled Fourth. Amid chaotic scenes the Bolsheviks attempted to fight their way out of the trap, although very few succeeded. Some 44,000 of them crossed the frontier into East Prussia, where they were disarmed; a further 66,000 became prisoners of war. Among the booty captured by the Poles were 231 artillery weapons, 1,023 machine guns and 10,000 assorted vehicles. This series of engagements, known collectively as the Battle of Warsaw, has been described as one of the decisive events of the 20th century since it effectively halted the drive of Bolshevism into eastern and central Europe for a generation.

Immediately following the rout of West Front, Pilsudski turned his attention to the southern sector of the war, despatching Sikorski to deal with Budyenny's First Cavalry Army. This, the Bolsheviks' pride and joy, narrowly escaped destruction when it was all-but encircled and cut to pieces by the Polish cavalry east of Zamosc on 31 August, and took little further part in the war.

After Zamosc the Polish armies on the southern sector continued to drive eastwards and crossed the Bug river. Their next objective was the town of Kowel, which contained the HQ of the Soviet Twelfth Army and was also an extremely important railway junction since it was the point where the Russian broad-gauge railway system began. Obviously the acquisition of as much Russian rolling stock as possible was essential to support a further advance and, as the Bolsheviks were also aware of its value, it would have to be secured before the enemy had time to remove it. For this reason, therefore, it was decided to use the same kind of motorised force that had operated successfully against Zytomierz, in conjunction with frontal attacks by the 7th and 18th Infantry Divisions.

Deception was to play an important part in the overall plan and on 9 September the 16th Infantry Division advanced from Wlodawa in the direction of Mokrany, capturing the town two days later. Mokrany lay on the approximate boundary between the Soviet Twelfth and Fourteenth Armies, and the commander of the former, interpreting the move simply as a demonstration prior to a Polish attack on his main front, despatched his reserve westwards. He was only partially correct in his assessment for the Poles were displaying considerably more subtlety and had decided to adopt an indirect approach to their objective, using their

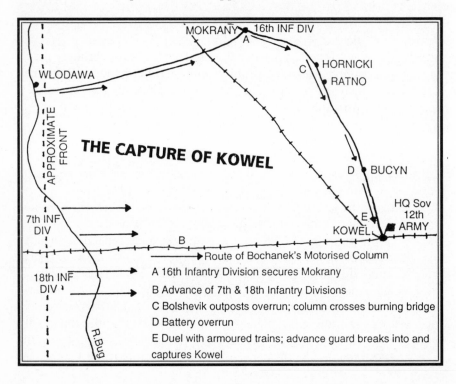

THE CAPTURE OF KOWEL

Route of Bochanek's Motorised Column
A 16th Infantry Division secures Mokrany
B Advance of 7th & 18th Infantry Divisions
C Bolshevik outposts overrun; column crosses burning bridge
D Battery overrun
E Duel with armoured trains; advance guard breaks into and captures Kowel

motorised troops to drive south-east down the lightly defended highway connecting Mokrany and Kowel. This meant that the attackers would be following a long and roundabout route, for while Kowel lay just 44 miles east of the Bug, the distance from Wlodawa to Mokrany was 41 miles and that from Mokrany to Kowel 60 miles. Against this, by launching their assault from a totally unexpected direction, they would achieve complete surprise.

The force detailed for the operation began assembling at Wlodawa on 10 September under the command of Major Bochanek. It consisted of an armoured car squadron containing eight Fords, two Whites and a Packard, two infantry battalions from 7th Division riding in 43 lorries, and two motorised field artillery batteries. At 1000 the following day it moved off along the road to Mokrany with an advance guard of three Ford and one White armoured cars, a half-battalion of lorried infantry and a half-battery of artillery. Approximately one mile behind was a link troop of two Fords, and a similar distance behind that the main body with one-and-a-half battalions of lorried infantry, the rest of the artillery and the column's supply vehicles, with close protection being provided by one Ford and the Packard. The rearguard, travelling one mile behind the tail of the column, consisted of two Fords and the remaining White. According to the original account there were several 'cisterns' in the supply element and the term has subsequently been interpreted as a reference to water trucks. This is almost certainly incorrect as water supply was not a problem; on the other hand, as Bochanek had a long way to go and no other means of replenishing his vehicles, it seems more probable that the 'cisterns' were actually small petrol tankers.

Although the first leg of the journey lay through what had recently become friendly territory, frequent stops had to be made to repair damaged bridges, although once again the Bolshevik demolition parties had skimped their work and no serious obstacles were encountered. During the evening the column reached Mokrany, where it carried out replenishment and maintenance tasks. At 0100 on 12 September it moved off down the road to Kowel and an hour later reached Hornicki, the first of three villages it would have to pass through. Here the garrison was quite literally caught napping when the advance guard drove in with its machine guns spitting fire. Most of them scattered into the darkness but a score or so were captured, as were two guns. The second village, Ratno, lay a few miles further on, and it seems that the Bolsheviks were alert, for they put up a brief but stiff fight during which they set fire to a timber bridge and only retired when this was burning fiercely. As neither the means nor the time existed to bring the blaze under control, Bochanek ordered the entire column to cross as quickly as possible. Only minutes after the rearguard had passed the entire structure crashed into the stream below in a sudden eruption of flame and sparks.

From this point onwards it had to be assumed that the Soviet Twelfth Army, having lost contact with two of its northern outposts in rapid succession, would take appropriate counter-measures, and such was indeed the case. With the return of daylight the column was able to make even better progress, but as the advance guard was approaching Bucyn, approximately three-quarters of the way between Mokrany and Kowel, it found an artillery battery drawn up across the road outside the village. Fortunately the gunners were unused to engaging moving targets and their first salvo screamed over the vehicles to explode well beyond. Unsettled by the return fire of the cars, they were unable to adjust their lay properly and were cut down when the battery was overrun.

The commander of the advance guard, Captain Przyborowski, now had the bit firmly between his teeth and headed for Kowel at top speed, inadvertently opening a gap between himself and the main body of the column. His armoured cars stormed into the town, spreading confusion as they fired long bursts down every street. Behind, the infantry left their vehicles and, supported by the guns, began fighting their way towards the railway station. The Poles estimated that the town contained the equivalent of two Soviet divisions, but the Bolsheviks were badly shaken by the suddenness and ferocity of the assault, which they understandably believed was being delivered by a much larger force, and they fled in disorder. With them, in his car, went the commander of the Twelfth Army, leaving behind all his maps, codes and papers; these were later studied with interest. Only at the railway station was determined resistance encountered, but this was captured after heavy fighting and held against several counter-attacks.

Although he was unaware of it at the time, Przyborowski was out on a limb, for Bochanek and the main body had become involved in a battle-royal of their own. As part of its counter-measures, Twelfth Army had summoned three armoured trains to protect the approaches to Kowel, one from the north and two from the west. These monsters, armed with guns and machine guns, had converged on the junction north of the town after the advance guard had passed but in time to intercept the main body, and they promptly opened fire on the latter, setting fire to several vehicles and causing a number of casualties. While the Polish infantry took cover, their motorised artillery unlimbered and went into action. The duel that followed was nothing if not spectacular.

During the Russian civil war, armoured trains had played the bully-boy and generally had things all their own way. However, they had never met the sort of opposition they were now encountering, consisting of one-and-a-half batteries equipped with the French 75, one of the best field guns in the world with a potential output of 20 aimed rounds per minute. Not even the combined resources of all three trains could match such firepower, nor had their armour been intended to withstand punishment on such a scale. Nevertheless, they stood their ground for a considerable time until one, seriously damaged, its armour dented, holed and torn, limped off into Kowel trailing smoke and steam. Its arrival at the station, where fighting was still going on, must have caused temporary alarm among Przyborowski's men. Another battle, however, was not what the train's surviving crew were looking for, and it passed through to vanish down the track to the east. Its departure was followed by that of the two remaining trains, which withdrew down the line to the west, pursued by shellfire as long as they remained in range; they were later found abandoned and taken into Polish service.

Re-assembling his column, Bochanek drove on into Kowel, reaching the town at 1600 to find it securely in Przyborowski's hands. Worried that the Bolsheviks would counter-attack once they discovered the size of the tiny force that had ejected them, he established a defensive perimeter incorporating numerous captured weapons and sent out the armoured cars to patrol the surrounding roads. At first light on 13 September the Bolsheviks did mount a counter-attack but it was a half-hearted affair and was easily driven off. At 1000 that morning elements of the Polish 7th and 18th Infantry Divisions, which had been fighting their way eastwards throughout the previous day, reached Kowel and Bochanek's mission was at an end.

In addition to the capture of the two armoured trains and Twelfth Army's HQ, the booty yielded by the operation was immense. It included several score artillery weapons and machine guns, tons of ammunition, 12 aircraft and, best of all, hundreds of railway wagons loaded with war material. The Soviet Twelfth Army had sustained a blow from which it never recovered and it was still retreating when the war ended.

To the north Tukhachevsky had managed to rally the wreckage of his army group and, reinforced, had managed to re-establish some sort of line between Grodno and Brest-Litovsk. Pilsudski, however, was hard on his heels and on 23 September the Polish Nieniewski Cavalry Group, consisting of 11 regiments, cut the vital Vilna-Grodno railway at Druskienniki. Three days later Pilsudski smashed through the Bolshevik defence lines in what has become known as the Battle of the Niemen, capturing Grodno on 26 September. The following day Tukhachevsky was again defeated at the Battle of the Szczara and his routed horde streamed eastwards. On the 29th the Nieniewski Cavalry Group captured the important road and railway junction of Lida, some 60 miles east of the Niemen, effectively trapping the Soviet Third Army, most of which was forced to surrender. Elsewhere, the Soviet First Army was again routed and, reduced to the lot of fugitives, driven in disorder into the Pinsk swamps. During this series of engagements the Poles took 50,000 prisoners and captured 160 guns.

Minsk, the capital of Belorussia, was taken on 15 October. By then the Bolshevik administration in Moscow, humiliated in the eyes of the world and beginning to lose credibility at home, was more than ready to sue for peace. It requested an armistice which Pilsudski, cautioned by Weygand on the dangers of over-extending himself, granted. At the Treaty of Riga, signed in March 1921, Poland recovered all but a fraction of her 18th century territory.

Pilsudski became President of the Polish Republic, which he ruled as a virtual autocrat until his death on 12 May 1935. Tukhachevsky survived him by two years. Of the campaign in which he had been so decisively beaten he wrote, 'Had we succeeded in disrupting the Polish army of bourgeoisie and lords, the Polish workers would have broken out in revolution and Bolshevism would have spread to the whole of Western Europe.' This, of course, was simply the Party line, for he knew perfectly well that his invading army had encountered little but hostility from the Poles. He had also been made painfully aware that the concept of the horde had no place in modern warfare, for time and again the nerve centres of his armies had been paralysed by the Polish combination of initiative, surprise, mobility, indirect approach to an objective and the imaginative use of motorised troops. The more he considered the subject, the more he was forced to acknowledge inwardly that the Red Army must undergo a profound change. In this he was greatly influenced by a Soviet artillery officer, V. K. Trianadafillov who, in 1927, published a book on mechanised warfare entitled *The Character of the Operations of Modern Armies*. He was also influenced by the writings of Major-General J. F. C. Fuller, for whom he expressed a sincere admiration, which was not reciprocated. In the mid-1930s, having been created a Marshal of the Soviet Union, he began forming large mechanised corps. These suffered from a number of organisational defects which, given time, could probably have been eliminated. Josef Stalin, however, had begun to see Tukhachevsky as a dangerous rival and in June 1937 he had him arrested, court martialled and shot for allegedly permitting himself to be seduced by bourgeois ideas; he was merely the first of many thousands who vanished during the Great Purge.

As for the Poles who had taught Tukhachevsky his first lessons, they were never to be forgiven by the Bolsheviks. In 1939, while Poland was fighting for her life against Hitler's Germany, the Red Army rolled across her eastern frontiers to recover the territory which had been surrendered in 1920. Stalin, determined to destroy Poland's prewar establishment, murdered thousands of Polish officers in cold blood and, when the Polish Home Army rose in 1944, he cynically left it to fight itself to destruction as a step on the road to imposing his own puppet regime.

Now, the wheel of history has taken another turn. Poland has once again achieved freedom and independence, although whether Pilsudski would rest content with her modern frontiers is another matter; and the Soviet Union has disappeared from the map.

CHAPTER 4

The Third Dimension: Holland and Belgium 1940

As finally drafted, the German plan for the invasion of Western Europe in 1940 contained three major elements. In the north, General von Bock's Army Group B, consisting of 29 divisions including, for the moment, three armoured, was to invade neutral Holland and Belgium not only with the ultimate object of occupying them but also enticing the British Expeditionary Force (BEF) and the best French armies northward into a trap. This was to be sprung by Colonel-General Gerd von Rundstedt's Army Group A, the 45 divisions of which, spearheaded by seven armoured divisions, would outflank the fixed defences of the Maginot Line by breaking through the Ardennes and cutting a swathe across northern France to the Channel coast, thereby isolating all Allied troops in the Low Countries within a pocket. The third element of the plan consisted of General von Leeb's Army Group C, at the southern end of the line, employing its 19 divisions in diversionary holding attacks against the Maginot Line itself.

In overall terms, the plan was based on the probable Allied reaction to German violation of Dutch and Belgian neutrality, a reaction reinforced by an inherited fear that any German offensive would be based on the old Schlieffen Plan which had failed so narrowly in 1914 and commenced with the German armies making a huge wheel across Belgian territory. In such an event the intention of the Allied Commander-in-Chief, General Maurice Gamelin, was to march rapidly northwards and join the Belgian Army of 23 divisions in halting the invaders' advance along the line of the Dyle river, simultaneously prolonging his own line to effect a junction with the Dutch Army which, though only 11 divisions strong, would prove a useful addition to his strength when he was ready to mount a counter-offensive.

It can therefore be seen that, long before the first shot had been fired, the Germans were well on the way to attaining their principal strategic objective. There were, however, a number of problems associated with operations in the Low Countries that Army Group B would have to solve, preferably in advance, and the majority of these centred on major waterways which provided the Dutch and Belgians with a series of natural defence lines. The Dutch, in fact, were sufficiently confident in the ability of these to delay an invader that they designated the area between the Zuider Zee and the Waal, including such cities of national importance as Amsterdam, Rotterdam and The Hague, as Fortress Holland.

In making their own plans the Dutch were, not unnaturally, anticipating a war fought very much along the lines of the battles of 1918, using up-dated equipment. They could hardly be blamed for failing to recognise that the Wehrmacht now possessed the ability to overfly such defences and establish itself in critical rear areas, for although parachute and airlanding operations had taken place during the German occupation of Denmark and Norway in April 1940, these were comparatively small in scope, little was known of their effect and, in any event, even had they been thoroughly evaluated, there was insufficient time to devise counter-measures.

The German intention was to remove Holland very quickly from the Allied order of battle and, since the country was obviously unsuited to the large-scale employment of armoured formations, von Bock was allocated almost all of Germany's parachute and airlanding troops to that end. These would operate under the overall command of Colonel-General Albert Kesselring's Second Air Fleet and were formed into a provisional Airlanding Corps under Lieutenant-General Kurt Student, consisting of the 7th Air Division, which would operate under Student's personal command, and Lieutenant-General Graf von Sponeck's 22nd Infantry Division. The former contained four parachute battalions plus three airlanding battalions of the 16th Infantry Regiment, and the latter one battalion of the 2nd Parachute Regiment and six airlanding battalions drawn equally from the 47th and 65th Infantry Regiments. In both formations the paratroopers were Luftwaffe troops and the airlanding battalions were provided by the Army, the usual system of co-operation being that target airfields were first secured by the parachute troops and then used to disembark the airlanding battalions, who arrived in tri-motor Junkers Ju 52 transports, the effect being to produce a very rapid build-up close to the designated objective.

The role assigned Student's corps in the forthcoming offensive was nothing less than to provide an airborne carpet into the very heart of Fortress Holland. 7th Air Division was to secure the bridge across the Hollandsch Diep at Moerdijk, the bridge over the Old Maas at Dordrecht, Waalhaven airfield south of Rotterdam and the bridges over the

New Maas in the centre of Rotterdam itself. 22nd Infantry Division was to capture the airfields of Valkenburg, Ockenburg and Ypenburg, all of which lay within striking distance of the The Hague, where the Dutch royal family and government were to be seized. The various elements of the airborne corridor were to be relieved in succession by Major-General Ritter von Hubicki's 9th Panzer Division, which was to drive straight across Holland from the German frontier. This aspect of the operation required careful timing as Hubicki's tanks had to reach Moerdijk bridge before the French, advancing from the south, could

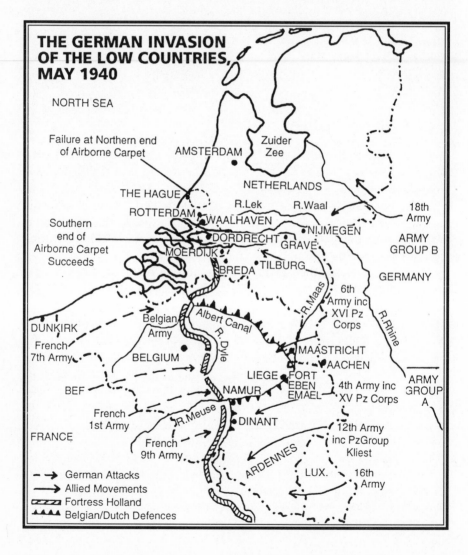

THE GERMAN INVASION OF THE LOW COUNTRIES, MAY 1940

re-capture it and effect a junction with the Dutch troops to the north. During the early stages of its advance 9th Panzer would have the assistance of Trojan Horse groups, operating in captured uniforms or civilian clothes, who were to secure bridges over the Maas close to the German frontier, where its course ran from south to north; these groups were provided by a covert operations unit known as the Bau- und Lehrkompanie (Construction and Training Company) Brandenburg, whose members were simply known as Brandenburgers. After the target airfields had been softened up by preparatory bombing, close tactical air support for the ground troops would be supplied by Junkers Ju 87 Stuka dive-bomber squadrons, heavily escorted by fighter aircraft.

Preceded by the bomber squadrons, the large formations of Ju 52 transports crossed the German coast during the early hours of 10 May, then wheeled to the south, intending to surprise the Dutch by making their approach runs from the North Sea, thereby creating an additional element of surprise. The Dutch, however, were not surprised, and were not only fully awake but also standing to, for during the previous week their military attaché in Berlin had received a series of warnings from anti-Nazi elements within the Abwehr, the German High Command's major intelligence organisation, that Holland was to be attacked on that date. As a result of these, and the monitoring of German troop movements beyond the frontier, the Dutch Army assumed a state of immediate war readiness on 8 May. At 2200 on 9 May the border was closed and five hours later, just 60 minutes before the German H-Hour, troops manning forward defences were brought to full alert.

Nevertheless, the speed, weight and ferocity of the airborne assault proved to be too much for some units. At Moerdijk 2nd/1st Parachute Regiment, commanded by Captain Prager, landed simultaneously at both ends of the 1,400 yard-long road and rail bridges, quickly overwhelmed the opposition and neutralised the demolition charges. At Dordrecht the lack of suitable drop zones meant that only a single company of 1st/1st Parachute Regiment, commanded by Lieutenant von Brandis, was available, although this succeeded in capturing the bridges in the first few minutes of the battle. The Dutch, however, quickly mounted a counter-attack and recovered the railway bridge. Unaware that the Dordrecht bridges were a vital element in the German airborne carpet, they did not demolish them, believing that they were needed for the passage of reinforcements from Fortress Holland to the south. Brandis was killed in the heavy fighting and for several hours the remnant of his company was pinned down, still contesting possession of the bridges but unable to make progress.

The lack of drop zones near the road/rail bridge in central Rotterdam had presented Student with a number of problems, and the solutions he applied to these were nothing if not ingenious. One company of the 16th Infantry and a handful of combat engineers, a total of some 120 men commanded by Lieutenant Schrader, were crammed aboard 12 Heinkel He 59C-2 air-sea rescue floatplanes which simply touched down on the Maas and taxied to the north bank of the river near the bridge. The sheer impertinence of the scheme produced its own reward, for early morning workers began to form an interested crowd which, believing that the large twin-engined biplanes were British, watched the soldiers inflate their rubber dinghies and paddle ashore, then obligingly helped them to climb the steep embankment. Within minutes both ends of the bridge were firmly in German hands. Simultaneously, 50 paratroopers under Lieutenant Kerfin had dropped into the small open space provided by the South Rotterdam football stadium. Emerging, they commandeered several trams, ejected the indignant passengers and, bells clanging, drove through the streets to join their comrades at the bridge.

Waalhaven airfield, to the south of the city, was marked by columns of smoke from the preparatory air attack when 3rd/1st Parachute Regiment, commanded by Captain Karl-Lothar Schulz, arrived overhead. The battalion dropped near the field's eastern perimeter and were immediately engaged by the defenders, drawn mainly from the Queen's Grenadiers. At this point 3rd/16th Infantry began airlanding on the field itself and the Dutch, caught between two fires, were overwhelmed after a sharp struggle. The rest of 16th Infantry landed in quick succession enabling the regiment's commander, Colonel von Choltitz, to despatch his 3rd Battalion to reinforce the bridge in Rotterdam while 1st and 2nd Battalions headed south to Dordrecht in captured or commandeered trucks.

Student also landed at Waalhaven and established his HQ. When, after fierce fighting, the bridges at Dordrecht were finally wrested from the Dutch, the 7th Air Division had completed its end of the airborne carpet, but now it was necessary to hold its isolated positions against mounting opposition until 9th Panzer Division arrived. The airfield was raided repeatedly throughout the day by Dutch, British and French aircraft, as well as being shelled by artillery, but remained operational. Counter-attacks against all the captured bridges were held off by the lightly armed Germans, whose ability to call in dive bomber squadrons partially offset their complete lack of artillery. Those in Rotterdam were hardest pressed, being confined to a very small area around the bridge by the attacks of tough Dutch Marines and shelled from the river by naval craft. The latter included patrol boat Z-5 and torpedo boat TM-51, which quickly reduced the tethered He 59 floatplanes into exploding, blazing, sinking wreckage before engaging the landing force's positions from 100 yards range until 1100 when they withdrew with their ammunition expended. Fortunately for the Germans the destroyer *Van Galen*, ordered up-river from the Hook of Holland to engage them with her 4.5in main armament, was intercepted by dive bombers and, unable to manoeuvre in the narrow waterway, was seriously damaged and had to be run aground before she could intervene in the battle.

While these events were taking place, attempts to establish the northern end of the airborne carpet had begun and ended in complete disaster. The principal reason for this was that 22nd Infantry Division had only one parachute battalion with which to suppress the defences of the three target airfields before the airlanding regiments arrived. This was demanding a great deal of the paratroopers, even if all went according to plan, but in the event two-thirds of the drops went astray.

At Valkenburg the parachutists dropped on their objective but were still engaging the well-entrenched and alert defenders when the first airlanding echelon began its approach run. Consequently the Ju 52s became the focus of anti-aircraft fire and several were burning even as they landed. Together the paratroopers and infantrymen completed the capture of the airfield only to find that their troubles had only just begun. The surface of the field consisted of soft mud and the Ju 52s were unable to take off. Soon it had become so jammed with aircraft that no more were able to get in. Some pilots reacted by making forced landings in fields or along the shoreline. Others, finding nowhere to put down, flew back to Germany with their troops still aboard. A second battalion lift to Valkenburg was cancelled.

An even worse situation had developed at Ockenburg. The paratroops destined for this objective had actually been dropped near the Hook, which meant that the first airlanding echelon had to capture the airfield on their own. This they succeeded in doing, covered by the machine guns of the aircraft. A similar situation to that at Valkenburg then developed, compounded by a British bomber attack which left the runways cratered and blocked with wrecked transports.

At Ypenburg, too, the parachutists had been wrongly dropped. The airfield had been selected as the site for 22nd Division's HQ but von Sponeck was forced to watch in horror as, one after another, the leading group of airlanding Ju 52s became the target of heavy and extremely accurate anti-aircraft fire. Having seen 11 of the group's 13 aircraft smash into the runway in flames, Sponeck aborted the operation and flew to Ockenburg where his own aircraft was hit and forced to crashland. Ten aircraft from the second group, with about 200 infantrymen aboard, managed a difficult landing on the Rotterdam motorway.

Unable to contact Student directly, Sponeck described the situation to Kesselring by radio. He estimated that only 2,000 widely scattered men of his division had been landed, while a further 5,000 had been forced to return to Germany. Kesselring took the only decision possible, cancelling the attack on The Hague, and ordered Sponeck to collect such troops as he could and advance in the direction of Rotterdam where he should attempt to establish a link with the 7th Air Division. This remnant managed to cover the few miles to Overschie, where it remained cut off until the fighting in Holland ended, the only crumb of comfort being that it absorbed the attention of three Dutch divisions which might have been better employed elsewhere. In the process it sustained over 600 casualties, including over 40 per cent of the officers present.

In the meantime, the northern wing of Army Group B had rolled across the Dutch frontier. Despite the elaborate provision of local support, including motor-cycle troops, tanks and even armoured trains, the Brandenburger parties enjoyed mixed fortunes. In many areas, including Maastricht, Nijmegen, Neerbosch, and Grave, the Dutch defenders blew the bridges at the first hint of trouble. In other places, notably along the Maas-Waal Canal, and at Gennep on the Maas, the Brandenburgers secured sufficient bridges for the invasion plan to proceed without serious check. The party at Gennep, led by a Lieutenant Walther, adopted the guise of German prisoners of war being escorted to the rear by three policemen. Unfortunately for the detachment guarding the bridge, who were quickly overpowered, the 'prisoners' had machine pistols and grenades concealed beneath their greatcoats, and the 'policemen' were in fact Dutch Nazis dressed in stolen uniforms. The success was quickly exploited by the 256th Division, which passed two trains across the bridge, these carrying sufficient troops and artillery to establish a deep bridgehead, and through this in turn passed the 9th Panzer Division.

In terms of striking power, 9th Panzer was comparatively weak in that of its total of 229 tanks only 54 (36 PzKw IIIs and 18 PzKw IVs) were mediums while the remainder were light PzKw Is and IIs armed only with machine guns. Speed, however, was the primary requirement, as it was of critical importance that Hubicki's tanks should reach Moerdijk before those of General Giraud's Seventh French Army. In its original form the plan had made the fast motorway between Nijmegen, Grave and s'Hertogenbosch available to them, but the failure to secure bridges at the first two meant that while the Gennep bridgehead offered an alternative, the going over much of this distance was along narrow, crowded country roads, and this consumed priceless time. However, when the 1st Division Légère Mecanique (DLM), leading the French advance, reached Breda it found that the Dutch troops it was to contact had already been withdrawn northwards. 1st DLM was now within easy striking distance of Moerdijk but its commander suddenly became cautious and split his advance guard into a reconnaissance screen. At about noon on 11 May part of this unexpectedly brushed with 9th Panzer between Breda and Tilburg. Other elements succeeded in reaching Moerdijk, where Student called down his dive bomber formations on them, and soon the whole division found itself under air attack. Believing that he had stuck his head into a hornet's nest, the French commander ordered his troops to fall back on Antwerp. 9th Panzer was therefore able to break through to the embattled paratroopers at Moerdijk at first light on the 12th and, with motorised infantry units following in its wake, passed along the airborne corridor to Rotterdam.

Here, and indeed throughout Holland, the Dutch were putting up a much tougher fight and inflicting far higher losses than had been anticipated. Hitler, worried, ordered his generals to bring the matters to a conclusion quickly. During the evening of 13 May a warning was passed to the Dutch commander in Rotterdam, Colonel Scharroo, that if he did not surrender the city would be razed to the ground by air attack. The Luftwaffe was ordered to deliver a concentrated raid the following afternoon, but in case the Dutch did surrender a procedure for cancelling the attack was worked out.

The following morning Scharroo did agree to a parley. By the time word of this had passed through the various channels the bombers were airborne and, having retracted their trailing aerials, they did not receive the recall signal. As a fail-safe, the Germans in the area of the bridge had been ordered to put up red signal flares, on seeing which the bombers would make for an alternative target near Antwerp. This choice of colour was to have tragic consequences, for it was too close to that of anti-aircraft tracer to distinguish easily. When it approached the target area at 1500 less than half of the bomber force spotted the flares and the rest went on to deliver a devastating attack on the city's commercial quarter, the damage caused by the bombs themselves being multiplied many times as fires raged through warehouses packed with petroleum products and other highly combustible materials. About 1,000 civilians died in the raid, which caused widespread revulsion abroad, not least in the United States.

Even if the raid had not been mounted, Holland could not have continued to resist for much longer. In the north German troops had reached the Zuider Zee; in the south the drive of 9th Panzer Division had ensured that no further assistance from Allied ground troops could be expected. The Dutch Air Force had courageously fought itself to destruction and without its support the Army would be compelled to fight at a fatal disadvantage. The royal family, some of whom had wished to remain for a final stand on the island of Walcheren, had reluctantly sailed for England from The Hook at noon on 13 May. Later that day the government, lacking the stomach of its soldiers, followed suit. In the circumstances the General Staff could only reach the conclusion that with no hope of repelling the invaders it would not be justified in exposing the population to the horror of further air attacks. Scharroo surrendered Rotterdam at 1700 on 14 May and at 2030 that evening Holland formally capitulated.

There could be no denying that, in addition to the losses sustained by 22nd Infantry Division, the casualties incurred by Student's troops had been heavy. Of the original coup de main parties which secured the bridge at Rotterdam only 60 men were still on their feet when the fighting ended, some so shaken and exhausted after five days and four nights of fighting that von Choltitz wondered whether they could ever be used on operations again. During the closing stages of the battle Student himself was severely wounded by a trigger-happy member of the SS Division Leibstandarte Adolf Hitler, a motorised formation which had followed up 9th Panzer's drive across Holland. In terms of equipment, too, the operation had been very expensive, the Luftwaffe reporting 170 aircraft of various types destroyed or written off, a similar number seriously damaged and proportionally severe casualties among aircrews. Nevertheless, the new form of warfare had proved itself capable of producing results quickly and it was decided to expand the German airborne arm.

Belgium presented the Wehrmacht with a different set of problems, for not only did the Belgian Army also rely on water barriers for defence, it was also much larger than that of Holland and would be reinforced by those of the Allies long before a decision was reached. In the event of a German invasion the Belgian intention was to hold a forward defence line along the Albert Canal to its junction with the Meuse (Maas) and thence southwards along the river itself through Liège, Namur and Dinant to the Ardennes, enabling the BEF and the French armies to establish a continuous front along the line of the Dyle river to the east of Brussels. In 1914 General Alexander von Kluck's German First Army had crossed the frontier east of Liège and, using specially designed heavy siege howitzers, quickly pounded the city's ring of forts into submission. Despite this, the Belgians did not lose their faith in fixed fortifications and in 1932 they decided to construct a fort at Eben Emael, some miles to the north of Liège. This dominated the point at which the Albert Canal was connected to the Meuse by a lock and was therefore of critical strategic importance since German possession of the area would obviously destroy the value of both elements in Belgium's first line of defence.

When completed in 1935 Fort Eben Emael was considered to be the last word in fortification technology and proof against every known form of artillery. In shape the fort, measuring 900 metres from north to south and 800 metres from east to west at its widest point, resembled a kite with the tail pointing north. As the southern end of the Maastricht Appendix, a strip of Dutch territory interposed between Belgium and Germany, lay opposite on the east bank of the Meuse, most of the fort's offensive armament, known as No 1 Battery, was trained north and south. Gun Positions Maastricht 1 and 2 and Vise 1 and 2, each armed with three 75mm guns, were ranged respectively on the routes westward from Maastricht to the north and Vise to the south. In addition No 1 Battery possessed two retractable revolving turrets, each with two 75mm guns, known as Cupolas North and South, and one revolving but non-retractable cupola containing two 120mm guns.

The local defence of the fort was the responsibility of No 2 Battery. This consisted of seven casemates, each containing a 60mm anti-tank gun, two machine guns, searchlights and, in some cases, grenade dischargers, set at intervals into the surrounding wall, including the gatehouse. On the roof were two blockhouses known as Mi-North and Mi-South, each armed with three machine guns and searchlights, as well as an anti-aircraft battery with multiple machine gun mountings. At the northern end of the roof were two dummy cupolas intended to decoy the enemy's artillery fire.

Externally, the eastern wall was protected by the canal, which at that period ran through a deep cutting, although this has been subsequently widened and is no longer apparent. The northern part of the western wall was protected for more than half its length by a water-filled moat running from the canal, and the little Geer river, the remainder of the perimeter being covered by a deep anti-tank ditch. The fort's outer defences consisted of extensive barbed wire entanglements, minefields and steel anti-tank obstacles, all of which were covered by fire from the main structure.

The real bulk of Fort Eben Emael, however, lay beneath the surface of the ground and was located on three levels, with No 1 Battery's gun positions and observation cupolas uppermost. If any one of these positions became untenable the crew could retire down a stairway to the intermediate level and seal it off by closing an inner steel door, then insert steel beams into slots on either side of the entrance to form a barricade which would be backed by a sandbag wall, and finally close an outer steel door leading into the access tunnel. The intermediate level

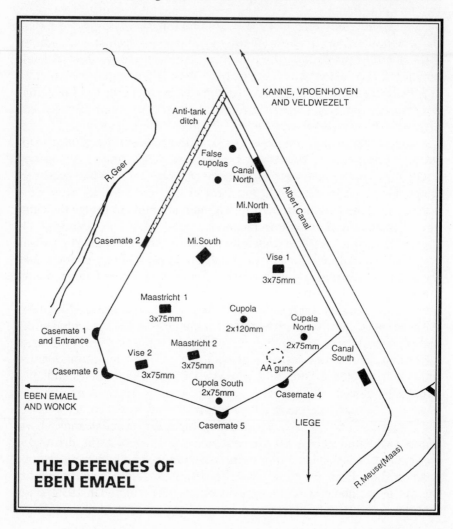

THE DEFENCES OF
EBEN EMAEL

also housed the fort's command post, communications centre, electric generators, water pumps, water pumps, hospital and individual magazines with shell hoists for the guns positions above. The bottom level contained barracks accommodation, including washrooms, showers and kitchens. Heated air was circulated by ventilation units throughout all these installations, which were connected by four-and-a-half miles of tunnels incorporating gas locks. All in all, Fort Eben Emael was considered by many of the leading military engineers of the day to be quite impregnable and capable of holding out indefinitely.

On 9 May 1940 the fort was commanded by Major Jean Jottrand and its garrison consisted of 17 officers and 632 other ranks; because of leave, absence on courses and sickness, this was about one-third short of the official establishment, but in the event it was to make little difference. Should the Germans invade, Jottrand's responsibilities included destroying the bridge over the Albert Canal at Kanne, north of the fort, and the bridge and locks at Lanaye, lying directly under the fire of one of his casemates, all of which had been previously prepared for demolition. To the north of Kanne two more bridges crossed the canal at the villages of Vroenhoven and Veltwezelt, and although these lay outside Jottrand's immediate area of responsibility and had also been prepared for demolition, he was expected to take them under the fire of his guns and destroy them if they fell into enemy hands intact; and, as a matter of course, his guns would also disrupt German attempts to bridge the canal or the Meuse anywhere within range.

From the outset it was appreciated by the German High Command that Fort Eben Emael was likely to prove a thorn in their side, imposing unacceptable delays on their carefully prepared timetable for the invasion of Belgium. It must, therefore, be eliminated as quickly as possible, but the question was how? The answer was provided by Adolf Hitler, whose keen interest in weapon systems and their potential application often surprised his generals. While studying plans of the fortress his infantryman's eye had noted that, with the exception of the cupolas, its roof resembled a large grassy field on which no obstacles whatever had been erected. If, then, this was the Achilles Heel of mighty Fort Eben Emael, how best might it be exploited?

Speed and total surprise were obviously essential and a parachute drop would certainly provide these. Against this, the drop zone was tiny, the risk of the troops being dispersed was high, and adverse weather conditions might make it impossible to mount such a mission on the very date it was required. At the end of October 1939, some months before the form of Germany's offensive in the west had been finalised, Hitler summoned Student to Berlin and asked him whether it would be possible to land assault gliders on top of the fort. During the years prior to the Fuhrer's repudiation of the Treaty of Versailles, Germany had been denied military aircraft and had resorted to providing potential Luftwaffe pilots with primary training in gliding clubs, to such good effect that she led the world in the field of sport gliding. Student had flown gliders since the 1920s and, knowing their capabilities, he confirmed that such a landing would be possible at dawn or in daylight. At this point his thoughts doubtless turned to what an inevitably small assault group was expected to do on the roof of a fortress sealed tight against attack, but again Hitler provided the answer. They would blow in the cupolas and gun positions with hollow charges, thereby neutralising the entire fort, then hold their positions until relieved by ground troops advancing across the Maastricht Appendix from the German frontier. It was breathtakingly simple, yet obviously practical.

The hollow charge principle had been discovered by C. E. Monroe, an American scientist, as long ago as 1888. Monroe found that if a cone was hollowed out of the base of a block of explosive, the blast wave was focussed into a jet of high temperature gases powerful enough to blow a hole through any obstacle in its path. For many years the Monroe Effect was regarded as being nothing more than a scientific curiosity without any apparent military application. In the 1920s it was discovered that if the cone was lined with thin-gauge metal the effect was multiplied many times and in 1938 two Swiss engineers, Matthias and Mohaupt, finally solved the problems of incorporating the device into munitions. Ultimately, it became the basis of light infantry anti-tank weapons such as the PIAT, the Bazooka and the Panzerfaust, and of many fin-stabilised missile systems. For the moment, however, the German Army's experiments into its potential uses were being conducted in total secrecy. Two demolition charges weighing 25lb (12.5kg) and 110lb (50kg), respectively capable of penetrating seven and 12 inches of armour plate or concrete, had been perfected, and the intention was that Student's assault groups should use these against the fortifications at Eben Emael.

Student's task, therefore, was to raise, train and equip the unit which would neutralise the fort and simultaneously capture the bridges at Kanne, Vroenhoven and Veldwezelt by glider assault. The officer selected for operational command was Captain Walter Koch and the unit's establishment was set at 11 officers and 427 men. Most were volunteers drawn from Student's airborne division, joined by a handful of internationally famous glider pilots who had been persuaded to offer their services. Appropriately, the group which would assault Eben Emael was based on a parachute engineer platoon commanded by Lieutenant Rudolf Witzig, who was himself a qualified engineer. The glider to be used was the DFS 230, which had a wingspan of 72 feet and was capable of transporting a section of 10 fully-equipped infantrymen.

Once formed, Assault Force Koch found itself completely isolated from the rest of the world. All leave was cancelled, off-duty contact with other troops was forbidden, outgoing mail was rigorously censored, telephone calls were strictly prohibited, insignia was removed from uniforms and everyone in the unit signed a declaration acknowledging the risk of being sentenced to death if any detail of the training was communicated to outsiders.

The training was as intensive as the security. The entire unit practiced entering and leaving the gliders, stowing them and landing techniques, again and again. The bridge parties rehearsed their attacks at locations in Germany which closely resembled their objectives. In February 1940 Witzig's assault engineers went to Czechoslovakia where they perfected attack drills against the casemates of the unblooded Benes Line using bangalore torpedoes to cut through wire, flamethrowers and pole charges which were thrust into embrasures - in fact, every weapon in their armoury except the hollow charges. These, and their 10-second delay fuses, they learned to handle on level ground, where the explosion left only a small crater without revealing the secret of the device or its purpose. They studied every aspect of the Belgian defences on full-scale replicas and a scale model. Each glider section was allocated a numbered objective the location of which, and that of its neighbours, became familiar with endlessly repeated training assaults. The one thing they were not told until the last minute was that they would be attacking Eben Emael.

At length Assault Force Koch moved to the airfields of Ostheim and Butzweilerhof near Cologne, where elaborate precautions ensured that it remained concealed from prying eyes. During the evening of 9 May it received the order to load its gliders. For Witzig's team at Ostheim this meant stowing 56 hollow charges, half 110lb and half 25lb, bangalore torpedoes, flamethrowers, pole charges, radios, collapsible ladders, air recognition flags and personal weapons and equipment. An interminable delay followed, but at length the gliders were hitched to their Ju 52 tugs and by 0335 the last DFS 230 was airborne. For the whole of the 45-mile route between Ostheim and the release point north-west of Aachen the tug pilots simply had to follow pre-positioned light beacons.

It seemed that every contingency had been allowed for save human error. Suddenly the Ju 52 pilot towing Witzig's glider was forced by a converging aircraft to take violent evasive action and the tow rope, unequal to the additional stress, parted. Fortunately, the glider pilot was able to make a good landing in open country and, commandeering a car, the furious Witzig returned to Ostheim to round up a fresh tug. Eight minutes after the first mishap another of Witzig's gliders was prematurely released, thereby keeping its occupants out of the battle for the fort and, somewhat later, two glider pilots from the bridge teams mistook their positions in the half light and came down in the wrong place. These four mishaps still left 38 gliders homing in silently on their objectives from 8,500 feet.

During the release a number of Ju 52s had penetrated Dutch air space over the Maastricht Appendix and attracted anti-aircraft fire. This, it was thought, would provide advance warning for the Belgians, but the latter were as aware as the Dutch that a German invasion was imminent and, having observed troop movements beyond the frontier, had placed the garrison of Fort Eben Emael on full alert as early as 0030. Most of the men lived in barracks or rented houses in the villages of Eben Emael and Wonck, four miles to the west, and it took some time for them to reach the fort. Even then, the procedure left much to be desired. Jottrand's standing orders required him to fire one blank round at 30 second intervals over a period of 10 minutes to warn troops and civilians in the surrounding countryside that a state of emergency existed. This task was allocated to Cupola North, but the gun crew had already been detailed for the purely domestic business of clearing the barracks closest to the fort and bringing their contents within the fortifications. Jottrand did not bother to investigate the prolonged silence until 0230, then ordered Cupola South to start firing, only to be told that the blank rounds were consistently malfunctioning. Not until 0315, presumably after a fresh supply had reached the position, did the regular banging of the warning gun commence, and by then Assault Force Koch was preparing for take-off.

At 0407 Jottrand became conscious of anti-aircraft fire from the direction of Maastricht and he ordered his own anti-aircraft gunners, commanded by Lieutenant Longdoz, to man their positions. After that events happened in rapid succession. Outposts near Kanne reported up to 50 aircraft approaching from the east, adding that their engines had stopped and that they had begun to circle at between 4,000 and 5,000 feet. Telephone monitors picked up a transmission from Regional HQ in Liège granting a request from the Vroenhoven bridge guard for permission to open fire on aircraft which were landing nearby. Jottrand could hear machine gun and small arms fire erupting from Belgian positions along the canal to the north, while far above long-winged shapes could be seen circling in eerie silence. Suddenly aware that their target was the fort itself, he ordered the demolition charges at Kanne and Lanaye to be blown at once. This action was to be the fort's sole major contribution to the war.

In their gunpits on the roof, the anti-aircraft gunners were simply staring skywards in the half-light, mesmerised by the strange sight. Longdoz, unable to identify the aircraft taking part in the noiseless ballet above, was torn by an agony of indecision until a telephone jangled and the speaker sharply ordered him to open fire. The multiple mountings burst into life but by then it was too late for them to inflict much damage, for the glider pilots had completed their descent spiral and, having verified their bearing, were breaking away to make their final approach run. One after another the gliders swooped below the level at which the defenders' machine guns would bear, then came soaring up over the walls to touch down in a long skid across the grassy surface of the roof. Within seconds the anti-aircraft gunners were under attack from squads of flat-helmetted, besmocked troopers who closed in remorselessly with blazing machine pistols and grenades. Those of the Belgians who did not surrender at once were cut down. The time was 0425.

It took just 30 minutes to neutralise Fort Eben Emael's offensive capacity, and in the process render obsolete every similar fortress in the world. So thoroughly trained were the assault squads, and so familiar were they with their individual objectives, that despite the absence of Witzig they simply set about their work without the need for further direction, such leadership as was required being ably provided by Sergeant Major Helmut Wenzel.

Maastricht 1 was attacked by Sergeant Arendt's squad, whose glider came to rest only 30 yards away. Unable to find a suitable surface to emplace their 110lb charge, they fixed a 25lb charge to the ball mounting of one of the 75mm guns. Totally unprepared for the violence of the explosion, they were blown off their feet. Within, the effect was devastating. A foot-square hole was blasted in the surrounding concrete, the gun was flung from across the chamber and down the stairwell, the power supply failed and some propellant charges caught fire, filling the interior with choking smoke. Those Belgians who could staggered down the stairwell, but some were killed when Arendt and two of his squad wriggled their way into the interior and tossed a charge down the shaft.

Arendt followed the stairs down only to find that further access into the fort's interior was barred by steel doors. Of all those manning the position, only one Belgian escaped death or serious injury.

Maastricht 2 was the objective of Sergeant Niedermeier and his men. This position incorporated an observation cupola which was blown in with a heavy charge, killing the two men below. A light charge was fastened to a steel door just below one of the gun barrels. This threw the weapon itself across the gun chamber and blasted the gunners off their stools, killing two. The remainder, wounded or burned by the explosion, made their escape, pursued by Niedermeier, who fired his machine pistol down the stairwell, but nevertheless managed to close the steel doors behind them.

Wenzel's own target was Mi-North, where the Belgian machine guns had already opened fire. Climbing to the top of the bunker, Wenzel dropped a 2lb explosive charge into a periscope shaft on the observation cupola, the effect being to leave the gunners without vision or direction. A hollow charge failed to penetrate the steel cupola but unseated it and caused casualties. A second hollow charge placed against a machine gun embrasure blasted a huge hole in the concrete and killed those remaining within. Picking his way over the tangle of wreckage and bodies in the shattered interior, Wenzel answered a ringing telephone. The caller demanded to know what was happening and the sergeant major told him: 'Mon Dieu!' said the voice, then the line went dead.

Mi-South was unusual in that it was surrounded by a wire entanglement through which Sergeant Neuhaus and his squad had to cut their way under fire before they could reach the structure. A blast from a flamethrower temporarily drove the Belgians from their weapons. A small hollow charge was placed against an embrasure but was dislodged and exploded harmlessly on the ground when an alert gunner thrust a cleaning rod through the barrel of his weapon. Neuhaus then placed a large hollow charge against a steel door, blowing it and part of the concrete surround into the interior, where some of the defenders were found alive but stunned and incapable of further resistance.

Vise 1 and Vise 2 were not priority targets as their guns were trained to the south and therefore presented no threat to the German troops advancing across the Maastricht Appendix. At Vise 1 the observation cupola was blown in and the ventilation system was wrecked, forcing the Belgians out of the gun chamber. However, they returned at intervals throughout the morning to fire instantaneous fused shells which exploded on leaving the muzzle, and did not finally abandon the position until 1130. Vise 2 was not attacked at all.

Inside the large cupola housing the fort's two 120mm guns the crew discovered that neither the ammunition hoist nor the power rammers would work and that crowbars needed to open ammunition crates had mysteriously vanished. As everything had been working and in place when the crew had carried out a drill only 14 hours earlier, sabotage by a pro-Nazi member of the garrison may well be an explanation, although nothing was ever proved. While the crew endeavoured to overcome their difficulties the big cupola continued to revolve menacingly. The German squad detailed to neutralise the position was the one whose glider had been released prematurely so, for a while, the Belgians remained unmolested. At length, despite a painful wound, the pilot from another squad, Heiner Lange, fetched a hollow charge from his glider and placed it on the summit of the dome. The explosion burst his eardrums but did not penetrate the thick steel. Wenzel appeared shortly after and thrust a 2lb demolition charge down each of the 120mm barrels. When, in due course, the Belgians attempted to fire the right hand gun the back-blast from the double explosion in the shattered weapon flung men in every direction, wrecked machinery and filled the interior of the chamber with choking smoke. The position was evacuated and sealed off.

Together, the squads of Sergeant Haug and Sergeant Unger blew in the dome of the retractable Cupola North, causing such severe internal damage that the 75mm guns were no longer workable, and buried an exit door with a second charge. This operation was complicated by heavy fire from a nearby workshop which caused casualties in both squads before it was suppressed. Unger was killed by shellfire as his men withdrew towards cover.

Cupola South had not been a designated target because the Germans had believed, incorrectly, that its field of fire lay below the level of the fort's roof. In the event it was assaulted by men from Niedermeier's and Haug's squads but its dome survived an attack with a heavy hollow charge and it remained in action, sweeping the surface with shrapnel and engaging targets around Kanne.

Jottrand had requested the Belgian forts at Pontisse and Barchon, both some miles distant, to fire on Fort Eben Emael with the intention of destroying the attackers on its surface. The first shells began falling while the Germans were clearing the last of their objectives and Wenzel got as many men as possible under cover inside the shattered fortifications, which were then marked with air recognition flags. Shortly after, additional ammunition supplies were dropped by parachute. At 0630, to everyone's surprise, Witzig's glider touched down.

The situation he found on assuming command was both satisfactory and alarming. On the one hand his men had completed their mission and although the casemates around the walls were still in the enemy's possession, the fort's real teeth had been drawn; on the other, there was no telling when the German advance would catch up. For the moment his little force was pinned down by shellfire and anticipating an infantry counter-attack which it would have to meet with very limited resources. It was, however, of comfort to know that although the Luftwaffe's dive bomber squadrons, on call above, were making no impression on the fort's unsubdued defences, their effect on troops in the open would be very different.

In the meantime the Belgians were considering their response. It was decided that the abandoned gun positions could not be re-occupied and Jottrand turned his mind to the question of a counter-attack. The problem was that his garrison did not contain an infantry element. His men were fortress troops, gunners and technicians untrained in basic infantry skills and certainly lacking in the necessary aggression. They had been un-nerved by the Germans' method of arrival and were severely shaken by the terrible new weapons which had inflicted horrific blast and burn injuries on their comrades. Most were unwilling either to volunteer or even be detailed for the counter-attack role. Jottrand sent out several parties under officers during the day but their efforts were half-hearted and they simply dispersed when they ran into opposition or came under dive bomber attack. By 1300 he had reached the decision that only a major counter-attack would suffice. The garrison's reserve was ordered forward from the barracks at Wonck. The column, more than 200 strong, was immediately pounced upon by dive bombers and scattered across the fields. At 1600 its men began to trickle in and by dusk half of them had arrived, no longer a relief force but frightened fugitives.

Elsewhere, Assault Force Koch had also captured the bridges at Vroenhoven and Veldwezelt intact. The gliders had touched down close enough to their objectives for the Germans to overcome the local defence quickly and disarm the demolition charges, assisted by a pin-point dive bomber attack which neutralised the local sector HQ before orders could be given to blow the latter. At Kanne the gliders landed too far from the bridge and the attackers were held off long enough for it to be blown, as Jottrand had ordered. All three parties were counter-attacked throughout the morning but despite sustaining casualties they managed to hold their positions. Some artillery support became available from about 1015 onwards and at 1430 the leading infantry elements of the German advance caught up with the detachments at the bridges.

Koch, however, was concerned that because the Brandenburgers had failed to capture the Maastricht bridges before they were blown by the Dutch, the 4th Panzer Division's advance was behind schedule, and with it that of the 51st Motorised Engineer Battalion, which was to relieve Witzig's men and complete the reduction of Eben Emael. By late afternoon an engineer platoon commanded by Sergeant Josef Portsteffen had reached a position on the canal near the northern end of the fort but was repeatedly prevented from launching its rubber assault boats by heavy fire from the waterside casemate known as Canal North. The glidermen attempted to neutralise the casemate by lowering charges onto it from above, without result, but at length hit upon the idea of using the explosions to dislodge earth from the cliff face in such quantities that the observation cupola was buried. Portsteffen, noting that the Belgian fire had become irregular and inaccurate, immediately launched his boats and gained the opposite bank of the canal where his platoon worked their way round to the north-western sector of the defences.

Inside the fort the Belgians could hear Witzig's troopers moving about beyond the barricaded steel doors of the abandoned gun positions. In response to well founded fears that the Germans would use their terrible explosive devices to blast their way into the interior of the structure, Jottrand ordered barricades to be erected and manned in the intermediate level tunnels. Throughout the night a series of heavy explosions took place in the captured positions, blowing the doors off their hinges and sending a concussive blast wave through the confined passageways. In many areas the lighting failed and smoke began to fill the interior, its effect compounded by fumes from ruptured drums of chloride of lime. Sometimes, the Germans fired machine pistols along the tunnels, adding to the mounting terror and confusion. The Belgians began to withdraw towards the command post and when Portsteffen shattered Casemate II in a spectacular flamethrower and pole charge assault they had virtually lost control of the northern part of the defences. Some of the southern casemates and gun positions continued to fire at targets outside but as the morning of 11 May wore on their embrasures came under direct fire from German anti-tank guns and artillery and one by one most of them were silenced. For the garrison it seemed as though the great fortress of Eben Emael was a prison which, sooner or later, would become their tomb.

At 0945 Jottrand consulted his superiors and was informed that they were unable to help. He summoned his Defence Council and, reminding its members of the Articles of War which prohibited the surrender of a fortress unless its defensive means had been destroyed or its garrison was starving, he asked their opinion as to the possibility of continued resistance. Although neither condition existed - seven positions were still in action and there was adequate food available - the unanimous recommendation of the council was for surrender. Jottrand made a last appeal direct to his troops, suggesting a breakout, but was howled down. There remained nothing to do but destroy as many of the remaining positions as possible with demolition charges and negotiate terms with the enemy. At 1215 a bugler accompanying an officer with a white flag sounded Cease Firing at the entry casemate. Shortly after, while negotiations were still in progress, the garrison streamed out and was willingly disarmed. Its losses were comparatively light, amounting to 23 killed and 59 wounded, but its will to fight had been utterly destroyed.

Of the 55 men of Witzig's platoon who had carried out the assault, six had been killed and 15 wounded. After the surrender Witzig marched the remainder into Eben Emael village for a beer, then on to Maastricht to rejoin Assault Force Koch for the journey back to Germany. Several days later Hitler personally decorated the unit's officers with the Knights' Cross; the same award was made to Sergeant Portsteffen as commander of the relief engineer platoon. The remainder of Koch's men were paraded before Kesselring and awarded the Iron Cross; with one exception, who had rendered himself drunk with a rum-filled water bottle during the attack, they were also promoted one grade. Koch, Witzig and Wenzel all took part in the airborne invasion of Crete. In 1942 Koch's love of fast cars led to his death in an autobahn accident. Witzig served on the Russian Front and as a staff officer in France; in 1956 he resumed his military career as an engineering specialist and rose to the rank of colonel. Wenzel was commissioned and was a captain when he became a prisoner of the Americans in Tunisia.

The capture of Fort Eben Emael after only 36 hours fighting was a brilliant coup which dealt a shattering blow to Belgian morale and focussed the Allies' attention yet more firmly on the Low Countries during the critical period that von Rundstedt's armoured divisions were threading their way through the allegedly tank-proof Ardennes. By 20 May the German armour had cut a swathe 40 miles wide across northern France and had reached the Channel coast, trapping the BEF, the French First and Seventh Armies and the Belgian Army in a contracting pocket to the north. On 26 May the Dunkirk evacuation commenced and two days later Belgium capitulated.

In the bitter recriminations following defeat many wild explanations were offered for the debacle at Eben Emael. Sabotage was suggested, and may well have taken place, but not on a scale that would have affected the outcome. One widely circulated story had it that local German chicory growers had tunnelled secretly beneath the fort and detonated a huge cache of explosives, wrecking the interior. The truth was too simple and too painful to reveal until it no longer mattered.

CHAPTER 5

The Road to Beda Fomm

T he letter which Benito Mussolini received in the last week of January 1941 was scarcely phrased in the diplomatic language which might have been expected of Italy's Foreign Minister, Count Galeazzo Ciano. However, since Ciano was also the Duce's son-in-law a degree of plainer language than usual was permissible, the more so since its purpose was to restore some sense of perspective to Mussolini's wildly optimistic view of the war he had so unwisely initiated in North Africa. The letter, in fact, contained little more than a list of reverses sustained by Italian arms since the beginning of December and to which no end was apparently in sight.

'At Sidi Barrani, they spoke of surprise,' wrote Ciano. 'Then, you counted upon Bardia, where Bergonzoli was, the heroic Bergonzoli. Bardia yielded after two hours. Then, you placed your hopes on Tobruk because Pitassi Mannella, the King of Artillerymen, was there. Now, you speak with great faith of the escarpment of Derna. I beg to differ with your dangerous illusion. The trouble is grave, mysterious and deep.'

The causes of that trouble, as any of Mussolini's generals in North Africa could have told him, was that the small British force to which they were opposed was better equipped and trained to fight a mechanised war in the desert than the much larger but mainly infantry army they had at their disposal. Whenever the Italians attempted to fight in the open, they were cut to pieces by the enemy's 7th Armoured Division; and when they attempted to fight behind fixed defences, they were overwhelmed by aggressive British, Australian and Indian infantry, spearheaded by terrifying Matilda tanks which no weapon in the Italian armoury was capable of penetrating. As no third alternative existed, one defeat inevitably followed another.

In May and June the previous summer the sweeping German victories in Western Europe had left the then neutral Mussolini a largely irrelevant spectator. It was not a role he was prepared to tolerate and, ignoring the advice of his Chiefs-of-Staff, who warned him that the Italian armed forces could not be adequately equipped for a modern war before 1942 at the earliest, he declared war on France and Great Britain on 10 June. In so doing he gambled on a short victorious war at the end of which he could 'sit at the conference table as a man who has fought' and so share in the spoils of the conqueror.

At the time the risks probably seemed minimal, for France was on the verge of collapse and Britain could hardly be expected to continue the fight alone. Even if she foolishly attempted to do so, she apparently represented no danger whatever to Italian interests in the Middle East and Mediterranean. After all, there were only 50,000 British and Imperial troops spread across the entire area, of whom some 36,000 were in Egypt, and according to intelligence sources they were seriously short of armour and artillery; superficially, they were in no position to threaten either Marshal Italo Balbo's 250,000-strong Italian army in Libya, or the Duke of Aosta's 200,000 men in East Africa. At sea, it seemed unlikely that the British would wish to contest possession of Mare Nostrum, as Mussolini liked to call the Mediterranean, for while they might oppose seven battleships to Italy's six, in other classes of warship the Royal Italian Navy's strength was overwhelming. That the British had two aircraft carriers in the area was not considered to be very important, as it was planned to support the fleet's operations with the 2,000 land-based aircraft of the Regia Aeronautica, numbers which the over-stretched British could not hope to match. All in all, it seemed that the time for adventurous expansion would never be better, especially as the Spanish dictator, General Francisco Franco, who had received German and Italian assistance during his country's civil war, was understandably sympathetic to the Axis powers and might, in appropriate circumstances, be persuaded to throw in his lot with them by closing the Straits of Gibraltar to British shipping.

Unfortunately for Mussolini, he was more impressed by show than substance. General Sir Archibald Wavell, the British Commander-in-Chief Middle East, was not, and he immediately gave orders for the war to be carried to the enemy. On the night of Italy's declaration of war elements of Major-General O'Moore Creagh's 7th Armoured Division, thoroughly familiar with the desert and trained to the highest pitch of efficiency, crossed the Libyan frontier and began a three-month campaign of harassment which included snapping up convoys, raiding outposts and capturing senior officers. These skirmishes, so one-sided in their results that the British captured large quantities of equipment and inflicted 3,000 casualties at the cost of 150 of their own, demoralised the Italians and led them to abandon the frontier zone and its forts.

On 28 June Marshal Balbo was shot down and killed by his own anti-aircraft gunners as his aircraft approached Tobruk. His replacement, Marshal Rodolfo Graziani, was prone to histrionics but professional enough to recognise that the army he had inherited was quite unsuited to the war it was required to fight. The infantry divisions of which it consisted were dangerously short of mechanical transport and relied on pack animals to make good the shortfall; furthermore, the divisional tank battalions were equipped with L3 tankettes which were little more than tracked machine gun carriers and barely able to hold their own against the British armoured cars.

Early in July, 1st and 2nd Battalions of the Italian 4th Tank Regiment equipped with 70 M11/39 medium tanks reached North Africa and were designated the Libyan Tank Group. In theory, this gave the Italians approximate parity with 7th Armoured Division's cruiser tanks, but as the M11/39 was badly designed, prone to breakdown and only senior officers' tanks were fitted with radios, the formation lacked both mechanical stamina and flexibility, so that in practical terms such a comparison was far from valid. The artillery gave less cause for concern, for although it was partially equipped with vintage weapons dating from World War 1, so too was that of the British; rather more worrying was the lack of a good anti-tank gun. Of the intangibles which would affect his army's performance, Graziani, himself a dedicated Fascist, would have accepted the preferment of political appointees to senior posts as a matter of course, and he would also have accepted as normal the system under which, even in the field, officers lived a privileged existence far removed from that of their troops, despite the corrosive effect this would have on the morale of the latter, especially in adversity.

Although Graziani was aware that Balbo had promised to invade Egypt in July, he was too aware of the dangers involved and had no intention of doing so save under compulsion. While visiting Rome on 8 August he prophetically outlined to Ciano the consequences of such an undertaking: 'The water supply is entirely insufficient. We move towards a defeat which, in the desert, must inevitably develop into a total disaster.' Mussolini swept his reasoned objections aside. Thus far, with the exception of some minor successes in East Africa, the war had brought him none of the glory to which he felt entitled. Whenever the British and Italian navies had clashed at sea, it was the latter who turned for home; and from Libya there had come nothing but reports of petty but irritating reverses. The Duce was losing patience and early the following month Graziani was told that he would be dismissed unless he mounted an offensive immediately.

On 13 September the Italian Tenth Army, commanded by General Berti, crossed the frontier and four days later reached Sidi Barrani. There, some 60 miles short of the main British defence line at Mersa Matruh, it halted and established a front consisting of a chain of fortified camps stretching south-west from the coast onto the escarpment. After this, no further advance was undertaken and the war subsided into patrol activity in which the British soon dominated the wide No-Man's-Land between the two armies. By this time the Luftwaffe had conceded defeat in the Battle of Britain and, with the threat of a German invasion of Great Britain removed, Churchill was able to despatch three sorely-needed armoured regiments, including one equipped with Matildas, around the Cape to Egypt, which they reached in early October.

Events elsewhere now began to have a direct bearing on the war in North Africa. Mussolini returned from his meeting with Hitler at the Brenner Pass ignorant of the latter's decision to occupy Romania. Not to be out-done, he pettishly announced that he would 'occupy' Greece. The Greeks had other ideas and inflicted a series of crushing defeats which forced the Italians to retreat into Albania. Then, during the night of 11-12 November, Swordfish aircraft flying from the carrier HMS *Illustrious* crippled the Italian battle fleet in Taranto harbour. The effect was to alter the naval balance in the Mediterranean, placing Graziani's seaborne communications at risk and enabling the Royal Navy to support the Army's operations in North Africa with the dramatic weight of its gunfire.

Churchill was anxious that military assistance should be despatched to Greece as quickly as possible but to Wavell the defence of Egypt and the Suez Canal, Great Britain's vital link with her Far Eastern possessions, held the higher priority. Tired of waiting for Graziani and Berti to renew their offensive, he decided to mount a major spoiling attack intended to destroy such preparations as they had made and force them onto the defensive. The troops detailed for the task included Creagh's 7th Armoured Division and Major-General Noel Beresford-Peirse's 4th Indian Division, known collectively as the Western Desert Force. In overall command was Lieutenant-General Richard O'Connor, who had commanded the important Peshawar Brigade on the North West Frontier of India between 1936 and 1938 and more recently held the post of Military Governor of Jerusalem.

During World War 1, O'Connor had served on the Italian Front, where he had been awarded the Italian Silver Medal for Valour. He was, therefore, fully aware of the strengths and weaknesses of his former

85

allies. They were, he knew from personal experience, a cultured and intelligent people who would fight hard and courageously for a cause they believed in. The evidence provided by recent events, however, suggested that the Italian armed services as a whole were merely lukewarm in their enthusiasm for the present war and that disillusion with the bombastic Mussolini and his clique was growing steadily. He was also aware that many Italians adopted a pragmatic attitude to defeat and were not inclined to squander their lives after an issue had apparently been decided. It would, nevertheless, be dangerous to take anything for granted, for some elements within Graziani's army, notably the artillery and the Fascist Blackshirt divisions, were likely to prove much tougher opponents than the rest. Above all, O'Connor knew that surprise was the weapon the Italians disliked most and, as Egypt was riddled with informers, his preparations for the spoiling attack, codenamed 'Compass', were made in the greatest secrecy.

During the night of 8-9 December the Western Desert Force penetrated a wide gap in the Italian chain of fortified camps. At dawn the 4th Indian Division, spearheaded by the Matildas of the 7th Royal Tank Regiment (7 RTR), launched a series of attacks which cleared the major camps to the north of the gap. During the first of these the Matildas destroyed a battalion of M11/39s before their crews could man them and, as the remainder of the Libyan Tank Group had already been withdrawn for refitting, the effect of this action was to eliminate the enemy's entire medium tank strength in the forward area. Sidi Barrani was similarly stormed the following day and on 11 December the Italians abandoned their remaining camps south of the gap. Having thus removed the threat to the Canal, Wavell was anxious to despatch 4th Indian Division to East Africa and withdrew it from Western Desert Force, leaving O'Connor to exploit his victory with 7th Armoured Division and 16th British Infantry Brigade until Major-General Iven Mackay's 6th Australian Division could be brought forward. On 12 December Berti's rearguard was overrun at Buq Buq.

In just four days' fighting the Western Desert Force had destroyed four Italian divisions, taken 38,000 prisoners including four generals, and captured or destroyed huge quantities of equipment which included 237 guns and 73 tankettes or medium tanks. O'Connor's men were now seriously outnumbered by their captives but the latter, recognising that their survival in the waterless desert depended upon their co-operation, caused no trouble and in some cases used their own lorries to run a shuttle service between the front and the rapidy expanding prisoner of war compounds.

The Italian invasion of Egypt had turned out very much as Graziani had predicted it would so perhaps it is surprising that, when only 10,000 survivors of Berti's army straggled back into Libya, he should have given way to hysterics. In his signal to Rome he spoke of abandoning the whole of Cyrenaica and withdrawing hundreds of miles to Tripoli. He was, he complained, compelled to 'wage the war of the flea against the elephant', and to his wife he sent his will and a note explaining that 'one cannot break steel armour with finger nails alone'. Mussolini, unable to believe that the truth could possibly be as bad as Graziani suggested, was nonplussed. 'This man has lost his mind or at least his senses,' he commented to Ciano. 'Here is another man with whom I cannot get angry, because I despise him.'

In the meantime Wavell, encouraged by the spectacular success of Operation 'Compass', had decided to expand the spoiling attack into a general offensive. The 6th Australian Division joined O'Connor on 20 December and, with 7 RTR, immediately began training for an assault on the heavily fortified port of Bardia across the Libyan frontier, while 7th Armoured Division isolated the objective to the west. On 1 January 1941 the Western Desert Force was re-designated XIII Corps.

The assault on Bardia commenced on 3 January. The combination of invulnerable Matildas, belligerent Australians and heavy naval gunfire support proved unstoppable and two days later the last areas of resistance were overwhelmed. Of the 45,000-strong garrison some 38,000 were captured, together with 400 guns, 120 tankettes and tanks, and some 700 vehicles; the last were very welcome acquisitions as the strain on XIII Corps' logistic services had become all but insupportable. Among those who managed to evade capture and find temporary sanctuary in Tobruk was the garrison commander, General Bergonzoli, an elderly, unimaginative but brave and popular officer who, unlike many of comparable rank in the Italian service, shared his men's hardships.

Tobruk possessed a better harbour than Bardia and therefore became O'Connor's next objective. It was similarly fortified but when it was assaulted on 21 January its defence lasted barely 24 hours. Another 25,000 demoralised prisoners were taken and this time the booty included 200 guns, 90 armoured vehicles including the last remnant of the Libyan Tank Group, a refrigeration and water distillation plant and 10,000 tons of drinking water. Hardly had the town fallen than the 7th Armoured Division began probing westward towards the Wadi Derna, where the re-formed Tenth Army, now commanded by General Tellera, had established itself in a strong defensive position between the sea and the foothills of the Djebel Akhdar.

The nature of the campaign now underwent a number of subtle but profound changes. The Italian reinforcements shipped hurriedly to North Africa in the wake of the disaster at Bardia included approximately 150 M13/40 medium tanks, the design of which corrected the major fault of the M11/39 in that the 47mm main armament was housed in a turret with all-round traverse instead of in a fixed sponson. Some of these vehicles had been encountered at Tobruk but most of the new arrivals were formed into an ad hoc armoured brigade under the command of Major General Babini. The presence of this formation was not suspected by the British as Graziani and Tellera were reluctant to commit it to offensive operations in its semi-trained state, and instead used it to cover the open southern flank of the Derna position.

In contrast, months of constant hard usage had so reduced the tank strength of Creagh's 7th Armoured Division that the personnel of two of its armoured regiments were sent back to Egypt after handing over their remaining vehicles. This left Creagh with some 80 thin-skinned Vickers light tanks which, being fast and armed with machine guns, were handy for beating up the enemy's convoys but of no use at all in a tank battle. In such a situation the only vehicles which counted were the division's remaining A9, A10 and A13 cruiser tanks, some 40 in number, armed with a 2pdr gun, and the mechanical reliability of some of these was very dubious. The overwhelming advantage in armour, therefore, now rested firmly with the Italians.

The two formations clashed during the morning of 24 January. A 7th Hussar light tank squadron, with three cruisers in support, was counter-attacked by fourteen M13s as it attempted to cut the track between Derna and Mechili. Two cruiser squadrons belonging to 2 RTR were ordered to intervene but before they could do so the Hussars lost several light tanks and one cruiser during a running fight in which they knocked out two M13s in return. It is possible that the Italians might have inflicted greater loss had they not indulged in the flashy but inefficient practice of firing on the move. As it was their success, combined with inexperience, made them over-confident and they drove into an ambush laid by 2 RTR, losing a further seven of their tanks, including one abandoned in running order, before the remainder broke contact and withdrew.

Next day Mackay's Australians assaulted the Wadi Derna line. To their surprise, they made no progress, being met with determined resistance, heavy artillery fire and fierce local counter-attacks. This, perhaps, was the cause of the Duce's restored confidence which Count Ciano so deplored. Certainly the events of these two days provided

O'Connor, Creagh and Mackay with considerable food for thought and to break the apparent impasse 7 RTR's Matildas, refitting in Tobruk, were ordered forward.

Before they could arrive, the course of this extraordinary campaign again changed direction. The loss of its tactical airfields near Tobruk meant that the Regia Aeronautica had withdrawn from Cyrenaica to Tripolitania and, because of the distance involved, it was no longer able to provide Tellera with the close support the Italian army had once enjoyed. Tellera, in fact, was even more concerned by the presence of 7th Armoured Division at Mechili and, as the 11th Hussars' armoured cars were already operating in the Djebel Akhdar, he was especially worried that this would develop into an encirclement through the mountain massif. To avoid this he asked Graziani's permission to withdraw, a decision which in effect would mean abandoning all that remained of Cyrenaica since neither Benghazi nor anywhere else short of the Tripolitanian border offered a tenable defensive position. Graziani, who had recently moved his own HQ from Cyrene to Tripoli, had also been informed by his agents that the British 2nd Armoured Division had begun arriving in Egypt and that its leading elements would reach the front some time in February. In the circumstances, therefore, he sanctioned Tellera's withdrawal, hoping thereby to keep his army in being and at the same time leave his opponents exposed at the end of a long and difficult line of communications.

The British, too, were examining their own position. In the eyes of the War Cabinet, now that the immediate threat to Egypt had been removed, aid to Greece held a higher priority than the fighting in Libya. The Greeks, however, politely declined the offer for the moment, commenting that the size of the proposed force was inadequate to counter the probable German intervention which its despatch from Egypt was likely to provoke. Indeed, as General Papagos, the Greek Commander-in-Chief, commented with irrefutable common sense, it would be of greater benefit to all concerned if the British concluded the business in hand rather than embarking on a fresh venture which would merely disperse their painfully gathered resources. To those on the spot there was another good reason why O'Connor should continue his advance, for it was considered essential that the RAF should establish bases in the Benghazi Bulge to counter Luftwaffe squadrons which Hitler had already despatched to assist his battered ally and which, flying from airfields in Sicily, had begun attacking Malta and British shipping in the central Mediterranean. It was decided, therefore, that O'Connor should be allowed to capture Benghazi and complete the occupation of Cyrenaica, thus forming a wide buffer zone between Egypt and the remaining Italian troops in North Africa.

Tellera commenced his retreat during the night of 28-29 January. The local Arab population, between whom and the Italians little love was lost, quickly passed on the news but it was the withdrawal of the Babini Armoured Brigade to the north-west that told O'Connor all he needed to know, namely that it would be providing the rearguard while Tellera's army withdrew round the Benghazi Bulge on the coast road; furthermore since Benghazi itself was untenable, Tellera was unlikely to halt before he reached Tripolitania.

Armed with this knowledge, O'Connor had a choice of alternatives to consider. The first involved a direct pursuit along the coast road, during which his troops would enjoy the benefits of support by the Royal Navy and a reasonable supply line. Against this, the narrow strip of land between the mountains of the Djebel Akhdar and the sea inhib-

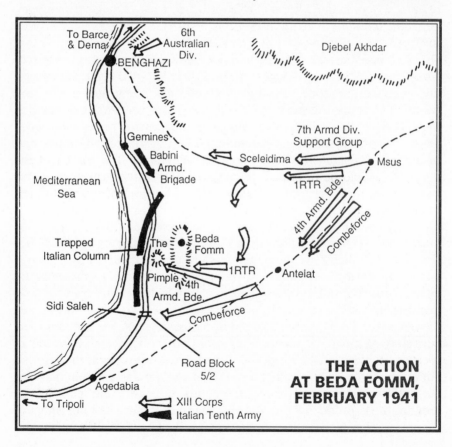

THE ACTION AT BEDA FOMM, FEBRUARY 1941

ited deployment and provided the enemy with the opportunity of fighting a series of delaying actions. Such a course might be slow and sure, but there was the risk of high casualties and there would be no decisive result at the end of it as Tellera's army would reach Tripolitania more or less intact.

The second contained so many risks that a less determined commander would have rejected it out of hand, but it did offer a reasonable chance to entrap and destroy the Italian Tenth Army as it withdrew from Benghazi. South of the Djebel Akhdar a desert track ran across the base of the Benghazi Bulge from Mechili to Msus and thence to the coast, a distance of approximately 150 miles. The terrain was unknown and unmapped, a supply of water could not be guaranteed, and the going was said to be so bad that the Italians never used the route. Conversely, if a mechanised force was passed along the track a roadblock could be established across the path of the retreating enemy. Yet even if this succeeded, the risk existed that the blocking force itself might be trapped between the Tenth Army and reinforcements which Tellera might bring forward from Tripolitania.

Having weighed all these factors in the balance, and taken into account the poor mechanical state to which 7th Armoured Division's vehicles had been reduced, together with the enemy's superior tank strength, O'Connor decided to combine the two alternatives by sending the 6th Australian Division to follow up the Tenth Army's withdrawal along the coast road and despatching the 7th Armoured Division across the desert to establish a block south of Benghazi. The timing of the operation would be of critical importance, for the window of opportunity would only remain open for a matter of hours. If Creagh's division reached the coast too early the enemy would have ample time in which to prepare effective counter-measures, but if it was seriously delayed for any reason the Italians might have passed through the ambush site. The progress of Tellera's army was regularly reported by air reconnaissance and while this assisted O'Connor in making his plans, the one factor for which he could not legislate was the going on the desert track and its possible effect on progress.

Even if the movement went according to plan, the outnumbered and under-strength 7th Armoured Division would become involved in severe and protracted fighting with only limited resources at its disposal. On paper, the outcome was far from clear. O'Connor, however, believed that the combination of surprise, his troops' will to win and poor Italian morale would produce a decisive result and in this he had not only the support of his divisional commanders, but also of Wavell, who had flown up to the forward area.

Early on the morning of 4 February the 7th Armoured Division began moving off along the track from Mechili to Msus. At this period in its history the division retained the same basic organisation with which it had begun the campaign, namely two armoured brigades, a support group with an artillery regiment and two motorised infantry battalions, and divisional troops including armoured car and anti-tank units and supporting services. By now only the 4th Armoured Brigade, commanded by Brigadier J. A. L. Caunter, retained three armoured regiments, these being the 3rd and 7th Hussars and 2nd Royal Tank Regiment. The 7th Armoured Brigade contained only the 1st Royal Tank Regiment, which Creagh designated as divisional reserve. In theory, each armoured regiment consisted of three squadrons, at least one of which was equipped with cruiser tanks, but all were seriously understrength; 2 RTR, the strongest regiment in the division, possessed two cruiser squadrons with a total of 19 tanks. Altogether, the maximum number of tanks which Creagh could hope to pit against the enemy's 100 mediums amounted to a mere 32 cruisers and 50 lights.

The Support Group contained the 4th Royal Horse Artillery (4 RHA), equipped with 25pdr gun-howitzers, the 1st Battalion King's Royal Rifle Corps and 2nd Battalion Rifle Brigade. These motor battalions were somewhat smaller than conventional infantry units but possessed greater firepower, and their organisation consisted of three rifle companies and a support company with heavy weapons.

It had been discovered early in the war that towing the small anti-tank guns of the day across the desert caused extensive damage to the weapons, and a solution to the problem had been found by mounting them on 15cwt lorries, the idea being that they would be dismounted in action; in practice, they seldom were. The arrangement was known as a portee and 7th Armoured Division possessed two regiments so equipped, their batteries being allocated as required by the operation in hand. The first, 3rd Royal Horse Artillery (3 RHA), was armed with the standard 2pdr anti-tank gun. The second, 106th Royal Horse Artillery (Lancashire Yeomanry) (106 RHA), a Territorial unit, had a combined anti-tank/anti-aircraft role, two batteries being armed with the Bofors 37mm anti-tank gun, the performance of which was only marginally inferior to that of the 2pdr, and two with captured 20mm Breda anti-aircraft guns.

Leading the advance was the divisional armoured car regiment, the 11th Hussars, commanded by Lieutenant-Colonel John Combe. The 11th, equipped with vintage Rolls-Royce armoured cars, had become the phantoms of the desert and their wide-ranging operations had made them a thorn in the Italian side since the first day of the war. There was always a heavy demand for their services and Combe had been forced to detach two of his squadrons, A to operate with the Support Group and B with the Australians. In their place he was given a squadron of the recently arrived King's Dragoon Guards and No 2 Armoured Car Company, an experienced RAF unit brought forward from Palestine, equipped respectively with Marmon-Herrington and Fordson armoured cars.

The first part of the route from Mechili traversed a vast boulder field made up of loose slab rock. This extended for approximately 20 miles and provided the armoured car drivers with some of the worst going in their wide experience. Nor did the absence of maps help, since troop leaders were unable to report their positions with any degree of accuracy. However, once the boulder field ended the cars were able to report much better going and accelerated towards Msus.

For the main body of the division, led by 4th Armoured Brigade with the artillery and 2nd Rifle Brigade behind, progress through the boulder field was a slow-motion nightmare. A feature of the light tanks' performance was a tendency to pitch even on the best going, caused by the comparatively short length of track in contact with the ground. On bad going such as this the movement was aggravated by constant violent jerks for which the vehicle commander in his sling seat could not always allow, the result being an accumulation of bruises and contusions to the shins, hips, elbows, forearms, chin and face. Fuel consumption rose dramatically and radiators began to boil. These last developments caused serious concern not only because the supply lorries were falling behind but also because the continuous crashing, banging and shaking was jostling the tin petrol and water containers so badly that the seams of many split and their precious contents drained away.

During the day Creagh received an air reconnaissance report suggesting that the Italians had already started to pull out of Benghazi. He therefore made two decisions, subsequently approved by O'Connor, which were to have a critical effect on the success of the operation. The first was that the division's axis of advance, previously designated as westwards from Msus, would now follow a south-westerly direction in order to increase to chances of interception. The second, induced by the 11th Hussars' reports of better going ahead, was to form a flying column with wheeled vehicles, which would make better time than the tanks, and use this to establish and hold a roadblock until the armoured regiments arrived. The flying column, commanded by Colonel Combe and therefore known as Combeforce, would consist of the 11th Hussars, 2nd Rifle Brigade, 106 RHA, C Battery 4 RHA with 160 rounds per gun, and an anti-aircraft detachment.

Assembling Combeforce and getting it on its way became the responsibility of Brigadier Caunter. This was more easily said than done, for most of the vehicles were far back down the divisional column and at its simplest the task involved moving over 140 lorries, towed guns, portees and tracked carriers along the atrocious track past the now stationary tanks of 4th Armoured Brigade, then forming them in the correct order of march. There were also numerous logistic and administrative complications caused by the change of plan. For example, 4 RHA lorries carrying reserve ammunition had to dump this and reload with petrol; simultaneously, separate radio communications had to be established for the component elements of Combeforce so that the divisional command net could function unhindered. After what seemed like a deliberately planned night of chaos the last units in the flying column moved off at 0800 on 5 February. Even then, an atmosphere of black farce persisted when the tanks caught up with the lumbering lorries and for a while were actually held back by them. Nevertheless, once the boulder field was left behind a gap quickly opened and Combeforce disappeared somewhere beyond its own dust cloud.

Contact with 11th Hussars was established near Msus and Combeforce, now complete, headed for Antelat, led by its armoured cars. The Regia Aeronautica had sown part of the track with air-dropped mines, known as 'thermos bombs' because of their appearance, and some care had to be taken in avoiding these as they exploded on contact. On two occasions CR42 Falco biplane fighters strafed the column briefly without result. After their appearance it had to be assumed that the Italian Tenth Army had been alerted to the presence of the force, but since it was comparatively small and lacked tanks Tellera evidently did not attach much importance to it. Creagh came through on the radio to emphasise that the need for speed held priority over every other consideration. Halts were therefore infrequent and of short duration. Combe was encouraged to find Antelat unoccupied and directed his cars to head for the coast road near Sidi Saleh. At this point the Rifle Brigade's tracked carriers, which had experienced difficulty keeping up, ran out of fuel one by one and had to be left behind. The bulk of the battalion, however, was travelling aboard its lorries, only one of which failed to complete the journey.

The Eleventh's C Squadron, commanded by Major Payne Gall-wey, reached the coast road shortly after noon. As the rest of the regiment came in Combe directed the King's Dragoon Guards squadron, under Major A. P. C. Crossley, to the south, where it could provide advance warning of any attempted intervention from the direction of Tripolitania. The remainder of Combeforce was brought in by Lieutenant-Colonel J. C. Campbell, the commander of 4 RHA and originator of the small all-arms 'Jock Columns' which had so harried the Italians during their invasion of Egypt.

At this point the road passed through an area of scrub-covered, gently rolling desert; to the west lay a parallel sandy track, then a belt of dunes with the sea beyond. Under the direction of its commanding officer, Lieutenant-Colonel J. M. L. Renton, the Rifle Brigade began to dig in with A Company on and to the east of the road, and the remaining companies adopting a position of all-round defence some way to the rear. Eight of 106 RHA's nine anti-tank guns were dispersed among them with the portees hull-down in defiladed positions, the ninth being dismounted, dismantled and carried to a position in the sandhills; the location of all the regiment's 20mm Breda guns is uncertain, although one is known to have been positioned, hull-down, on either side of the main road. Suitable fire positions were also adopted by the armoured cars and C Battery 4 RHA established its gun line some way to the south. Everything had been done to make the roadblock secure, but in the final analysis just one infantry battalion, two armoured car squadrons and some 20 artillery weapons of various types, a total of less than 2,000 men, were available to hold a front of three-and-a-half miles against an army.

For a short while doubts may have existed as to whether the Italians had already escaped. Yet, whatever it was that the RAF had reported leaving Benghazi the previous day it was not the main body of Tenth Army, for at approximately 1430 a large convoy was sighted approaching Combeforce from the north. As soon as the range had closed suffiently the head of this was engaged by the Rifle Brigade, the armoured cars and the artillery. Lance-Bombardier Larry McDermott, serving as a gun-layer on one of 106 RHA's 20mm Breda portees, retained a vivid impression of lorries bursting into flames, reversing flat out into each other or becoming bogged in the soft sand as they left the metalled highway in frantic attempts to flee.

The Italians seemed to be afflicted by a panic paralysis. They belonged to administrative units that were leading the withdrawal, escorted by a battalion of Bersaglieri, and they had believed themselves to be well beyond the reach of the enemy. Now, inexplicably, they found themselves being ambushed in strength some 70 miles south of Benghazi, just when they felt they had reached safety. Despite their ample resources they seemed incapable of co-ordinating a response which would turn the British flank and instead mounted a series of weak infantry attacks, all of which were easily contained. Latterly, these were made west of the road, causing Renton to extend his front by bringing up B Company to hold the ground between the road and the track. In the meantime, the length of the stalled column was growing by the minute. A handful of motorcyclists, irritated by the delay, threaded their way through the tangle and roared straight down the highway into the roadblock where, to their surprise, they were made prisoner.

For the moment, all seemed to be going according to plan. Combe had already informed Creagh that the trap had been sprung and at approximately 1630 the latter asked him where Caunter's 4th Armoured Brigade could best help. Combe suggested that the tanks should engage the flank of the ever-lengthening enemy column from a series of parallel ridges east of the road at Beda Fomm, some miles to the north of the roadblock. By now 4th Armoured Brigade was passing through Antelat and the conversation was intercepted by its HQ radio operators. Caunter immediately ordered the 7th Hussars and A Squadron 2 RTR, the latter equipped with six A13 cruisers capable of a maximum speed of 30mph, to head for the area while the rest of the brigade followed on and 3rd Hussars screened tracks to the north and north-west of Antelat.

At approximately 1700 the 7th Hussars reached Beda Fomm itself, a windmill on high ground, from which the trapped enemy column could be seen stretching away in both directions. The light tanks of the regiment's B and C Squadrons closed in to savage the Italians with their machine guns, being joined at about 1750 by 2 RTR's fast cruiser squadron. The light was fading fast but for a while it was possible to continue the engagement by the flames from a burning petrol tanker.

Before the tanks withdrew into leaguer for the night two M13s were captured by the unusual technique of boarding. A cruiser commanded by Lieutenant Plough of 2 RTR came across them broadside-on as it reached the end of a line of shot-up transport. They were firing at distant targets and were completely oblivious of Plough's presence, so that at pointblank range they were the most helpless of sitting ducks. At this period, however, the desert war was still being fought with a degree of chivalry and Plough simply told his operator, Trooper Eldred Hughes, to get the crews out. Clambering over the engine decks of both, Hughes rapped on the turret hatches with his revolver and, when these were opened, made his intentions clear. One by one the Italians emerged,

OPENING THE IRON GATE

Above: Despite the impression given by this photograph, the Romanian Army was inexperienced, badly led and under-equipped. *Imperial War Museum IWM*

Right: Romanian signallers tap into the civilian telephone system. Careless use of this means told Picht everything he needed to know. *IWM*

YOUNG MISTER ROMMEL

Above: Typical mountain strongpoint on the Isonzo Front.
Bildarchiv d. Ost Nationalbiblioth

Left: Mountain troops demonstrate the method of carrying a medium machine gun. No 1 (centre) carries the weapon itself; No 2 (right) carries the sledge mounting; No 3 (left) carries four boxed ammunition belts.
Bildarchiv d. Ost Nationalbiblioth

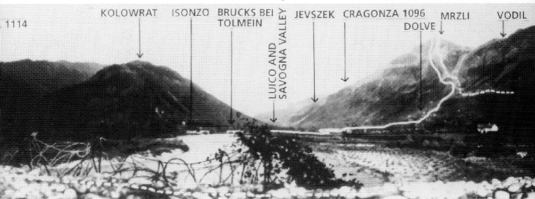

| 1114 | KOLOWRAT | ISONZO | BRUCKS BEI TOLMEIN | LUICO AND SAVOGNA VALLEY | JEVSZEK | CRAGONZA 1096 | DOLVE | MRZLI | VODIL |

Top: The peak of Monte Matajur (centre) with Monte Mrzli to its left. Luico lies in the entrance to the valley on the extreme left. Seen from the direction of Karfreit. *Bildarchiv d. Ost Nationalbiblioth*

Above: The Tolmino sector of the Isonzo Front showing the area in which the Rommel Detachment was employed. *Heeresgeschichtlichen Museums.*

POLISH EAGLE RUSSIAN BEAR
Below: Polish Model T Ford light armoured cars. *Janusz Magnuski*

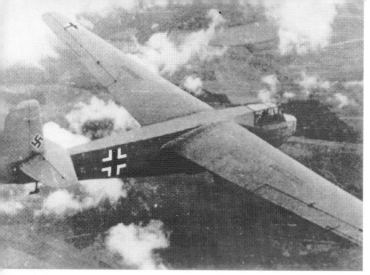

HOLLAND AND BELGIUM

Left: The DFS 230 glider, used to land troops within the defences on Fort Eben Emael. *IWM*

Left: An aerial view of Fort Eben Emael (left) showing the Albert Canal and part of Lanaye Lock. *Bundesarchiv*

Below left: Eben Emael. The effect of hollow charges on the embrasures of Mi-North. The cupola in the background was unseated but not penetrated. *Bundesarchiv*

Below: Eben Emael. Army and Waffen SS officers examine the results of Sergeant

Portsteffen's flamethrower and polecharge attack on Casemate II. *Bundesarchiv*

Right: The Ju 52 was the mainstay of the German airborne forces. Large numbers were lost during the attempt to lay an 'airborne carpet' across Fortress Holland. This example came to grief while attempting a forced landing on the highway north of Amsterdam. *Rijksinstituut voor Oorlogsdocumentatie (RIOD)*

Right: German paratroopers taking up positions around the Moerdijk bridges. *RIOD*

Below Right: A PzKw III of 9th Panzer Division breaks through to the paratroopers at Moerdijk. *RIOD*

THE ROAD TO BEDA FOMM

Left: Cruiser Tank A10. By the time they reached Beda Fomm most of 7th Armoured Division's tanks were in poor mechanical condition. *IWM*

Left: A Bofors 37mm portee anti-tank gun of the type used by 106 RHA at Sidi Saleh. *IWM*

Left: Beda Fomm. Some of the Italian M13 tanks captured during the battle; many had been abandoned in running order. *IWM*

Right: Beda Fomm. Italian guns abandoned on The Pimple. *IWM*

JITRA AND SLIM RIVER

Right: The 2nd Argyll & Sutherland Highlanders was the only battalion to have received realistic jungle training prior to the Japanese invasion of Malaya. In the background is one of the unit's Lanchester armoured cars. *IWM*

Right: The bulk of Malaya's garrison consisted of Indian troops, many of whom were only partially trained. *IWM*

Left: The Japanese Type 97 Medium Tank was obsolete by Western standards but in Malaya its presence was decisive against an enemy who had no tanks at all. *RAC Tank Museum*

Left: The Japanese Type 95 Light Tank. It performed the role of road-runner after the initial penetration at Slim River, thereby preventing the shattered 12th Brigade from conducting an orderly withdrawal. *RAC Tank Museum*

HILL 309 AND THE BRIDGE AT 637436
Left: The Souleuvre bridge. Though insignificant in itself, its acquisition was to play a vital part in the conduct of subsequent operations.
Household Cavalry Museum

Above: The recently disembarked C Squadron 2nd Household Cavalry Regiment prepares for action at Graye-sur-Mer, Normandy. The officer with folded arms is Lieutenant D. B. Powle, who captured the Souleuvre bridge. Some of the cars in the background are fitted with the Littlejohn adapter, which improved the armour-piercing performance of their 2pdr guns. *Household Cavalry Museum*

Below: Churchills of 6th Guards Tank Brigade lift infantry forward during the fighting in Normandy. *IWM*

MEIKTILA
Above: Shermans of Probyn's Horse approaching Kaing during the drive on Meiktila. *IWM*

Below: Indian infantry assault the blazing village of Seywa as they close in on Meiktila. *IWM*

Above: British troops advance warily through the streets of Meiktila. The Japanese fought to the death, many digging themselves into the foundations of buildings. *IWM*

Below: Stuarts of 7th Light Cavalry, part of Stilettocol, drive past the site of an earlier ambush on the road to Mandalay. *IWM*

LUDENDORFF BRIDGE

Left: An air reconnaissance photograph of the Ludendorff bridge the day after its capture. The crater blown by Friesenhahn in the western approach ramp is clearly visible. *IWM*

Left: German prisoners and light traffic cross the bridge at Remagen in opposite directions shortly after its capture. Temporary decking has been installed over the crater. *US Army Military History Institute (USAMHI)*

Left: Tanks and infantry stream across the bridge to consolidate the American's hold on the east bank of the Rhine. *USAMHI*

Above: The eastern end of the Ludendorff bridge. The left-hand tower was damaged by tank gunfire while the bridge was being stormed. *USAMHI*

Below: Friesenhahn's secondary demolition charge failed to destroy the bridge, although it caused serious damage to several of its critical members. Increased stresses resulted in the failure of these on 17 March and the whole structure collapsed into the river. *IWM*

THE INCHON LANDINGS
Opposite page, top: Tank dozer on Wolmi-do Island at the entrance to Inchon harbour. Those North Koreans who refused to surrender were walled up inside their bunkers. *USAMHI*

Opposite page, centre: Amtracs and LSTs close on Red Beach during the Inchon landings. *USAMHI*

Opposite page, bottom: Prisoners pass the wrecks of two T34s, knocked out during an abortive North Korean counter-attack along the Seoul-Inchon highway. *USAMHI*

IA DRANG VALLEY CAMPAIGN
Above: 1st Cavalry Division troopers saddle up prior to lift-off from their base camp. *USAMHI*

Below: A Chinook helicopter hovers above a recently cleared landing zone with an M102 105mm howitzer and ready-use ammunition. *USAMHI*

Above: A battery of M101 105mm howitzers firing in support of 1st Cavalry Division operations. *USAMHI*

Below: Bombs cascade from the belly of a Boeing B-52 Stratofortress. The codename for tactical strikes by these huge aircraft, each of which carried a 60,000lb bombload, was "Arc Light". *US Air Force*

encouraged by machine gun bursts fired over their heads by Plough's gunner, and were disarmed. While marching them back Hughes encountered a senior officer in a 'beautiful powder-blue uniform with gold braid everywhere', who was brusquely told to 'fall in' and did so under protest. Hughes was to be awarded the Distinguished Conduct Medal, although the dramatic events of the next 36 hours were to drive the episode temporarily from his mind.

The night was one of heavy rain and high winds during which both sides considered their situation. The Italian column was now 11 miles long and Tellera was aware that he was confronted by something far more serious than a simple roadblock. He was also acutely conscious that the Australians would enter Benghazi the following day and that it was only a matter of time before they closed in on his rear. It was essential, therefore, that the Tenth Army should break out of the trap at the earliest possible moment.

The task was entrusted to General Bergonzoli, who had left Tobruk before it was stormed the previous month. While artillery and infantry began concentrating for the breakout the Babini Armoured Brigade, now under the command of Major-General Cona, began moving forward along the column from its position in the rearguard. What Bergonzoli envisaged was that the Italian armour, under cover of massed artillery fire, would attack eastwards in the area of a low hill subsequently known as The Pimple, break through 4th Armoured Brigade and then swing south to overrun Combeforce, already pinned down by holding attacks, from the flank and rear. The Tenth Army would then resume its march before the Australians could come within striking distance. The plan was sound enough and, provided it was executed in accordance with established military principles, no logical reason existed why it should not have worked.

Creagh's orders for the following day were simple. From Msus the rump of the Support Group and 1 RTR would head for Sceleidima and thence towards to the coast road where they would fall on the enemy's rear; the 4th Armoured Brigade at Beda Fomm was to maintain its grip on the flank of the Italian column; and Combeforce was to hold its ground at all costs. In the event, the fighting on 6 February took the form of two separate but related battles, fought around the roadblock at Sidi Saleh and east of the road at Beda Fomm.

Combeforce had a quiet night during which several hundred Italians wandered into its lines and gave themselves up. At length their numbers were such that a prisoner of war compound had to be set up some way to the east of C Battery's gun position. More were escaping as individuals and in small parties past the seaward flank and to counter any possible threat from this direction Renton extended his front still further by positioning his Support Company between the track and the shore. Many of these escapees were picked up by the King's Dragoon Guards squadron to the south, which reported some opposition from that direction but nothing amounting to a serious threat; its principal worry, in fact, was the constant drain on its radio batteries. Combeforce as a whole was beginning to suffer from shortages of food, water, fuel and ammunition because its supply lorries had not arrived. C Battery 4 RHA, down to 30 rounds per gun, requested re-supply as a matter of urgency but was told to make the best of what it had got.

At first light the growing thunder of battle to the north told Combe that 4th Armoured Brigade was heavily engaged, although his own troops were not attacked until approximately 1000 when three tanks began probing the position to the west of the road. Two were knocked out by portees and the third withdrew. Some 40 minutes later three columns, each led by a strong force of infantry and containing numerous vehicles, were spotted approaching the position along the road, the track and near the dunes. The last two were halted as soon as they came within range and promptly indicated their willingness to sur- render. The road column, however, included tanks and guns and for a while seemed prepared to make a fight of it. Having evidently identified 106 RHA's anti-tank guns as being a major source of their troubles, the Italians brought forward a 75mm field gun to engage one over open sights. The ensuing duel, known to have been fought at exactly 1,000 metres as both weapons were positioned beside kilometre stones, was short and sharp; no damage was sustained by the portee and the Italian crew headed for cover when two 37mm holes suddenly appeared in their gunshield. After an hour the third column, too, surrendered.

Throughout the day the position remained under shellfire. The Rifle Brigade had always conducted itself with a certain style and the commander of the battalion's HQ Company, having little else to do, decided to erect its white mess marquee several hundred yards behind C Company, which remained in reserve. There the tent performed a quite different function from that intended, attracting the attention of the Ital- ian gunners and in so doing diverting them from more worthwhile tar- gets. As the afternoon wore on the enemy mounted three of four more attacks, similar to those of the morning, but all were easily contained. By dusk Combeforce had several thousand prisoners on its hands, including a general and his staff, and was hard pressed to find sufficient men to guard them.

The Italians decided to continue their breakout efforts under cover of darkness. A major attack, spearheaded by tanks, was launched at 2100. For some reason mines laid on the road the previous night had been lifted and the attackers were able to come to such close quarters that C Battery's 25pdrs were compelled to cease firing. The crew of a 37mm portee covering the road were killed or wounded when a shell-burst penetrated the gunshield. A handful of tanks and other vehicles roared past and managed to break right through the roadblock. The infantry who had accompanied them, some 500 in number, were not so fortunate as the penetration was quickly sealed off and, now isolated, they were soon rounded up by Renton's riflemen.

Mines were hastily laid to prevent a repetition of the occurrence. To the surprise of the defenders, Lieutenant Kernan of 106 RHA appeared out of the darkness with two more 37mm portees, bringing the total available to 11. Shortly after, a further enemy attack along the road foundered when the leading vehicle struck a mine, another 150 prisoners being added to the growing multitude. A final attack, put in on the seaward side of the road about midnight, was broken up, its course being described by Major R. S. Burton, commander of 1st Anti-Tank Battery 106 RHA:

'Lieutenant K. Pinnington did extremely well with the guns he commanded and knocked out many vehicles and guns at extremely close range. The Italian attempt to break through was foolishly carried out; they appeared to be completely unable to avoid the herd instinct and large groups of bunched vehicles afforded good targets in the moonlight.'

To the north, Bergonzoli had selected The Pimple as the point for his attack because, having seen the enemy armour apparently withdrawing eastward from this area the previous evening, he concluded that it would be used in direct support of the roadblock at Sidi Saleh. In fact, the British tanks had merely pulled back into their night leaguers and it was in the sector of The Pimple that Caunter was strongest, although the term was relative in the extreme. What 4th Armoured Brigade's strength actually amounted to was two cruisers and three light tanks in Brigade HQ; 3rd Hussars with seven cruisers belonging to 2 RTR (these regiments having exchanged their B Squadrons at the beginning of the campaign), six lights of its own and one troop of 2pdr portees manned by 3 RHA; 7th Hussars with one cruiser and 29 lights; 2 RTR with 12 cruisers and eight lights, the latter belonging to 3rd Hussars; and F Battery 4 RHA with 25pdrs. When dawn revealed that the Italian column was even longer than it had been the night before, Caunter despatched 7th

Hussars northwards to locate and harry its rear while 3rd Hussars, detaching a squadron to guard the brigade's right rear, attacked the centre, leaving 2 RTR alone to meet the attack on The Pimple. No immediate reserve existed, for although Creagh had ordered 1 RTR, with 10 cruisers and eight lights, to move south from Sceleidima to Antelat, the regiment had no direct contact with Caunter and its progress was delayed by a sandstorm.

The Italian attack commenced shortly after 0830 and would have stood a reasonable chance of success had adequate artillery support been provided and the tanks not been committed piecemeal in comparatively small numbers as they arrived from the north. The M13 crews showed more determination to come to grips than at any time previously, but were hampered by the absence of radios in all but company commanders' tanks so that once an attack was launched it was difficult to control. Failure to observe the elementary principles of fire and movement was further aggravated by the practice of shooting on the move, which was useless against the small and constantly shifting targets presented by the turrets of the hull-down British cruisers.

The two cruiser squadrons of 2 RTR, commanded by Lieutenant-Colonel A. C. Harcourt, were in an entirely different class. Their gunnery was steady, controlled and accurate, tanks changing their fire positions regularly as part of the normal battle drill and in so doing giving the Italians the impression that their numbers were greater than they were. As each attack rolled in six, eight or 10 M13s were killed. At one point pressure forced the regiment off The Pimple and back to the next ridge, known as The Mosque because it was surmounted by a small tomb. Covered by the fire of A Squadron under Major Gerald Strong, C Squadron, commanded by Major James Richardson, executed a fast-moving counter-attack into the enemy's flank and rear and recaptured the feature, the combined efforts of both squadrons destroying a further 18 enemy tanks. Harcourt then despatched A Squadron, together with the light tanks of B Squadron 3rd Hussars, in pursuit of a portion of the trapped column which had begun to move south while the battle was in progress. During a five-mile running fight 10 more M13s were destroyed and numerous lorries wrecked or set ablaze, some 350 survivors being rounded up by the Hussars.

A Squadron returned to The Pimple at 1115. By now the Italian artillery was at last making its presence felt, plastering the feature with shellfire and obtaining direct hits on four of C Squadron's cruisers. Simultaneously, the continuous firing had all but emptied the tanks' ammunition bins; Plough, for example, had reached Beda Fomm with

112 rounds of 2pdr aboard and was now down to his last two, both of which had to be punched into an M13 at 600 yards as a matter of urgent necessity. Fortunately, Harcourt was aware of the situation. Once the most immediate threat had been dealt with he combined both squadrons under Richardson and ordered them back to The Mosque, where he had arranged for ammunition lorries to be waiting in the lee of the ridge. During the withdrawal three cruisers had to be abandoned, two with battle damage and one with a seized engine.

That 2 RTR were granted a pause for replenishment was largely due to the efforts of the 3rd and 7th Hussars to the north. Both regiments launched attacks against the flank of the column and in the poor visibility the Italians were uncertain whether their assailants were equipped with lights or cruisers. Unwilling to take the chance, local commanders diverted M13s destined for the battle around The Pimple to deal with the threat. The 3rd Hussars were driven back when 24 of the Italian mediums counter-attacked from the centre of the column. B Squadron 2 RTR claimed three but lost one of its cruisers when a track was shot away; the crew of this vehicle became the only prisoners taken by the Italians at Beda Fomm, although their captivity was brief. Despite its complete lack of armour, D Battery 3 RHA's attached 2pdr portee troop also waded into the battle and destroyed two M13s. The 7th Hussars' lights found the rear of the column and began snarling round it like a pack of hounds. A Morris armoured car, captured from 11th Hussars the previous July, attempted to escape but was rammed to destruction by the 7th's only cruiser; later the tank broke a track and its crew spent 25 nerve-racking minutes repairing it within view of the enemy, less than 2,000 yards distant.

By 1415, 2 RTR had completed its replenishment and, as The Pimple was now occupied by Italian artillery, took up a position one mile to the south of the feature. At 1530 intense pressure caused the composite squadron to retire still further to the south but, shortly after 1600, F Battery silenced the guns on The Pimple and it was able to return, eliminating several more enemy tanks at the cost of one of its own.

In the meantime Creagh had finally agreed to Caunter's repeated requests for 1 RTR to be despatched to the assistance of the hard-pressed 4th Armoured Brigade. The regiment, commanded by Lieutenant-Colonel G. J. N. Culverwell, had reached Antelat but was temporarily halted while it replenished its fuel. When it began moving Culverwell was handicapped by the lack of a direct radio link with Caunter. In fact, the only possible channel of communication between the two was through Creagh and HQ 7th Armoured Brigade. Consequently Culverwell had no knowledge of local conditions and was worried by the possibility of engaging friendly troops. Nevertheless, 1 RTR advanced towards the sound of the guns and entered the battle on 3rd Hussars' sector shortly after 1600. It drove off the Italian counter-attack force, destroying two M13s, then proceeded to shoot up the now defenceless column until dusk. The real effect of the regiment's arrival, however, was on the enemy's morale. Until then the Italians had believed that they were making progress, albeit at a high price, yet now the British were committing fresh troops to the battle and seemingly had ample reserves in hand. Brittle hopes raised at the cost of so much blood and effort were suddenly shattered.

As the light began to fade 2 RTR, its ammunition again all but expended and now reduced to a mere handful, observed the force of M13s recently engaged by Culverwell's squadrons moving down the column to the west of the road. Caunter had already requested that 1 RTR be sent south to the area of The Pimple but because of the communication difficulties outlined above the regiment did not arrive before nightfall. 2 RTR, hopelessly outnumbered, withdrew under cover of a smokescreen to replenish near The Mosque. The Italian tanks, however, were not seeking a fight and in any event the onset of darkness would have made one impossible.

O'Connor had been present at Creagh's HQ throughout the day, anxiously watching the progress of the battle. The Support Group, consisting only of the 1st Battalion King's Royal Rifle Corps and a few guns, reported the capture of Sceleidima and was ordered to close in on the enemy rear next day. Mackay, whose Australians, much to their bewilderment, had entered Benghazi through cheering crowds, was ordered to send forward two infantry battalions in lorries and do likewise.

The Tenth Army's column now presented a spectacle of mechanical carnage. Everywhere there were wrecked or burning lorries, knocked out tanks and smashed artillery weapons, lying thickest in the area of The Pimple, and amidst the wreckage lay the dead and injured, including the mortally wounded General Tellera. Bergonzoli, now in command, decided that he would concentrate his 30 remaining tanks as the spearhead of an attack which, supported by artillery, would smash its way through the roadblock at Sidi Saleh at dawn. The day's fighting had won the Italians a little elbow room in the area of The Pimple and past this during the night ground long lines of vehicles, some on the road, others on the track to the west.

Combe, informed of the danger, could only warn his men what to expect. Little had happened since the last breakout attempt had been foiled at midnight but at about 0400 on 7 February two tanks approached an isolated platoon of the Rifle Brigade near the sand dunes. The platoon already had its hands full guarding over 400 prisoners. The Italians, scenting freedom, stampeded towards the tanks and swarmed over them, with Platoon Sergeant Major Jarvis and Rifleman O'Brien in hot pursuit. Accounts vary slightly as to what happened next, but it seems that Jarvis and O'Brien fired their rifles through the vision slits at close quarters, wounding some at least of the crews. The officer commanding the leading tank opened the sponson hatch and fired at Jarvis with his pistol; he missed and received a butt-stroke to the head in return. Both crews then emerged to surrender and the prisoners settled down once more, covered by the machine guns of the captured tanks. Jarvis was philosophical about his achievement, commenting that it had enabled him and O'Brien to spend the rest of the night in the relative warmth of their interiors.

At 0630 the enemy artillery opened a heavy but largely ineffective fire on Combeforce's position. Shortly after, the Italians came on in two columns, led by their tanks. The latter displayed the utmost determination and, regardless of their losses, overran the forward companies. C Battery, having obtained permission, brought down their fire on the Rifle Brigade's own position. With the exception of those men armed with anti-tank rifles, the Riflemen could only keep their heads down while 106 RHA's portees fought it out with the M13s. Major Burton later wrote in *The Royal Artillery Commemoration Book*:

'All our anti-tank guns did very well. Two tanks were knocked out a few yards from 2nd Rifle Brigade Battalion HQ and a number were now burning fiercely on the main road. Two of the anti-tank guns put up a gallant fight there before being knocked out at a few yards range by the tanks, but these were all dealt with by other guns soon after... Sergeant Gould knocked out six tanks at extremely close range – he handled (his portee) very cleverly, getting some of the tanks in the rear as they ran down the road past his position. He received an immediate DCM.'

Burton does not say so in his account but, together with his batman and a cook, he formed a scratch crew for the portee which had been damaged the previous afternoon and also scored heavily. After the battle ended Renton asked Burton to parade his battery and personally thanked all the men on behalf of the Rifle Brigade, whose total casualties amounted to only three killed and four wounded.

Once the tanks had been dealt with the rifleman had surfaced to engage the infantry and lorries which were following in their wake. The Italians surrendered immediately and white flags began to flutter along the length of the column, hastened by the appearance of 2 RTR which, sent south by Caunter at first light to assist in the defence of the road-block, arrived just too late to take part in the battle. As a fighting force, the Italian Tenth Army had ceased to exist. Bergonzoli, who had been well forward during the attack, surrendered to Combeforce. His forked beard had earned him the nickname of Electric Whiskers among his peers and this had delighted O'Connor's troops when they learned of it. Yet the curious stares he attracted revealed not the expected figure of fun, but rather an elderly man of some presence who accepted his defeat with a philosophical dignity. Sympathetic, Combe provided him with breakfast while arrangements were made to fly him and his senior officers to Cairo. The Tenth Army's Staff had not taken part in the attack; brilliantined and shiny-booted as ever, they presented themselves to Caunter some hours later.

O'Connor's signal to Wavell read: 'Fox killed in the open.' No amplification was necessary. Some 25,000 prisoners were taken at Beda Fomm, as well as 216 guns and 1,500 wheeled vehicles. Of the 101 Italian tanks left on the battlefield, 48 had been penetrated by 2pdr or 37mm guns, often more than once (in some instances the shot had passed straight through); eight had been destroyed by other weapons; in the case of six the cause of destruction was uncertain; and 39 had either been captured or abandoned intact by their crews.

Between Beda Fomm and Tripoli there remained only a single Italian division and such fugitives as had escaped the disaster. O'Connor believed that, using captured supplies, he could have reached Tripoli, but it was not to be. Once the threat to Egypt had been removed, the War Cabinet's attention turned again to Greece and it was to that theatre that Wavell was required to commit his resources next. In the meantime a distraught and greatly humbled Mussolini had accepted Hitler's offer of assistance and on 14 February, just one week after the Tenth Army had surrendered, the first German ground troops began landing at Tripoli. More than two years were to pass before the Axis powers were finally ejected from North Africa. Because of this, O'Connor's remarkable victory, which did so much to restore the morale of the British public at the time, has tended to become obscured by later events.

Fate was to deal with the victors of Beda Fomm in its many and divers ways. O'Connor himself was captured during the first German drive into Cyrenaica; he was to escape in due course and, as we shall see, command VIII Corps to good effect in Normandy. 106 RHA, which had administered the coup de grace to the Tenth Army, sustained so many casualties in Greece and Crete and the evacuations therefrom that the regiment had to be disbanded, a sad end for so excellent a unit. 2 RTR and 7th Hussars were to fight in further desert battles in 1941, notably Operation 'Crusader' resulting in the relief of Tobruk, and the following year performed prodigies covering the British withdrawal from Burma. On 27 October 1942 the 2nd Rifle Brigade was to earn immortality with its epic defence of Outpost Snipe during the decisive Second Battle of El Alamein.

CHAPTER 6

Deep Strike: Jitra and Slim River, Malaya 1941–2

For the many thousands of Britons who had elected to spend their working lives in Malaya, the country offered a standard of living far higher than that which most could expect to afford at home. They included rubber planters, tin miners, engineers, civil administrators, railway officials and business and professional men of every kind, the great majority of whom were decent, hard-working people, often on such good terms with their native servants that they became God-parents to their children and even made provision for their education. In Malaya the races lived together in harmony and prospered. Yet the good life, which had lasted so long, and seemed set to continue, had over the years become a soft life, simply because it had neither been challenged nor threatened since it began.

Until 1941 the war was remote from Malaya and life continued as before. Even when Japan began to present a potentially serious threat few believed that war was likely and fewer still that any real danger existed. After all, Singapore was considered to be impregnable to an assault from the sea, and as so much of the Malayan mainland consisted of tangled mountain ranges, jungle and swamp, an invader was unlikely to make much progress there before the Royal Navy arrived with reinforcements to redress the balance. Together, the good life and a totally false sense of security inhibited the vital transition from a peace to a war psychology among either the civil or military authorities, with fatal results.

The General Officer Commanding Land Forces in Malaya was Lieutenant-General Arthur Percival, who had enlisted as a private soldier during World War 1. Despite an excellent regimental record which included the award of his commission and a decoration for gallantry, his greatest virtues were those of the staff officer. Indeed, personally courageous and perceptive though he might be, he lacked the charisma needed to inspire his troops, the drive necessary to impose his will on the battle and, above all, the all-important will to win. It is at Percival's door that much of the responsibility for the subsequent catastrophe has been laid yet, in fairness to him, it is merely just to point out that he accurately predicted that if the Japanese chose to invade they would do so through southern Thailand, which was accepted, and that the jungle was not the impenetrable barrier it was thought to be, which was not.

Again, as the storm clouds began to gather, such steps as he attempted to take for the greater security of the peninsula were regularly thwarted by his political and military superiors. Thus, while several new airfields were constructed in 1940 and 1941, the RAF was only prepared to base squadrons of obsolete Brewster Buffalos on them, and these were no match for the latest generation of Japanese fighters; nevertheless, in spite of the obvious inadequacy of his air cover, Percival became responsible for protecting the airfields and denying their use to the enemy, an additional and unwelcome burden involving the diversion of troops who could be more usefully employed elsewhere.

A suggestion that prepared defence lines should be dug was howled down on the grounds that it was defeatist, would interfere with economic, commercial and social interests, and therefore have an adverse effect on civilian morale. The only armoured vehicles at Percival's disposal were a number of tracked weapons carriers and ageing Lanchester armoured cars, the latter armed with machine guns but so thin-skinned as to be vulnerable to anything heavier than small arms fire, but his request for two armoured regiments in August 1941 was firmly denied as the Establishment took the view that the Malayan terrain was tank-proof; even had this been true, the Malayan roads were not.

Simultaneously, a request for additional anti-tank guns was also denied, presumably on the same grounds; even less intelligible was the refusal to supply extra anti-aircraft guns. For these decisions, some of the blame must rest with Winston Churchill, who doubted whether Japan would resort to outright war with the West. In May 1941 he had been reminded by General Sir John Dill, Chief of the Imperial General Staff, that as Singapore was the cornerstone of the British presence in the Far East its security was therefore of paramount importance. Churchill's eyes, however, were firmly fixed on Egypt, where he had hopes of inflicting a defeat on the Axis powers, and it was to the Middle East rather than to Malaya that reinforcements and arms were flowing. Belatedly, as the Japanese became ever more belligerent, some reinforcements were sent to Malaya. So too were the battleship *Prince of Wales* and the battlecruiser *Repulse* in the ill-founded hope that a modest naval presence would avert the threat of invasion.

Even these eleventh-hour preparations took place in a dangerous climate of complacency which had its roots in a perverse and quite
illogical tendency to under-estimate – despise is not too strong a word –
the Japanese capacity for waging a modern war, notwithstanding the disturbing reports forwarded from Tokyo by Western naval and military
attachés. The truth was that, after years of fighting in China, the Japanese Army was experienced and battle-hardened. In the shock of the
defeat it was to inflict, wild rumours were to circulate that it had
received extensive training in jungle warfare, when the reality was that
while it had prudently studied some of the problems involved, it merely
adapted basic military principles to the environment. The Japanese
Army and Naval Air Forces were equally experienced and equipped with
modern high-performance aircraft. At sea, the Imperial Navy no longer
regarded big-gun battleships as its major striking force; that role was
performed by superbly trained aircraft carrier groups which would not
meet their equals until the middle of 1942.

On the eve of war the British garrison of Malaya numbered
88,000 men, including the 9th Indian Division (Major-General
A.E.Barstow), 11th Indian Division (Major-General D.M. Murray-Lyon),
each of two brigades, the 8th Australian Division (Major-General
H.Gordon Bennett), also of two brigades, the independent 12th and
28th Indian Brigades, the 1st and 2nd Malaya Brigades, and a number of
independent Indian infantry battalions performing guard duties. Both
Indian divisions and the 28th Indian Brigade were formed into III Corps
under Lieutenant-General Sir Lewis Heath, and this was made responsible for the defence of northern Malaya. The 8th Australian Division and
12th Indian Brigade were retained in southern Malaya as army reserve
and the two Malayan brigades were stationed on Singapore Island.

Superficially, this was an impressive force, even allowing for the
complete lack of tanks and the shortage of anti-tank and anti-aircraft
guns. Below the surface, however, there were grounds for serious concern. There was, throughout Percival's command, a general shortage of
officers and men with active service experience. A large proportion of
his strength consisted of newly raised and incompletely trained Indian
formations with an unfortunate junior leadership problem. In normal
times British officers had to pass an examination in Urdu, the official
language of the Indian Army, before they were finally accepted for service in an Indian regiment, but the formations serving in Malaya contained considerable numbers of recently commissioned British officers
who had yet to master the skill and were therefore unable to communi-
cate properly with their men. The sepoys themselves, all volunteers and

anxious to do well, would in time have become as formidable soldiers as their countrymen who were to win telling victories in North Africa, Italy and Burma, but for the moment the majority had not progressed far beyond their recruit training and were barely used to the ways of the Army. Very few of them had ever seen a tank, let alone faced one, but they knew what they were and what they were capable of.

For the invasion of Malaya the Japanese had formed the Twenty-Fifth Army under the command of Lieutenant-General Tomoyuki Yamashita. This consisted of the 5th Division (Lieutenant-General Takuro Matsui), the 18th Division (Lieutenant-General Renya Mutaguchi), the Imperial Guards Division (Lieutenant-General Takuma Nishimura), the 3rd Tank Brigade with 80 tanks, two field artillery regiments and a strong engineer element, a total of approximately 60,000 men who were to remain outnumbered throughout the campaign.

Of these formations elements of the 3rd Tank Brigade, containing the 1st, 6th and 14th Tank Regiments, were to play the leading role on a number of critically important occasions. In itself, this is surprising in that within the infantry-dominated Japanese Army the Armoured Corps was something of a Cinderella, all but permanently committed to supporting infantry operations and discouraged from developing a doctrine of its own. Furthermore, in China the enemy had possessed little or no armour worth speaking of and, since Japanese tanks had proved adequate for the demands made on them there, further design and development had been allowed to lag further and further behind that of the West, in spite of a salutary lesson administered by the Red Army at Khalkin Gol on the Manchurian frontier in 1939. Even if the reverse had been the case, tank production came low on Japanese industry's list of war priorities, as the Imperial Navy absorbed the lion's share of the country's steel production.

The types of tank used in Malaya were the Type 95 Light, a 1935 design with 12mm armour, armed with 37mm gun and a hull-mounted machine gun; and the more numerous Type 97 Medium with 25mm armour, armed with a 57mm gun and co-axial and hull machine guns, which had been introduced in 1937. The best features of these designs was their air-cooled diesel engines, which were suitable for use in widely varying climatic conditions, and the compatibilty of their maximum speed of approximately 23mph. In other respects they were poorly armoured, under-gunned, old-fashioned in their layout and impossibly cramped, but were a great deal better than no tanks at all.

Yamashita's invasion convoys left Hainan on 4 December, bound, as Percival had predicted, for the Kra isthmus in southern Thailand. In the event of an invasion seeming probable, Percival's plan, codenamed 'Matador', was to mount a pre-emptive strike across the Thai frontier with 11th Indian Division and secure the ports of Singora and Patani, together with their adjacent airfields, before the Japanese could establish themselves. Unfortunately, the Cabinet refused to sanction the operation, which it believed would be used by the Japanese as an excuse to declare war. On 5 December it relented, informing Air Chief Marshal Sir Robert Brooke-Popham, Commander-in-Chief Far East, that he could activate 'Matador' without further reference to London. Next day the Japanese convoys were sighted but Brooke-Popham still witheld permission, although the 11th Division was placed on 30 minutes' stand-by. That the invasion was a fact was not definitely established in Singapore until the morning of 8 December, and only then was Percival allowed to proceed. 'Matador' was now irrelevant, for Yamashita's troops were not only ashore but had begun to advance, bundling back such units of the 11th Division as had managed to cross the frontier. Sadly, this sequence of events was to set the tone for the whole campaign.

By the evening of 8 December more than half the British aircraft in northern Malaya had been destroyed, and rest were soon eliminated. On 10 December *Prince of Wales* and *Repulse*, having left Singapore with the object of destroying the invasion convoys, were sunk by swarms of bombers and torpedo aircraft at trivial cost to the enemy. The Japanese now possessed complete air and naval superiority and were able to develop the campaign as they wished.

In the meantime, Murray-Lyon's 11th Indian Division was falling back to occupy a defensive position at Jitra. Because of 'Matador' the division had been deployed for offensive operations and this was reflected in its order of march, which did not include an effective rearguard. This was most unfortunate as the commander of the Japanese advance guard, Lieutenant-Colonel Shizuo Saeki, was an officer of notable drive and aggression. On 10 December Saeki's troops had brushed with the battalion covering the withdrawal, 1st/14th Punjabis, and forced them back into a village named Changlun, where they made a stand. Next morning Saeki attacked and captured the village, although the Punjabis withdrew in good order and fell back towards the next village, Asun, where the 2nd/1st Gurkha Rifles had been moved up in support. In the meantime, Saeki had been joined by 10 tanks of the 1st Tank Regiment and, with part of the 41st Infantry Regiment mounted in lorries, he set off in pursuit. At about 1630 he caught up with the Punjabis' column and bore down on it with guns blazing. Terrified, those who were not cut down by the apparently unstoppable juggernauts scattered in every direction.

Ploughing through the wreckage of the battalion, Saeki's force suddenly came upon a sight which would have made any tank commander's heart miss a beat - a line of 10 2pdr anti-tank guns drawn up across the road. Though rapidly becoming obsolete themselves, they would have been quite capable of beating Saeki's tank company into a line of burning wrecks, had their crews not been sheltering from the heavy rain in a nearby rubber plantation. It took but a moment for the Japanese to realise that the weapons were not manned and the battery was quickly overrun.

In themselves, the destruction of an infantry battalion and the loss of so many anti-tank guns might be considered disasters enough for Murray-Lyon's division to have suffered, but its ordeal had only just begun. At about 1700 Saeki's continued advance brought him to Asun, where 2nd/1st Gurkha Rifles, unaware of what had happened, were also taken by surprise. The Gurkhas were able to block a bridge by knocking out the leading tank with an anti-tank rifle, but were overwhelmed and driven out of the village into the jungle by a combination of intense fire from the remaining tanks and a flank attack by the Japanese infantry. Of the entire battalion, less than 200 men succeeded in reaching their own lines; from 1st/14th Pubjabis only a handful got through. Some miles to the west, more anti-tank guns and many lorries had to be abandoned on the wrong side of a river, thanks to the premature demolition of a bridge.

During the night, Saeki's infantry probed the 11th Division's main position at Jitra but were unable to effect a breakthough. On 12 December, however, the remainder of the 41st Infantry arrived and pressure began to build up against the British right flank. By 2200 Murray-Lyon considered that the position had become untenable and issued orders for a general withdrawal; this was undoubtedly the correct decision as the Japanese had brought up a fresh regiment, the 11th Infantry, which they intended using against his left flank, a move that would have culminated in his virtual encirclement. Amid some confusion, disengagement was completed during the early hours of 13 December. Some units, fearful of the Japanese tanks, chose to retreat through swamplands rather than along the road, abandoning their transport and guns in the process. No doubt existed that the division had suffered a major defeat, having sustained over 2,000 casualties in contrast to enemy losses amounting to a mere 27 killed and 83 wounded. The Japanese took over 1,000 prisoners and captured 50 artillery weapons, some 300 vehicles and sufficient ammunition and rations to support a division for three months. Saeki's tank unit, which had played so important a part in the fighting, was rewarded with a Unit Citation.

In the weeks that followed the hapless 11th Division was harried steadily southwards and repeatedly foiled in its attempts to form fresh defence lines along the series of rivers flowing down to the west coast of the peninsula. To some extent III Corps as a whole was handicapped by Percival's own ambivalent strategy, which required formation commanders to impose the maximum delay on the enemy, yet simultaneously preserve as much of their commands as possible for the defence of Singapore Island until the arrival of reinforcements enabled a fresh assessment to be made. This in itself was a tacit admission that the battle on the Malayan mainland could not be won and meant that at times too much emphasis was placed on the second part of the directive. At the lower levels, it was the sheer speed of the Japanese advance that the men of the 11th Division found unsettling.

The first encounters had confirmed Yamashita's view that he was not opposed by a first class army. He therefore decided to deny the British time in which to consolidate their new positions by maintaining the momentum of his drive, and to this end his troops commandeered thousands of bicycles. On these they pedalled their way southwards along any available track, remaining comparatively fresh while covering far more ground than would have been possible with marching infantry. More bicycles, pack animals and impressed local labour were used to bring up ammunition; food was not a problem, so much having been captured that the men barely bothered with their frugal marching rations. Equally important was the speed with which the forward engineering detachments were able to repair demolished bridges, thereby enabling artillery and tanks to keep pace with the advance along the main roads.

It was also apparent that the British, in relying so heavily on motorised transport, were mentally road-bound and seldom extended their positions more than 500 yards on either side of the road. This was a situation that the Japanese found easy to exploit, for when they ran into opposition they would leave approximately one-third of their strength to mount a holding attack and use the rest to make a wide and generally unobserved detour through the jungle and rejoin the road some miles behind the British defences, where one or more roadblocks would be set up, preferably near a bend. More often than not, the basis of the block was an ambushed vehicle, sometimes supplemented by a felled tree or two, covered by mortars and machine guns; the more vehicles which attempted to drive through the block the better, as they would simply add to the resulting tangle when they were shot up. The local British commander, already engaged in fighting off the holding attack, which might be supported by tanks, could either request that the block be cleared by friendly troops beyond, a course of action seldom successful, or attempt to fight his own way out. If he was unable to break through himself the only alternative remaining was to try and regain his own lines by taking to the jungle, although this invariably meant abandoning his artillery, anti-tank guns, vehicles and supplies.

Within the 11th Division, which also had to cope with a series of small but potentially dangerous enemy landings to its rear on the west coast, growing exhaustion was compounded by falling morale induced by the deadly cycle of retreat and defeat. Nor did it help that it was the enemy's aircraft that dominated the skies. However hard the men fought, and they fought very hard on many occasions, the Japanese always seemed to be one move ahead. The division, beset by a sickening sense of failure, lost confidence in its leaders. Murray-Lyon was relieved on 24 December, his place being taken by Brigadier A. Paris, but by then the pattern had been set.

Percival visited the division and was shocked to find that the continuous fighting and lack of rest had reduced the troops' reactions to a level that he described as 'subnormal'. When orders were given, it could not be assumed that they were understood, absorbed or remembered, let alone acted upon, and in this condition it was inevitable that, sooner or later, it would be overtaken by a major disaster. As the 9th Indian Division in eastern Malaya was not under such intense pressure, it should have been possible to bring forward the as-yet unblooded Australians to man a defence line through which the battered 11th Indian Division could have retired to rest and reorganise. Unfortunately, it was not a course Percival chose to take.

On 4 January 1942 the division fell back to yet another defensive position, this time on the Slim river, the line of which was to be held until the night of 7/8 January in accordance with the timetable Percival had prepared to allow reinforcements on the point of reaching Singapore to acclimatise themselves and receive some training before being committed to the fighting on the mainland. This was considered to be particularly important in the case of the British 18th Division, which had been at sea for three months and was therefore unfit.

The position at Slim river offered certain advantages in that for several miles north of the river the railway and Trunk Road ran parallel to each other through a belt of plantations only four miles wide, bounded to the east by tangled mountain country and to the west by jungle and swamp, thereby confining the Japanese to a comparatively narrow frontage. Brigadier Paris's plan involved the forward edge of this defile being defended by his 12th Brigade, based on Trolak village, while some five miles to the south the 28th Brigade deployed along the north bank of the Slim around Slim River Station, the point at which the railway passed straight across the river and the Trunk Road turned east for five miles along the right bank towards a bridge at Slim village. The division still possessed more field artillery than the Japanese but, as a result of the engagements described above, 12th Brigade had only three anti-tank guns available and 28th Brigade only two. Most infantry battalions had sustained over 200 casualties and their rifle companies were operating at about half-strength. On the night of 6-7 January, 28th Brigade had still to complete its deployment by occupying a battalion

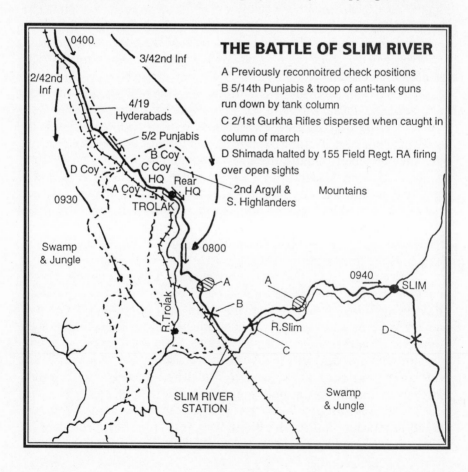

THE BATTLE OF SLIM RIVER

A Previously reconnoitred check positions

B 5/14th Punjabis & troop of anti-tank guns run down by tank column

C 2/1st Gurkha Rifles dispersed when caught in column of march

D Shimada halted by 155 Field Regt. RA firing over open sights position on the Trunk Road midway between the Slim river rail and road bridges.

The 12th Brigade consisted of the 2nd Argyll & Sutherland Highlanders, 5th/2nd Punjabis and 4th/19th Hyderabads. The Argylls were directly descended from the 93rd Highlanders, the original Thin Red Line which had repulsed the Russian cavalry at Balaclava, and indeed still referred to themselves as the 93rd. Thanks to the foresight and imagination of their commanding officer, they were the only battalion in Malaya which had been thoroughly trained in jungle warfare and, ably supported by their platoon of Lanchester armoured cars, they had repeatedly inflicted heavy casualties on the Japanese. Now, commanded by Lieutenant-Colonel L. B. Robertson, they were to become involved in the most tragic episode in their history.

The situation at Trolak on the evening of 6 January is described by the Argylls' historian:

'The position had been reconnoitred four days previously and since then wiring under divisional engineer supervision with native labour had been in progress. This work was continued by units as they arrived and weapon pits were dug. It was the only partly prepared position ever held by 12th Brigade. The position was designed in the case of the forward battalions to force the enemy into the defiles of the road and railway where they ran through the jungle, thus allowing economy of troops on our part, creating definite targets for our artillery and reducing the Japanese liberty of movement to a minimum.

'4th/19th Hyderabads and 5th/2nd Punjabis were disposed in company localities in depth for two and a half miles down the road and railway. The road had recently been modernised and was broad, flat and straight, running through deep cuttings that made admirable and comparatively tank-proof localities, well-wired and partially booby-trapped.

'The firm base of the brigade layout was 5th/2nd Punjabis. 4th/19th Hyderabads' purpose was the usual one of gaining time by making the initial enemy blow strike either the air, or at least a situation that had radically changed from the moment that he had initiated his plan. It was therefore given a directive to this effect, which included the liberty of withdrawal into depth behind the Argylls at Trolak.

'The anti-tank defence was the weakest point. The modernised road offered no place where a demolition would stop tanks until Trolak. This was prepared, as was one leading onto the western estate road. The railway was blocked by blowing a bridge in the same area. Some concrete pillars and about three dozen anti-tank mines arrived and were used to make slender obstacles in the two forward battalion areas. The three anti-tank guns were in depth over one and a half miles, inside infantry company localities and covering the obstacles.'

The Argylls' own company positions were located in the plantations on either side of the road and railway north of Trolak, and in Trolak itself, the idea being 'to use the good lateral communications for infantry and armoured cars in their area to engage any deep encircling attack through the jungle as soon as it emerged into the rubber, and before it could effect its purpose of cutting the road. '

By 1600 on the 6th it was apparent that the Japanese had begun to close up to the position. A Chinese refugee provided disturbing news that he had seen many tanks some 25 miles to the north and that in the intervening area the enemy was hard at work repairing demolitions. It seemed probable, therefore, that an attack could be expected the following day and 4th/19th Hyderabads were ordered to withdraw through 5th/2nd Pubjabis and the Argylls after dawn. The effect of this, it was thought, would create the necessary depth to thwart the enemy's encircling move and therefore compel him to develop a second attack, by which time the period set for holding the Slim river position would have elapsed.

The problem was that the enemy, consisting of Colonel Andoh's 42nd Infantry Regiment, with a field artillery battalion, one medium and one light tank company in support, were a great deal closer than anyone had imagined and had already begun to develop flank attacks in battalion strength. At 0730 on 6 January, 3rd/42nd had begun moving through the mountainous jungle to the east with the intention of cutting the Trunk Road south of Trolak in the area of Milestone 66. An hour later 2nd/42nd had set off through the swamp and jungle to the west, intending to strike somewhat deeper, into the area between Milestone 69 and Slim River Station.

As Paris had appreciated in deciding to defend the defile at Trolak, the neighbouring jungle was thick and extremely difficult going. Both battalions made very slow progress and it was soon apparent to an impatient Andoh, who had wanted to develop his regimental attack on 6 January, that the flanking troops would not be in a position to establish their roadblocks before the following morning. Aware of the situation, Major Toyosaku Shimada, his senior tank officer, proposed an alternative course of action which would, he believed, take full advantage of the dispositions already made yet produce far greater rewards.

Shimada, a career officer in the hitherto underrated armoured corps, was a company commander in the 6th Tank Regiment. He had clearly absorbed the lessons of deep penetration techniques demonstrated by the Germans in Poland, France and Russia and by the British in North Africa and, encouraged by Saeki's success at Jitra, he was anxious to demonstrate that Japanese tanks could be employed to similar effect. What he proposed was nothing less than using his own No 4 Company, equipped with 10 Type 97 mediums, reinforced with five Type 95 lights from No 1 Company and accompanied by an infantry company and an engineer platoon travelling in lorries, as the spearhead of an attack straight down the highway with the ultimate object of capturing the road bridge over the Slim. He doubted whether the British possessed the means to stop him and his intention was simply to fillet his way through the defences with the minimum of delay, leaving the mopping up to the flanking battalions and the second echelon of the attack, the latter consisting of the remainder of 1st/42nd, led by 10 Type 95s of No 1 Company. One of the most interesting aspects of the plan was the designated role of No 1 Company which, after Shimada's attack group had achieved its breakthrough, was to maintain continuous patrols along the road and so deny its use to the British. Andoh, having no alternative in mind and nothing to lose, gave his approval.

At about 0330 on 7 January mortar and artillery fire began erupting on the Hyderabads' positions. Some 30 minutes later a column of tanks, accompanied by infantry, drove slowly down the road towards the forward company, firing on the move. In view of the confused nature of the fighting in the darkness, it is understandable that the recorded details of the battle vary considerably, although its course remains clear. The factor dominating its opening stages arose directly from recent improvements to the Trunk Road, long sections of which had been straightened, leaving the now disused bends as a series of loops. In the months prior to the war Japanese intelligence gathering on such matters had been meticulous. Shimada, therefore, may have been aware of the existence of the loops, but even if he was not he did not hesitate to make good use of them.

After one tank had been knocked out by an anti-tank gun he swung his column into such a loop and outflanked the Hyderabads' position. In accordance with their orders, the Hyderabads broke contact and began withdrawing through the jungle towards their battalion rendezvous. At about 0430 the Japanese ran into the Punjabis' forward company in the area of Milestone 61. After one tank had been disabled by a mine, Shimada's lorried infantry company, consisting of 80 men under Second Lieutenant Morokuma, left their vehicles and launched an immediate attack. This eager reaction was ill-considered, for the task was not only beyond them but also deprived Shimada of their services for the rest of the day. Leaving the fierce free-for-all raging behind them in the darkness, the tanks took a second loop, then a third, which by-passed the Punjabis' battalion HQ and brought them out in the reserve company's position near Milestone 62. Here a second protracted struggle ensued, during which Shimada lost a further three tanks - one knocked out by an anti-tank gun, another disabled by mines and the third with a track shot off by anti-tank rifles. What finally overwhelmed the Punjabis was the arrival of Andoh's second attack echelon and its tanks. Lieutenant-Colonel Deakin, commanding 5th/2nd, believed that the Japanese employed a total of 30 tanks against his battalion, a figure not far in excess of the truth; only he and some 70 of his men managed to fight their way out of the battle, most being captured as they tried to regain their own lines.

So much signals equipment had been lost during the campaign's early stages that communications within 12th Brigade relied on the civilian telephone system, which ceased to function when the Japanese cut the wires at about 0500. The Argylls were therefore unaware of what exactly was happening to the north but had taken the precaution of preparing a minor road bridge for demolition at Trolak, together with an improvised roadblock covered by two armoured cars and an ambush party armed with Molotov cocktails. At 0530 four Type 97s, sent ahead by an impatient Shimada, appeared out of the darkness and engaged the defenders of the roadblock. One was enveloped in external flames from bursting petrol bombs but was otherwise unharmed. The remainder engaged in a brief and one-sided duel with the armoured cars which, armed with anti-tank rifles unable to penetrate their armour, were quickly knocked out. At this point it was decided to blow the demolition, but nothing happened. When the charge refused to explode it was believed that the wires had been cut by retreating vehicles; in fact a Second Lieutenant Watanabe had jumped from his tank under fire and severed them with his sword. The Japanese, however, possessed no monopoly of suicidal courage. Captain Turner, commander of the Argylls' armoured car platoon, quickly assembled a small group and pushed one of the knocked out Lanchesters onto the bridge, under continuous fire from the tanks. Sadly, this gallant act was to no avail, for the tanks were able to shoulder the vehicle aside and continue down the road.

At first light, some 30 minutes later, an attack was launched against Trolak village from the east. By 0730 this had been repulsed by the battalion HQ personnel and transport drivers. In the meantime 'B' and 'C' Companies, occupying forward positions in the rubber to the east of the road, had been forced to give ground under heavy pressure.

More tanks, followed by a large number of cyclists, could be seen streaming along the road in the direction of Trolak and as the situation was becoming increasingly confused both companies were withdrawn to a position 200 yards south of the village and the same distance from the highway. This was held until 1000 when it was decided to fall back to Slim River Station through the jungle.

To the west of the road 'A' Company ambushed and all but wiped out a Japanese company attempting to infiltrate down the railway, then withdrew successfuly along the line during the afternoon. 'D' Company beat off an attack by tanks and infantry during which the leading Type 95 was knocked out by an armoured car commanded by Sergeant Nuttall. Shortly after, the company was joined by elements of the Hyderabads and at 0930 the combined force was ordered to withdraw. It had not gone far when it found its path blocked by a strong enemy force, almost certainly belonging to 2nd/42nd Infantry. More Japanese converged on the firing from all directions and the situation became desperate. Captain Boyle, commanding 'D' Company, ordered Nuttall to break through along a plantation road in his Lanchester, then proceed to Slim River Station, which he succeeded in doing. Boyle managed to break out with his survivors but was left behind by the speed of the enemy's advance and forced to surrender several days later.

The fate of 'D' Company was shared by most of 12th Brigade. Unable to use the Trunk Road because it was being patrolled incessantly by the light tanks of Andoh's second attack echelon, groups already encumbered with wounded were forced to take to the jungle, where many were intercepted by the inwards wheel of 2nd and 3rd/42nd Infantry. By the time the remainder reached the Slim river they were far behind enemy lines. Some were still making their way south when Singapore fell. One party of Argylls headed for the west coast and joined the Dutch in Sumatra after a 150-mile voyage in fishing boats. Two Argylls, Privates Stewart and Bennett, remained at liberty in Malaya for the next four years, serving as instructors to Chinese guerrilla groups. The rest of their battalion, which numbered some 90 men and two armoured cars in the immediate aftermath of the disaster, was reinforced and took part in the final battles for Singapore island.

Meanwhile, Shimada's spearhead group had been rejoined by the rest of its tanks and was driving slowly but steadily southwards from Trolak along the Trunk Road. Brigadier Selby, commanding 28th Brigade, had been informed of the breakthrough at 0630. Leaving two of his battalions, 2nd/2nd and 2nd/9th Gurkha Rifles, to guard Slim River Station and the railway bridge, he despatched 5th/14th Punjabis north-

wards towards a previously reconnoitred check position in the wide gap
between 12th and 28th Brigades, and sent 2nd/1st Gurkha Rifles eastwards to establish a similar position near Milestone 72 which would
cover the road bridge.

Shortly before 0800 Shimada's tanks ran into 5th/14th Punjabis
between Milestones 68 and 69. The two leading companies were cut to
pieces on the road but the remainder of the battalion ran for cover into
the rubber plantations and took up covering positions, holding these
until driven out by the enemy's second echelon. Shimada did not halt
and almost immediately shot up and destroyed 28th Brigade's only troop
of anti-tank guns, which was caught driving forward to support the Punjabis in accordance with Selby's instructions.

Following the Trunk Road where it swung east at Slim River
Station, the Japanese drove straight through 2nd/9th Gurkha Rifles.
Fortunately, the latter's trenches were sited some way off the highway
and the Gurkhas remained where they were to meet the anticipated
infantry attack. Not far beyond, however, the tanks ran down 2nd/1st
Gurkha Rifles as they were marching in column towards their new position, and dispersed them with such heavy loss that the following day the
battalion could only muster five officers and 20 other ranks. Next, the
Japanese came across two batteries of 137 Field Regiment RA parked at
the roadside and raked these with their main armament and machine
guns before the startled gunners could fire a shot in return. Similar treatment was meted out to a field ambulance unit.

Shimada continued his career of destruction towards the road
bridge in Slim village, now only a mile or two distant. The only defence
consisted of one troop of 16th Light Anti-Aircraft Battery, armed with
Bofors 40mm anti-aircraft guns. The troop commander, alerted by a sig-
naller who had witnessed the recent massacre and raced back in his
truck, courageously decided to engage the tanks and, when they came
into view at 0840 he held his fire until they were only 100 yards distant.
It amounted to nothing more than a very gallant gesture, for while a rain
of shells burst all over the Type 97s, they were small calibre explosive
projectiles designed for use against aircraft and therefore quite unable to
make any impression on the enemy's armour. The guns crews were shot
down around their weapons and the tanks ground on across the bridge.

Leaving one tank to guard the bridge, Shimada continued down
the road for a further two miles. Near Milestone 78 he ran into the
unsuspecting 155 Field Regiment RA, driving towards the front. For a
few minutes all went as before, but then the gunners recovered from
their surprise and brought one of their 4. 5in howitzers into action at 30

yards range, blowing the leading tank apart. Shimada, sensible enough to recognise that at last his luck had run out, retired to the bridge where he was forced to endure heavy shelling for the rest of the day. From start to finish, he had lost only six tanks.

To the west, the Japanese infantry did not close up to Slim River Station until 1830. In the dusk, Selby withdrew his two remaining battalions, now swollen by fugitives from many units, and blew up the railway bridge. The battle of Slim river was over. It had cost the British 4,000 casualties, most of whom were captured, plus 33 medium and field artillery weapons, 15 anti-tank guns, six light anti-aircraft guns, 50 armoured cars and tracked carriers, 550 motor vehicles and large quantities of food and ammunition. With 12th Brigade destroyed and 28th Brigade so badly mauled that it was no longer fit for action, 11th Indian Division was finished for a while. This, together with the premature loss of the Slim River Line, meant that central Malaya, which provided reasonable going for tanks, could not be held for as long as Percival had required and, that being the case, no time remained for the reinforcements reaching Singapore to be trained and committed to the fighting on the mainland.

General Sir Archibald Wavell, the recently appointed Supreme Commander of all Allied forces in South-East Asia, otherwise known as ABDA (American, British, Dutch, Australian) Command, arrived in Singapore while the fighting at Slim river was in progress. Visiting the mainland, he recognised that the campaign there was lost. It was at his insistence rather than Percival's that the shattered 11th Division was taken out of the line, leaving the 8th Australian and 9th Indian Divisions to fight further delaying actions in Johore. Returning to Singapore island he found to his horror that, despite all that had happened, the poisonous Malayan malaise was still at work. No defences whatever had been prepared on the north coast, where the narrow Straits of Johore separated the island from the mainland, Percival's excuse being that their construction would have been bad for morale. Before leaving, Wavell angrily ordered him commence work at once; but it was too late.

By the end of January Percival had decided to abandon the mainland and his troops streamed back across the Causeway, weary, demoralised and with no confidence in leaders who seemed to regard defeat as inevitable. In some units, but by no means all, discipline was seriously affected. During the night of 8-9 February, the Japanese secured their first beachhead and once their tanks were ashore they made steady progress towards Singapore city. On 15 February, wishing to spare the civil population the massacres which had followed the

Japanese capture of Shanghai and Hong Kong, Percival asked for terms, little knowing that Yamashita was running dangerously short of ammunition. Yamashita demanded unconditional surrender, promising to respect the lives of the troops and civilians, and this was accepted, setting the seal on the greatest defeat in the history of the British Empire. Both sides had sustained about 9,000 battle casualties, but no less than 130,000 British, Australian and Imperial soldiers marched into captivity.

The spectacular successes achieved by Japanese tanks at Jitra and Slim river were never to be repeated. On 18 January, during the fighting in Johore, Australian anti-tank gunners of the 2nd/29th Infantry Battalion ambushed and destroyed an entire company of eight Type 95s attempting a similar breakthrough. A month after the fall of Singapore the 1st and 14th Tank Regiments were shipped to Burma where, with far fewer resources than Percival had possessed, the small British army, assisted by under-equipped Chinese troops, succeeded in completing a long and difficult retreat to India. The difference was that in Burma the British had the support of the veteran 7th Armoured Brigade, consisting of the 7th Hussars and the 2nd Royal Tank Regiment, which had belatedly been despatched from the Middle East to Malaya but diverted to Rangoon when Percival surrendered. In the first clash between the two armoured forces the Japanese discovered that they were outgunned and had everything to learn about tank versus tank fighting. After this their tanks were seldom encountered on the British sector. For the remainder of the Pacific war Japanese armour reverted to the more pedestrian role of direct infantry support, occasional attempts to divert from this ending in failure.

As for Shimada, his company was awarded a well-earned Unit Citation. In any other less conservative army his obvious ability and insight would have enabled him to play a prominent part in the development of his arm, but the Japanese were neither seeking nor wanted a Guderian of their own. On the other hand, his achievements at Slim river could not be ignored, although his reward was also carefully designed to remove him from the mainstream of active service military life. In 1942 he was appointed instructor in the Armoured Department of the Military Academy, where he remained for the rest of the war, doubtless preaching what would never be put into practice. He subsequently became a schoolmaster and died in 1988, aged 76.

CHAPTER 7

Hill 309 and the Bridge at 637436

From the outset, the Allied strategy for the campaign in Normandy had been to pin down the German armour opposite the sector held by General Sir Miles Dempsey's British Second Army while the US First Army, commanded by Lieutenant-General Omar N. Bradley, completed its preparations to break out of the beach-head. This was achieved not only by mounting major operations such as 'Epsom', 26 June–1 July, intended to force crossings of the rivers Odon and Orne, and 'Goodwood', 18-21 July, designed as a major offensive drive south-east of Caen, but also by continuous attritional fighting involving the British and Canadian infantry divisions and their supporting tank brigades, notably around Caen and the vital feature known as Hill 112. So effective were these tactics that when the break-out operations, code-named 'Cobra', commenced on 25 July the Germans could field only 190 serviceable tanks against the Americans, whereas no less than 645 were deployed against the British.

Both General Dwight D. Eisenhower, the Allied Supreme Commander, and General Sir Bernard Montgomery, commander of the 21st Army Group, were anxious to preserve this state of imbalance until the Americans had broken out into open country and ordered the British VIII and XXX Corps to mount a fresh offensive, codenamed 'Bluecoat', on 30 July, with the object of pushing the British line as far south as possible, thereby compelling the enemy to fight for more ground and forcing such armour as he wished to transfer from the British to the American sector to make a wide detour. XXX Corps, commanded by Lieutenant-General G. C. Bucknall, was to attack southwards along the axis Villers-Bocage – Aunay sur Odon – Mont Pincon, the last being designated as its principal objective. On the British right VIII Corps, commanded by Lieutenant-General Sir Richard O'Connor, the victor of Beda Fomm, was to attack along the axis Caumont – Vire, capturing Hill 309 in the process. The Guards and 7th Armoured Divisions were also made available, to be held in reserve and committed as the situation warranted.

Beyond the Army boundary on O'Connor's right was Major-General
Leonard T. Gerow's US V Corps, which would adjust its own left to
conform as the battle developed. The fortunes of war were to dictate

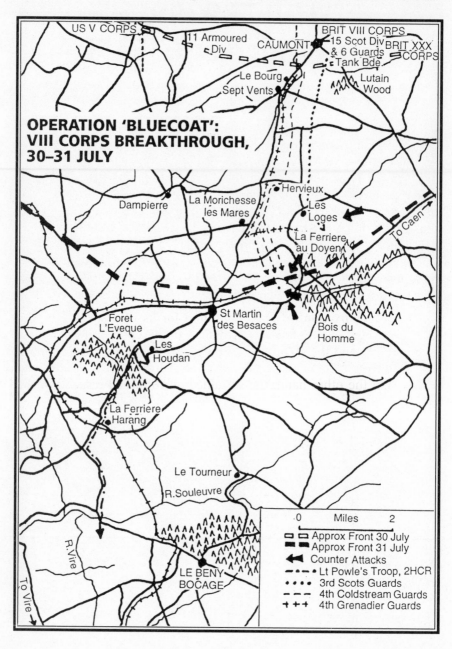

that on 30 July XXX Corps' advance was to be uneven while that of VIII Corps was to make unexpectedly good progress; and since the latter was to prepare the ground for the most remarkable coup of the campaign it is worth examining in some detail.

The terrain over which the battle was fought was typical Normandy bocage, consisting of small fields separated by earthen banks topped by hedges, close-planted orchards, woodland, sunken leafy lanes, streams running through deep tree-lined valleys, isolated farms and small villages. Picturesque as it was, the landscape favoured defence rather than attack, offering as it did so many opportunities for concealed positions which only became apparent once an attacker was well within killing range. Because of this, casualties among the British infantry divisions had been extremely heavy. Nor did the armour fare much better, as the bocage itself presented a serious obstacle to the passage of tanks, there were few adequate roads along the axes of advance, and often the only means of crossing the numerous streams was by timber bridges incapable of supporting even the lesser weight of an armoured car. In such circumstances, where vision was almost always restricted, it was only too easy for a sniper to pick off a tank commander or for a tank to fall victim to a Panzerfaust (the German equivalent of the Bazooka) fired at close quarters from the cover of a hedge.

Hitler's fixation on holding ground for its own sake apart, the bocage provided one reason why the Allies, despite possessing complete air superiority and the ability to call on crushing naval gunfire support, had only been able to make slow progress during the previous two months. On the other hand, the sustained attrition had resulted in the German armies in Normandy being bled white; they had received few reinforcements and were now close to exhaustion, although they were still capable of offering determined resistance. The troops opposite O'Connor's corps, in fact, belonged to the 326th Infantry Division, commanded by Lieutenant-General Viktor von Drabich-Waechter, and had only been in occupation of their positions since 22 July, having been moved to what was considered to be a quiet sector for a rest. They believed that they were opposed by an equally tired American division and were unaware that on 28 July O'Connor's troops had taken over the latter's positions, so extending the British line to the west in preparation for 'Bluecoat'. The division had been formed late in 1942 but, apart from the occupation of Vichy France that year, had not seen active service until after the Allied landings in Normandy. It was not, therefore, a high value formation, although it had acquired some experience and was quite capable of performing a defensive role.

Against this, Drabich-Waechter's task was rendered more difficult by the need to cover no less than 10 miles of front, which meant
that he could not be strong everywhere. Allied intelligence had already
identified his 751st and 752nd Grenadier Regiments in the line, with
753rd Grenadier Regiment in reserve, and estimated that the division's
heavy weapons included nine assault guns, 21 anti-tank guns of 50mm
calibre and over, and approximately seventy field and medium guns.
Also believed to be present on this sector were elements, at least, of
654th (GHQ) Tank Destroyer Battalion, equipped with up to thirty formidable Jagdpanthers, although the whereabouts of these remained
unknown.

O'Connor's VIII Corps was to mount its major attack with
Major-General G. H. A. MacMillan's 15th (Scottish) Division, which
would strike south from Caumont to Hill 309, its right flank being covered by the 11th Armoured Division under Major-General G. P. B.
Roberts. In direct support of MacMillan's division was the recently
arrived 6th Guards Tank Brigade under Brigadier G. L. Verney, with
which it had trained extensively in England prior to the Normandy landings. As its name suggests this formation, consisting of the 4th Grenadier
Guards, 4th Coldstream Guards and 3rd Scots Guards, was specifically
trained to support infantry operations and was equipped with a total of
174 Churchill tanks, slow and under-gunned by comparison with the
enemy armour, but heavily armoured and capable of crossing terrain
impassable to any other fighting vehicle. Normally, infantry tank units
were allocated on the scale of one regiment per infantry brigade or one
squadron per infantry battalion, but in this instance MacMillan's attack
was to be delivered on a one-brigade frontage and would therefore have
three times the usual amount of armoured support. Additional armoured
units had also been provided by the specialist 79th Armoured Division
to assist in the break-in phase, including Churchill-based Crocodile
flamethrowers from 141 Regiment RAC and Sherman Crab flail tanks
manned by crews from the 1st Lothians and Border Horse.

As planned, the assault involved three distinct phases. In Phase
I the Grenadiers, with assistance from the Crocodiles and Crabs, were to
capture Lutain Wood and the hamlets of Le Bourg and Sept Vents in
conjunction with 9th Cameronians and 2nd Gordon Highlanders, supported by an artillery programme firing concentrations on nine known
strongpoints from H-2 to H+20 minutes.

During Phase II the artillery would fire a rolling barrage on a
2,300-yard frontage lasting for 110 minutes, lifting 100 yards every four
minutes; three-quarters of the shells fired would be fuzed to air-burst, as

this had been found to be best way of keeping the enemy's heads down in the bocage. Under cover of this the Coldstream and 10th Highland Light Infantry would advance to Hervieux crossroads while the Scots Guards and 2nd Argyll and Sutherland Highlanders secured Hill 226, also known as Le Homme.

Phase III was to begin with a carpet-bombing attack on Hill 309, the divisional objective. As soon as this had ended the Coldstream, 2nd Glasgow Highlanders and 7th Seaforth Highlanders would advance under cover of a rolling barrage similar to that fired in Phase II and capture the hill.

The attack itself commenced at 0655 on 30 July. On the right the Grenadiers' No 1 Squadron and the Cameronians moved off towards their objectives, covered by the bombardment and direct gunfire support provided by the regiment's No 2 Squadron from the higher ground near Caumont. Heavy defensive fire was encountered at once and for a while a sunken lane barred the tanks' way forward until a way across was discovered. The Churchills immediately found themselves in the middle of a minefield which disabled seven of their number and two of the Lothians' Crabs. While the remaining Crabs flailed a way through, the Grenadiers' armoured recovery vehicles came forward and towed off those mine casualties which were blocking the axis of advance.

By now the infantry had gone ahead. As the tanks rejoined them they provided support wherever it was needed, disregarding the original plan which attached troops to specific companies. In this way the combined force fought its way forward in very close country, several tank commanders being hit by sniper fire. The Cameronians secured Le Bourg without difficulty, although Sept Vents proved to be a tougher nut and they requested tank support to assist in the street fighting. Major J. C. Gascoigne, commanding No 1 Squadron, sent in two troops, all that could be mustered until the repaired mine casualties came up. Fortunately, the Grenadiers' commanding officer, Lieutenant-Colonel H. R. H. Davies, was aware of the squadron's losses and had sent forward the regiment's under-employed Anti-Aircraft Troop. This, equipped with Crusader tanks mounting twin 20mm Oerlikon cannon, was also committed to fighting in Sept Vents and by 1030 the hamlet had been cleared.

On the left the Grenadiers' No 3 Squadron and the Gordons had taken Lutain Wood in a three-phase attack. Two infantry companies, each supported by two tank troops and one close-support Churchill armed with a 95mm howitzer, first captured the wood's corners. Then 141 Regiment's Crocodiles had closed in to flame the forward edge of the trees, burning up the hedgerows as they went. Finally, the remaining Gordon companies cleared the wood in an assault shot in from the flanks.

All of the operation's Phase I objectives had now been secured. When the infantry brought up their anti-tank guns and consolidated the captured ground Davies released his specialised armour and ordered the Grenadiers to carry out a forward rally at which fuel and ammunition could be replenished and casualties allowed to catch up.

Phase II had been activated before Phase I had been completed. It was true that the enemy's front had been broken, but there were still plenty of individuals and small groups in the area who, as yet, showed no signs of being intimidated. Thus, when the Coldstream and the HLI passed between Le Bourg and Sept Vents, and the Scots Guards and the Argylls between Le Bourg and Lutain Wood, both battlegroups ran into the enemy's defensive artillery fire, snipers and Panzerfaust teams, and were compelled to fight for their designated start-lines. The British infantry/tank battledrill was thorough and gained ground steadily but slowly. Verney, however, observed that the rolling barrage was drawing steadily ahead of the fighting and, anxious lest the benefit of this be lost, obtained MacMillan's approval for a daring and unorthodox change of plan which would involve sending the tanks ahead and leaving the infantry to catch up as soon as they were able.

The experience of both Guards regiments was identical. Probing the hedges and buildings ahead with their fire, the Churchills followed the barrage closely as it progressed across the chequerboard fields. No other tank then in service could have surmounted the continuous succession of hedge-topped embankments with which they were presented. For the crews, however, the incessant pitching as a tank mounted a bank, followed by the crashing descent on the far side, was both uncomfortable and dangerous. Most men were soon black and blue from their bruises, some were knocked unconscious, and radio sets were shaken off frequency. Even on level going tank commanders faced a further hazard in the orchards for, forced as they were by the restricted visibility to leave their hatches open, they were struck repeatedly across the face by branches and battered by a cascade of hard little apples.

On the right the Coldstream, commanded by Lieutenant-Colonel Sir Walter de S. Bartellot, reached Hervieux crossroads at 1130, where they were joined by the HLI at about 1400. On the left progress had been slower and at one point the Scots Guards commanding officer, Lieutenant-Colonel C. I. H. Dunbar, had halted for an hour to reorganise and allow the infantry to catch up a little. By 1430, however, the regiment had reached the summit of Hill 226 and during the next hour the Argylls also arrived.

At 1500 flight after flight of aircraft had passed overhead to carpet bomb Hill 309. Those now in possession of the Phase II objectives had a grandstand view as the forward slopes and summit of the hill erupted in clouds of smoke, dust, and up-rooted trees. To the Guardsmen and Scottish infantry it was a heartening sight which boded no good at all for the defenders. Dunbar expected some indication that the Coldstream and the Phase III infantry battalions would mount their attack shortly after, but nothing happened and at 1530 he asked Verney for permission to assault the hill with his own regiment. Verney, conversant with the overall context in which the battle was being fought, informed him that XXX Corps' progress had been seriously restricted by extensive minefields and because of this VIII Corps and 6th Guards Tank Brigade were now operating with an open and therefore exposed left flank. In the circumstances, therefore, the Scots Guards and the Argylls were to hold Hill 226 at all costs.

Verney, in fact, was becoming doubtful as to whether Phase III could be activated at all, so slow had been the progress of its infantry component. He conferred once more with MacMillan and the plan was again modified. The Coldstream were to push on alone and seize Hill 309 while the Grenadiers left Sept Vents and lifted the 2nd Glasgow Highlanders forward to their start-line; the second Phase III infantry battalion, 7th Seaforths, would continue on foot, making the best time possible.

Bartellot decided that his regiment would advance with two squadrons forward and one in reserve. An immediate complication arose when the right hand squadron, attempting to pass through La Morichesse les Mares, ran into an ambush. It was apparent that the village was held in strength and it was by-passed; later in the afternoon, one of the Coldstream's spare tanks and the Grenadiers' leading vehicle were knocked out by an anti-tank gun when, unaware of the situation, they drove straight in. By 1630, however, the Coldstream had deployed and were advancing on Hill 309, meeting much the same sort of sporadic opposition that they had encountered earlier in the day. The terrain actually presented more of a threat to success than the enemy. First, ways had to be found round such natural anti-tank obstacles as a deep ditch with a muddy bottom and a cutting which carried a local railway line across the lower slopes of the hill. Then, the slopes themselves were extremely steep and pitted with overlapping bomb craters in which several tanks shed their tracks. Nevertheless, the majority reached the summit with a sense of anti-climax, for it had been abandoned by the enemy.

At approximately 1800, while the Coldstream were taking possession of Hill 309, the wisdom of Verney's decision to hold Hill 226 in strength became apparent. As the Argylls' anti-tank guns had not yet arrived, the infantry had taken up position on the reverse slopes and in Les Loges, a nearby hamlet, leaving the Scots Guards on the hill itself. For some time the feature had been under intermittent artillery and mortar fire, but suddenly this intensified. Almost immediately tanks of 'S' Squadron which, under Major W. S. I. Whitelaw (later to pursue a distinguished political career) was holding the left-front area of the defences, began to burst into flames. Two troops were knocked out, followed by two squadron HQ tanks, without apparent explanation. Then, in the mistaken belief that they had eliminated all the British armour on the hill, three Jagdpanthers broke cover on the left and headed for the summit. They quickly discovered their error, coming under fire from Whitelaw, his reserve troop and other tanks, but succeeded in destroying a third troop before vanishing over the crest. Two were subsequently found abandoned with track damage in woodland on the slopes below.

Back on Hill 309, as the dusk began to gather, Bartellot was beginning to worry about the ability of his regiment to hold the feature, since unsupported tanks were most vulnerable at night, when they could be stalked with ease by infantry armed with close-range anti-tank weapons. Several anxious hours passed until at 2330 the Glasgow Highlanders, having been dropped by the Grenadiers short of La Morichesse les Mares and instructed to follow the Coldstream's tracks, arrived on the hill, to be joined about midnight by the Seaforths.

The day's fighting, including breaking the enemy's front and an advance of no less than six miles, was quite unlike anything experienced in the campaign so far. Casualties had been remarkably light, the 15th Division sustaining the loss of nine officers and 214 other ranks, while 6th Guards Tank Brigade lost 11 officers and 61 other ranks, a high proportion of these being tank commanders. The Grenadiers lost seven tanks, of which four rejoined next day; the Coldstream, most heavily involved of the three regiments, lost 14 of which seven caught up; and the Scots Guards also lost 14, including 12 totally destroyed. It was extremely rare for the regiments of a tank brigade to fight together in the manner of an armoured division, as did those of 6th Guards Tank Brigade at Caumont, but of their action O'Connor commented, 'No tank unit has ever been handled with greater dash and determination.' In recognition of this, Verney was to receive a quite unexpected reward a few days later.

To the right of 15th Scottish, the 11th Armoured Division, commanded by Major-General G. P. B. Roberts, had also made sustained if not quite so spectacular progress. Roberts had served throughout the North African campaign, having been present at Beda Fomm with HQ 4th Armoured Brigade and later commanded a regiment, then an armoured brigade, before returning home to take command of 11th Armoured after the fall of Tunis. The divisional order of battle included an armoured reconnaissance regiment (2nd Northamptonshire Yeomanry equipped with Cromwell cruiser tanks); 29th Armoured Brigade (23rd Hussars, 2nd Fife and Forfar Yeomanry and 3rd Royal Tank Regiment, equipped with Shermans and a proportion of 17pdr Fireflies, and 8th Rifle Brigade); and 159th Infantry Brigade (3rd Monmouthshire Regiment, 4th King's Shropshire Light Infantry (KSLI) and 1st Herefordshire Regiment). However, previous experience in the campaign had indicated the need for much closer co-operation between tanks and infantry and for 'Bluecoat' Roberts had re-organised his division into two self-contained brigade groups - 159th Brigade Group, on the right, with the Northamptonshire Yeomanry, Fife and Forfar Yeomanry, the KSLI and the Herefords; and 29th Armoured Brigade Group, on the left, with 23rd Hussars, 3 RTR, the Rifle Brigade and the Monmouths. By dusk the former was one mile beyond Dampierre while the latter was some two miles short of St Martin des Besaces.

On the German side of the lines the 326th Infantry Division had all but fallen apart. Drabich-Waechter had been killed during an air attack which destroyed his divisional HQ, and the regimental command posts of the two forward Grenadier units had been overrun by the British advance. For the moment, on their own initiative local commanders were attempting to establish a new front along the line of the main Caen-Avranches highway, which passed through St Martin. Field Marshal Gunther von Kluge, the German Commander-in-Chief West, was aware of the situation and ordered the 21st Panzer Division, then in reserve, to converge on the area and recapture Hill 309. In its move forward, however, the division was constantly harried by Allied air attacks so that by 2200 on the 30th its leading elements were still some miles short of the battle zone, having taken five hours to cover 20 miles.

O'Connor's instinct told him that the enemy front was on the point of crumbling. He ordered Roberts to maintain pressure during the night with a view to capturing St Martin. The KSLI, commanded by Lieutenant-Colonel Max Robinson, discovered a track leading south and, in the inky blackness of a moonless night, a company was sent along this in single file. Having made no contact whatever with the enemy, in due course the company reported itself in position astride the main highway west of the village, where it was joined by the rest of the battalion at first light and reinforced with tanks. On the 29th Armoured Brigade Group sector the Rifle Brigade had also advanced and established itself near the railway, which lay immediately to the north of St Martin.

Also moving towards the front through the darkness were the 2nd Household Cavalry, VIII Corps' reconnaissance regiment, which O'Connor had ordered forward to probe for the expected cracks in the enemy's defences. The regiment, commanded by Lieutenant-Colonel H. Abel-Smith, consisted of a HQ squadron and four armoured car squadrons; each armoured car squadron contained a HQ troop with four Staghound armoured cars; five troops each with two Daimler armoured cars and two Daimler scout cars; a heavy troop with two AEC armoured cars; and a support troop of riflemen in armoured half-tracks.

In 1944 the primary role of the armoured car was to obtain information and in this respect its radio was its most powerful weapon. Its armament was intended to give it a reasonable chance of escaping from trouble; the Daimler's 2pdr, for example, was still capable of destroying lightly armoured vehicles and could also fire high explosive and smoke shells, but was useless against the new generation of German tanks. In the vast spaces of the Western Desert armoured car crews, freed from direct supervision and with limitless horizons to scan, had lived the life of the beau sabreur to an extent impossible on the closer and more crowded landscape of a European battle. In the bocage, with its limited vision and limitless opportunities for ambush, their task sometimes bordered on the suicidal, for even negative information was of value to the planners. If a troop, sent to verify whether a bridge or crossroads was still in enemy hands, suddenly vanished from the air and failed to return, the answer would probably be in the affirmative; later, the burned-out hulks of the cars would be discovered and tell their own story. Yet, by thorough forward planning, anticipation, use of ground, speed and daring, some of the risks could be reduced.

The 2nd Household Cavalry, raised from the Life Guards and Royal Horse Guards, were recent arrivals in Normandy and their first impression was of the congestion within the beach-head, 'where entire divisions were moving along footpaths so narrow that even a Devonshire lane seemed like the Kingston By-pass'. For the majority of the men the night march into the forward area was their first experience of the sharp end of war, and if logic told them that the sights and sounds they encountered were encouraging, they were, as the regiment's historian recorded, none the less unpleasant.

'Little hamlets, existing in a world of their own and toned by the years to tranquil somnolence and peace, lay torn wide open, desecrated and burning. What had been but a few hours ago inhabited farms and cottages now crackled fiercely, casting eerie shadows across the path of the advancing cars as they lurched over the debris. The route led by taped detours across country where only with the greatest difficulty could the wheeled transport negotiate the deep ruts made by the previous passage of the tanks. Reaching the bed of a stream, we suddenly found ourselves squelching through mud. Two cars stuck and had to be dug out. At other times the column would scrape past the glowing carcass of a Sherman or have to avoid a burning truck whose stinking rubber tyres were a reminder that the battle had not long receded. A German tank, a Panther, had been hit and was still burning in the corner of a barn. Helmets, mess tins, mattresses, sheets and even a large oaken dresser lay scattered about the fields. Countless rifles had been flung aside, and belts of ammunition, strewn across our path, crunched beneath the wheels of the vehicles. The villages were deserted and what remained of livestock roamed terror-stricken about the wreckage. Two goats, still tethered to a burning outhouse, their horned shadows dancing against a whitewashed wall like a pair of bearded satyrs, were bleating piteously. A trooper ran across and cut them adrift.'

There had also been contact with batches of haggard and unshaven German prisoners being escorted to the rear. Some of them told the crews that Rommel had been mortally wounded; this was not true, although he had been seriously injured and evacuated to Germany when his staff car was strafed from the air. None of the prisoners were aware that an attempt on Hitler's life had been made only 10 days previously. When told, they merely shrugged, adding, 'Only the SS wish to fight!' This was not altogether true, either, for as the Household Cavalry would soon discover, even a broken division like the 326th was still capable of handing out some hard knocks.

Abel Smith had already detached his 'B' Squadron to operate with 15th Division. The rest of the regiment was placed under the command of 11th Armoured Division with 'C' and 'D' Squadrons working respectively on the sectors of 159th Brigade Group and 29th Armoured Brigade Group, and 'A' Squadron in reserve. The forward squadrons were ordered not to become involved in the developing battle for St Martin des Besaces, but to probe for a gap to the south. As the corps frontage was itself comparatively narrow, it was inevitable that squadron areas would overlap to some extent; it was inevitable, too, that while squadron commanders would attempt to guide the movements of their troops, in the final analysis it would be a troop leader's battle.

The cars began passing through their own lines at about 0700. Shortly after, squadron nets became congested with rapidly spoken contact reports, supplemented later by brief accounts of actions, ambushes, cars destroyed or bogged down and personnel missing. Methodically, the information gathered was entered on situation maps, but of the expected crack in the enemy's defences there was no sign.

Of the nature of this very confused series of actions, a few examples will suffice. Corporal-of-Horse Munn, commanding an armoured car of 'B' Squadron's 3 Troop, misinterpreting his orders, drove at speed into St Martin from the north and at 400 yards range fell victim to three shots from a Panther concealed among the houses, one passing between the driver's legs, one shooting away a front suspension assembly, and one passing straight through the vehicle from front to rear. Incredibly, all three of the crew escaped, Munn wounded by shards of metal, his driver with burns and his gunner unharmed.

To the west of St Martin 'C' Squadron's 4 and 5 Troops, commanded respectively by Lieutenant D. A. Corbett and Lieutenant C. Petherick, were ambushed shortly after they reached the main highway. Petherick's car burst into flames after it was penetrated by an anti-tank gun. All three of the crew were either burnt or injured, but they managed to crawl along a ditch and scramble aboard the engine deck of Corporal-of-Horse Cridland's car, which was turning round. In the process two wheels slid into the ditch, although they retained sufficient traction for the car to retire out of immediate danger, pursued by fire which further wounded Petherick and his gunner and caused their driver to drop off. With a lurch the car regained the road and, rounding a bend, came across Lieutenant Corbett's car similarly ditched. In some buildings nearby there were approximately 50 Germans, evidently eager to take advantage of the situation. Corporal-of-Horse Jenkins ordered his gunner to keep their heads down with his own car's co-axial machine gun while he closed up to his troop leader. Under fire themselves, Corbett and Jenkins dismounted and attached a tow rope to the ditched vehicle, enabling it to be hauled free, and both troops retired out of range. Corbett was then ordered to loop round the ambush site and try further west. He managed to by-pass a number of enemy positions, but every track he tried petered out and when one of his scout cars fell victim to an anti-tank gun it was apparent that any further advance in this direction was pointless.

Some troops, however, were operating south of the highway, including 'D' Squadron's 4 Troop, commanded by Lieutenant W. A.

Ainsworth. Having personally witnessed the fate of Munn's car, Ainsworth looped east around St Martin and, leaving his heavy vehicles behind, had pressed on with his two scout cars. Once across the highway he found himself on a forward slope with an excellent view across the Souleuvre valley. For a while he took to the fields, using the hedges for cover. In this way he was able to observe and report on enemy activity in the valley, including two Tiger tanks which retired into the hamlet of Le Tourneur, thereby blocking access to one of the bridges across the Souleuvre. Continuing slowly in a south-westerly direction, the cars entered another hamlet, named Les Houdan. There was no sign of life, which in itself was suspicious, although in an orchard there were slit trenches, some washing hung out to dry between the trees, ammunition boxes and Panzerfausts, all of which suggested that the occupants had gone.

Cautiously the cars probed through the houses and then reached a T-junction, where Ainsworth remained in order to cover Corporal Bugby in the leading car while he examined a bridge over a stream known to be less than 200 yards distant. After turning left at the junction, Bugby followed the road round to the right and immediately came to another T-junction. Nosing out to turn left towards his objective, now only 80 yards away, he observed a German company drawn up on the bridge itself. The scout car's armament consisted of a single poorly-mounted Bren light machine gun, with which Bugby began to create havoc without attracting one round of return fire. He was well into his fourth magazine when Ainsworth's voice suddenly yelled in his headset: 'Retire at once! Enemy tank advancing on you! Have laid down smoke!' Needing no further urging, Bugby rejoined his troop leader, observing with satisfaction the thickening screen across the road caused by the latter firing his multiple grenade dischargers, and the two retired through the hamlet. Seconds later the tank snarled past the mouth of the T-junction without suspecting their presence.

To Roberts at 11th Armoured Division and O'Connor at VIII Corps it began to seem, as the morning wore on, that for all their efforts the 2nd Household Cavalry would not find the anticipated gap in the enemy's defences. Indeed, although 159th Brigade Group was developing a major attack against St Martin from the west, it looked very much as though the Germans had, for the moment at least, succeeded in stabilising their front. Yet, through a combination of persistence and incredible luck, one armoured car troop had struck the purest gold.

For 'C' Squadron's 1 Troop, commanded by Lieutenant D. B. Powle, the day had begun badly. Shortly after leaving Dampierre, Corporal-of-Horse Brown's car, travelling third in the troop column, developed trouble with its accelerator in a narrow lane flanked by high banks, thereby blocking the passage of the rear scout car as well. Powle decided to proceed with the rest of the troop, consisting of a scout car manned by Corporal G. B. Bland and Trooper H. G. P. Read, and one armoured car crewed by himself, Corporal P. Staples as gunner-radio operator and Trooper Clarke as driver.

Shortly after, Bland, in the lead, came upon a German sentry. The man took to his heels but was killed by a grenade which Bland flung after him, believing that this would attract less attention than a burst of machine gun fire. This seems to have served well, for the troop was now approaching the highway on which Powle observed at least one 88mm anti-tank gun and several other weapons. Fortunately, their muzzles were pointing in another direction and the Germans seemed unaware of the cars' approach. Powle decided to use speed and surprise and both cars flashed across the highway to vanish down the lane opposite before the enemy could react; it is believed that it was these guns which subsequently engaged Petherick's troop.

It had been a tense moment. Now, Powle was anxious to put as much distance as possible between himself and the highway, shouting to Bland: 'We may as well try what's in front – it can't be worse than trying to neck it back through that lot!' Shortly after, a four-wheeled German armoured car, probably an SdKfz 222, which bore a passing resemblance to the Daimler family, turned into the lane ahead and began driving south at speed. Powle could have destroyed it, although this would merely have blocked the road, but instead he decided to follow it closely. Neither the German crew nor anyone else along the way gave the British cars a second glance. This was not perhaps as surprising as it might seem, for the enemy was still using quantities of Allied equipment captured in 1940 and to the casual observer there was no reason to suspect that the two dust-covered cars tearing along behind the unmistakably German vehicle were not part of the same unit.

Powle found himself on a track passing through woodland which his map told him was the Foret l'Eveque. His map also told him that in due course this route would bring him to a bridge across the Souleuvre, just above its confluence with the Vire. The track left the trees and when the German car turned left into a side road at La Ferriere Harang the British troop continued straight on. Reaching a wider road leading to the bridge, the cars turned along it. Powle received an unpleasant start when he was suddenly confronted by a dummy wooden tank, 'so well camouflaged that I didn't see it until I was only 20 yards away, so that it entirely lost its purpose'. Intermittent traffic was using the road in both directions, although most of the flow was from north to south, which suggested that the enemy was indeed pulling back. Still no one paid any attention to the two cars. The road wound downhill through trees to the bridge where, covered by Powle, Bland's scout car slipped across. Bland and Read then dismounted and killed an unsuspecting sentry. Powle crossed and the cars were concealed under cut bushes among trees to the south-west of the bridge. Only one pair of eyes had noted their arrival. They belonged to M. Desiré Papillon, owner of a nearby farm who, believing that his property would be fought over that day, had hidden in the woods beside the river.

It might have seemed strange to Powle and his men that the bridge had neither been guarded adequately nor prepared for demolition, but they had no intention of looking a gift horse in the mouth. What they could not possibly have guessed was that the road carried by the bridge had been designated by the enemy not merely as the boundary between the 326th and 3rd Parachute Divisions, nor even the boundary between LXXIV Corps and II Parachute Corps, but as the boundary between Panzer Group West and the German Seventh Army. Neither army had considered itself responsible for its security, with the result that an extremely sensitive sector lay virtually unprotected.

While Powle and the rest maintained watch on the bridge, Corporal Staples remained aboard his car and attempted to transmit details of the coup. Operating conditions were very difficult indeed, for the radio was working at the limit of its range, the net was crowded with traffic, and there was an overlay of transmissions from the American sector as well as severe interference. At length Staples got through to squadron HQ: 'At 1030 hours – the bridge at 637436 is clear of enemy and still intact. ' The message was relayed by rear link to Abel Smith who, observing from his map that the reference lay no less than six miles behind enemy lines, demanded immediate verification. At 1035 Staples repeated the message verbatim; there was no mistake.

As the news was passed up the chain of command its effect was electric. At Second Army, Dempsey decided that the emphasis of 'Bluecoat' would be shifted to VIII Corps' sector. For O'Connor this meant that 11th Armoured Division would exploit to the high ground beyond the captured bridge, which in turn would mean bringing the Guards Armoured Division forward to fill the gap which would thus be created between Roberts and MacMillan. Roberts himself was already engaged in the battle for St Martin, which was captured at about 1100, but he fully appreciated that the need to get troops forward was of paramount importance and he ordered the 23rd Hussars, with the Monmouths aboard, to drive hard for the bridge. Aware that this would take a little time to organise, and that the bridge had to be reinforced immediately, he further ordered two troops of 'C' Squadron Northamptonshire Yeomanry, which had covered the right flank of 159 Brigade Group's attack on St Martin and were already close to the Foret l'Eveque, to join Powle, following the route taken by the latter's cars.

The two troops, commanded by Lieutenant K. M. Dyson and Sergeant J. Taylor, possessed a total of five tanks, having lost one of their Cromwells to an anti-tank gun as they crossed the railway and main road earlier that morning. It seems that Staples had been able to provide details of the route, which in turn were passed to Major John MacGillycuddy, commanding the Yeomanry's 'C' Squadron. This enabled MacGillycuddy, otherwise known as 'Big Mac', to talk the two troops forward onto the correct track and through the forest. At La Ferrière the tanks were held up for a while by two self-propelled guns, but after these had been disposed of they pressed on at speed and joined Powle shortly after mid-day. Even when combined, the little force at the bridge could hardly be described as impressive, although the enemy made no attempt to eject it. As the afternoon wore on it shot up several vehicles, including a lorry, a staff car and a motorcyclist, and took a prisoner who had in his possession all of 21st Panzer Division's radio codes.

If, at the end of the day, the Household Cavalry had much to celebrate in Powle's achievement, its elation was also tempered by sadness. Anxious about the isolated handful of his men so far behind enemy lines, Abel Smith had also sent 'D' Squadron's 5 Troop forward along the same route to join them. All had gone well until the cars reached La Ferrière, where they found the Yeomanry's Cromwells temporarily held up. The troop leader, Lieutenant R. A. Bethell, decided to strike west along a track which joined the road leading down to the bridge. After this, the troop was neither heard from nor seen again. Next morning the burnt-out wrecks of an armoured car and a scout car were found on the road; of the crews and the other cars there was no sign. It was many months before the full story was pieced together. The troop had reached the road and turned south only to run into an ambush in which the two leading vehicles were immediately knocked out by Panzerfausts. The Germans had then burst through the hedges and swarmed over the remaining cars as they attempted to turn. The crews were taken prisoner and the wounded were driven on the backs of the captured cars to Le Tourneur, which was evidently an enemy rally-point. Bethell, who had lost a leg in the action, had his wound cleaned with local anaethetic and wrapped in paper bandages while the German doctor explained that his own men received just the same treatment.

Meanwhile, the 23rd Hussars and Monmouths had left St Martin and were moving towards the bridge. For the sake of speed, Roberts had directed them to use the wider road to the west rather than the forest track, but this brought them into contact with American units which were also advancing on the bridge, and the result was a traffic jam when it was needed least. The problem was resolved amicably when the Americans realised that the bridge they wanted actually lay a mile or two to the west and pulled out. However, valuable time had been lost and it was not until 2100 that the lonely vigil of Powle, Dyson and their men ended with the arrival of the first Shermans. Pressing on, the Hussars and Monmouths crossed the bridge to secure the high ground beyond, overlooking Le Beny Bocage. During the evening the Guards Armoured Division passed through St Martin but found the hills to the south defended by tanks and infantry of the 21st Panzer Division.

Although the operation as a whole did not result in a major breakthrough on the British Second Army's sector, several days' hard fighting being required to advance its line a further six miles to the south, many historians regard 'Bluecoat' in general, and the capture of the Souleuvre bridge in particular, as being a major turning point in the campaign. First, the seizure of Hill 309 by 6th Guards Tank Brigade had caused Kluge to pull 21st Panzer Division out of reserve and commit it, together with other troops including a Tiger battalion, in an attempt to restore the situation. None of the counter-attacks mounted to recover the hill made any progress, for although the Coldstream might have been alarmed to see their armour-piercing shot flying off the Tigers 'like ping-pong balls', the enemy's assaults were regularly broken up by concentrated artillery fire and air attacks; two wrecked Tigers and over 200 bodies were subsequently discovered in one wood alone. Secondly, the capture of the Souleuvre crossing and its exploitation by 11th Armoured Division presented Kluge with a potentially disastrous set of circumstances which would quickly run out of control unless immediate action was taken. There was, in fact, only one option open to him and that was to move II SS Panzer Corps (9th and 10th SS Panzer Divisions) from the Caen sector into the line opposite the 11th and Guards Armoured Divisions, even if this left his right flank seriously weakened. During the early hours of 3 August he received an order from Hitler telling him that all the Panzer divisions facing the British were to be withdrawn for a counter-stroke against the Americans, who had broken through into open country at Avranches. With no reserves whatever in hand, he knew that if he complied the front would collapse within a matter of hours, and he declined to do so.

On the Allied side of the line the odds had become yet more heavily stacked against Kluge. On 1 August Lieutenant-General George S. Patton's US Third Army was activated with the specific role of exploiting the American breakthrough; simultaneously, to the north, the First Canadian Army, commanded by Lieutenant-General H. D. G. Crerar, came into being on the Caen sector. In accordance with Hitler's specific orders, Kluge, who had managed to assemble four weak Panzer divisions with a total strength of only 185 tanks and self-propelled guns, mounted a counter-attack against the Americans at Mortain on 7 August and was decisively defeated. Patton's corps swung south, then east, then north towards the Seine, causing Kluge to withdraw and extend his now exposed left flank. On 8 August the First Canadian Army began to drive in his right flank in two operations codenamed 'Totalize' and 'Tractable'. By 16 August the German armies in Normandy were trapped within a pocket which was to take its name from the nearby town of Falaise; by 21 August they had ceased to exist. Kluge, dismissed by Hitler, had taken his own life two days previously; an unwilling conspirator in the July Bomb Plot, he was well aware of the probable fate which awaited him at the hands of the Gestapo if he returned to Germany.

Both Montgomery and Dempsey had every reason to feel satisfied with VIII Corps' performance during 'Bluecoat', although they were disappointed that XXX Corps had not produced better results during its early stages and many of its senior officers were moved to other appointments. One consequence of this was that Brigadier Verney, who had orchestrated 6th Guards Tank Brigade's dramatic seizure of Hill 309, suddenly found himself promoted and appointed to command the 7th Armoured Division. For their part in securing the bridge across the Souleuvre, Lieutenant Powle and Corporal Bland received, respectively, immediate awards of the Military Cross and the Military Medal. Within the 2nd Household Cavalry, Powle's nickname was Dickie and the bridge itself was subsequently referred to as Dickie's Bridge. VIII Corps HQ, not wishing to diminish the part played by the Northamptonshire Yeomanry, called it Cavalry Bridge. On 2 June 1984, almost 40 years after the event, a ceremony was held on the spot, attended by Major-General Roberts and Powle, by then a retired lieutenant-colonel. After describing the course of the action, Roberts asked Powle to open the bridge for the second time and then unveiled plaques recording the name by which it will be known to posterity: Le Pont du Taureau, chosen because of the 11th Armoured Division's symbol of a charging bull.

CHAPTER 8

Meiktila – The Master Stroke

Beaten, bitter, starving and diseased, the survivors of Lieutenant-General Renya Mutaguchi's Fifteenth Army straggled back across the Chindwin river, leaving behind them a grisly trail of wreckage which included all their heavy equipment and 53,000 of their comrades whose skeletons would be picked clean by the jungle's teeming life-forms. Never in its history had the Imperial Japanese Army sustained so decisive a defeat on such a scale.

Yet in March 1944, barely four months earlier, Mutaguchi's three divisions had advanced into Manipur supremely confident that they could isolate and destroy Lieutenant-General G. A. P. Scoones' IV Corps on the Imphal Plain and secure an impregnable defence line on the Naga Hills which would remove, once and for all, any prospect of a British re-conquest of Burma from the north. Then, there had seemed to be no reason why they should not defeat their British and Indian opponents just as easily as they had in Malaya or in the earlier fighting in Burma.

The old magic, however, refused to work. The British Fourteenth Army, commanded by Lieutenant-General William Slim, was trained, equipped and psychologically prepared for the encounter. Furthermore, it was now the Allies who possessed, and in even greater measure, the air superiority which had contributed so much to Japan's early victories. Ominously, in a battle which had lasted throughout February, a Japanese division had been cut to pieces in the Arakan by a British force which had been surrounded and was apparently on the verge of defeat. The force had stood its ground, being supplied by air, and tanks had played a major part in its defence and relief. (See *Last Stand!* Chapter 11, 'The Defence of the Admin Box'.) This, on a much larger scale, predicted the nature of the fighting in Manipur, for while Mutaguchi succeeded in isolating IV Corps at Imphal its divisions received all their requirements by air and their wounded were evacuated the same way. In addition, sustained counter-attacks by Scoones' troops imposed a rate of attrition which Mutaguchi could not afford. Finally, at the end of May Lieutenant-General Montagu Stopford's XXXIII Corps broke through the Japanese blocking position at Kohima and on 22 June effected a junction with IV Corps north of Imphal. Mutaguchi could do no more than extract what remained of his army.

The fighting had been savage in the extreme, with neither side willing to give or receive quarter, and it revealed a number of serious flaws in the Japanese military machine. The Fifteenth Army's three divisions, for example, fought what amounted to separate battles and were in no position to provide mutual support for each other, even if their commanders had not indulged in acrimonious, and occasionally insubordinate, squabbling. It was, however, in the field of logistics that the Japanese had proved to be most vulnerable. In the past, when their frugal marching rations had gone, their success had enabled them to feed themselves from the enemy's supplies. Now, denied success, they starved. Ammunition held absolute priority on the tenuous supply lines stretching back to the Chindwin, but these were under constant attack by Major-General Orde Wingate's Chindit columns. Wingate had been killed in an air crash on 24 March but under his successor, Major-General Walter Lentaigne, the Chindits tied down the equivalent of two-and-a-half Japanese divisions at the very time when Mutaguchi's manpower resources were stretched beyond safe limits.

During the closing stages of the battles of Imphal and Kohima the Chindits were directed northwards to assist Lieutenant-General Joseph Stilwell's Chinese-American army, which was fighting to re-open the only land route to China, the Burma Road. Initially, Stilwell's advance had gone according to plan, but at Myitkyina the Japanese resisted so stubbornly that the town did not fall until 3 August. Despite the fact that Lentaigne's men had already been decimated by casualties, disease and exhaustion, Stilwell opposed their withdrawal to the bitter end. As a result of this the health of many men was permanently affected and no further Chindit operations were mounted.

Fortune also favoured the Japanese in that the monsoon slowed down the British pursuit, so providing time in which General Hoyotaro Kimura, the new commander of the Japanese army group in Burma - known as the Burma Area Army - could rally his troops after the disaster in Manipur and re-establish a coherent strategy. Altogether, he had a total of approximately 250,000 men available, although this included units of the Indian and Burma National Armies, recruited from prisoners of war and those with a political axe to grind, which could not be relied upon. Discounting these and adminstrative personnel he could still field some 100,000 fighting troops, the bulk of which were deployed across a wide area in three armies: the Thirty-Third, with two divisions, under Lieutenant-General Masaki Honda, facing the Chinese-American army in northern Burma; the Fifteenth, with four divisions, now commanded by Lieutenant-General Shihachi Katamura, in central Burma and around Mandalay, still recovering from its defeats at Imphal and Kohima; and the Twenty-Eighth, with three divisions, under Lieutenant-General Seizo Sakurai, in the Arakan and southern Burma.

Kimura's strategy was to allow the British to cross the Chindwin, then the Irrawaddy, and fight a major battle in the area of Mandalay where his own troops would be close to their supply bases. In these circumstances, he reasoned, the British would be fighting at the end of over-extended supply lines, just as Mutaguchi had done in Manipur, and they would be defeated. Such a conclusion was totally illogical in that it ignored his opponents' now unchallenged air superiority, which would enable them to be supplied by air as easily in central Burma as they had been at Imphal. It also ignored the fact that central Burma contained arid open areas which would allow the British to use their armour to even better advantage than they had done in the difficult terrain of Manipur, where the intervention of a handful of tanks had often proved decisive.

Perhaps the latter risk might have been acceptable if he had possessed a comparable armoured force of his own, but the obsolete vehicles of his single tank regiment were no match for British Shermans and Lees and their crews were trained not for the tank battle but for local tactical operations in support of infantry. Nor could he trust his anti-tank weapons to provide an adequate defence, for although the Japanese 47mm anti-tank gun could and did inflict serious damage it was in very short supply; when the moment came, anti-tank defences would be improvised from whatever resources were to hand, and the nature of these would provide some extremely unpleasant shocks for the British and Indian tank crews.

All in all, Kimura's plan paid so little attention to his enemy's potential and intentions, and to the deficiencies of his own army, that it amounted to little more than a grand delusion. Yet, there was one factor on which he could rely implicitly and that was the spirit of his troops, who would willingly fight to the death rather than surrender. Unless the battle took a totally unexpected form, therefore, it would be a bloody business for both sides.

Allied plans for the next phase of the campaign involved maintaining the offensive on all fronts. Stilwell, recalled to the United States at the request of Chiang Kai-shek in October, had been replaced by Lieutenant-General Dan Sultan and on the northern sector the latter's Chinese-American army, reinforced by the British 36th Division, had succeeded in reopening the land route to China on 5 January 1945. In the centre IV and XXXIII Corps, the victors in the Manipur fighting, were advancing into central Burma. In the strategically sensitive Arakan, Lieutenant-General A. F. P. Christison's XV Corps would again take the offensive, assisted by a series of amphibious landings, pinning down Sakurai's Twenty-Eighth Army by threatening to break through the intervening mountain chain into central Burma.

Slim had no doubt that the Burma Area Army would be defeated in the forthcoming battle, but his intention was to destroy it where it stood rather than allow Kimura to withdraw his troops into Siam or even Malaya. To this end his eyes were fixed on the town of Meiktila, a

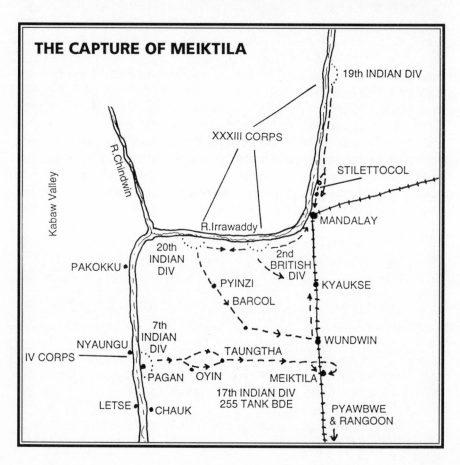

THE CAPTURE OF MEIKTILA

19th INDIAN DIV

XXXIII CORPS

R.Chindwin

Kabaw Valley

STILETTOCOL

R.Irrawaddy

MANDALAY

20th INDIAN DIV

PAKOKKU

2nd BRITISH DIV

PYINZI

BARCOL

KYAUKSE

7th INDIAN DIV

NYAUNGU

IV CORPS

TAUNGTHA

WUNDWIN

PAGAN OYIN

MEIKTILA

LETSE CHAUK

17th INDIAN DIV
255 TANK BDE

PYAWBWE & RANGOON

major road and rail communications centre with an important airfield. Through Meiktila passed the bulk of supplies destined for Katamura's Fifteenth Army, grouped around Mandalay, and Honda's Thirty-Third Army, further north. It followed, therefore, that if Meiktila could be seized and held against counter-attack, those armies would be deprived of the means with which to fight their battles and they would simply collapse, especially if they were kept under constant pressure.

It was, in fact, Wingate who had first recognised the supreme importance of Meiktila to the enemy. In March 1944 he had suggested that, after the Japanese had been defeated in Manipur, the town should become the objective of the next Chindit offensive. Wingate, however, was dead and, thanks largely to Stilwell, the Chindit force was no more. Slim and his staff therefore considered alternative means of securing Meiktila and in this they were materially assisted by Kimura's own strategy. At one point Slim had believed that, during the course of its retreat, the defeated Fifteenth Army would make a stand on the Shwebo Plain, between the Chindwin and Irrawaddy rivers. In such circumstances he would have moved IV Corps in alongside XXXIII Corps, which was leading his advance, but as contact with the enemy was restricted to clashes with his rearguards it became apparent that Kimura's intention was merely to deploy the Fifteenth Army beyond the Irrawaddy on either side of Mandalay.

This discovery was of immense benefit to Slim's plans, since it enabled him to commit the whole of IV Corps to the Meiktila operation. As finalised, therefore, the British plan involved several overlapping phases. During the first Stopford's XXXIII Corps, consisting of the 2nd British, 19th and 20th Indian Divisions and 254th Indian Tank Brigade, would close up to the Irrawaddy, just as Kimura anticipated, then cross and establish several bridgeheads with the deliberate intention of attracting Japanese counter-attacks.

Simultaneously an elaborate deception plan, codenamed 'Cloak', would be put into effect, intended to convince the enemy that IV Corps was present on the Shwebo Plain and conforming to XXXIII Corps' movements. The most important element of this was a dummy radio net which, day after day, transmitted the full range of IV Corps' radio traffic with just sufficient breaches of security to permit the Japanese intercept operators to identify units and monitor their imaginary movements.

Meanwhile, the real IV Corps, now commanded by Lieutenant-General F. W. Messervy and consisting of 7th and 17th Indian Divisions, 28th East African Brigade and 255th Indian Tank Brigade, would be moving in strict radio silence down the Kabaw and Gangaw valleys to Pakokku on the Irrawaddy, well downstream of XXXIII Corps' operational area. There it would secure a bridgehead on the far bank from which, at the earliest possible moment, a task force spearheaded by armour would seize Meiktila.

It was anticipated that the Japanese would react violently to the loss of their vital communications centre and that the task force would itself be isolated and besieged, in which event it would be reinforced and supplied by air. By this time XXXIII Corps would have gone over to the offensive, breaking out of its bridgeheads to drive on Mandalay. In these circumstances the enemy, already fragmented and denied the wherewithal to fight, faced being crushed between the two British corps and was not expected to offer protracted resistance.

The plan, brilliant in concept, was assisted by the fact that Kimura lacked the troops to defend the entire length of the Irrawaddy. Thus, while Slim's troops were faced with one of the world's greatest and widest rivers, which they would have to cross with nothing more sophisticated than infantry assault boats and motorised rafts for their tanks, artillery and vehicles, initially they would encounter nothing more serious than local opposition. In the event, none of XXXIII Corps' divisions experienced any difficulty in establishing a bridgehead. On 9 January the 19th Indian Division (Major-General Rees) secured a perimeter on the east bank some 60 miles north of Mandalay. On 12 February the 20th Indian Division (Major-General Gracey) landed 40 miles downstream of the city, where the river flowed west to its confluence with the Chindwin. On 24 February the 2nd British Division (Major-General Cameron Nicholson) established a third bridgehead between 20th Division and Mandalay.

Each of these landings had been carefully scheduled not only to keep the Japanese off balance on XXXIII Corps' sector, but also to coincide with a phase of IV Corps' movements far to the west. The intention, too, was to write down the enemy's strength before IV Corps made its presence felt so that when, as anticipated, Katamura's Fifteenth Army launched frenzied counter-attacks against each of the bridgeheads, these foundered with much slaughter in a storm of artillery, tank and infantry fire. The role played by the supporting armour of 254th Indian Tank Brigade (3rd Carabiniers and 150 Regiment RAC with Lees, 7th Light Cavalry with Stuart light tanks and two squadrons of 11th Cavalry with Daimler armoured cars), elements of which were allocated to each bridgehead, was of particular importance: once heavy casualties had forced the Japanese onto the defensive, they formed the spearhead of attacks directed at villages lying beyond their respective perimeters. These actions were designed to further pin down Katamura's troops and inflict even heavier casualties on them: in this they were entirely successful.

During bitterly contested day-long battles the Japanese fought to the bitter end as a matter of course and at dusk the British and Indian tanks and infantry were intentionally withdrawn within their own lines. Observing this, local Japanese commanders, under strict orders to hold their ground at all costs, would promptly insert new garrisons into the villages and these would simply re-occupy the identical bunkers and trenches in which their comrades had died. In the morning, the tanks and infantry would return and, as the layout of the defences was already familiar to them, they would systematically clear the objective at small cost to themselves. In such battles, which were sometimes repeated for days at a time, the Fifteenth Army allowed itself to be ruthlessly exploited and in consequence its manpower and equipment resources began to haemorrhage at an unacceptable rate.

During these actions the Japanese displayed the same suicidal courage in attack and the same dedicated tenacity in defence that they had always done. Recognising that the tanks were the principal cause of their defeats, they would resort to the most desperate measures in an attempt to destroy them or kill their crews. Perhaps the most notable example of this occurred when, breaking out of close scrub, an officer and a private scrambled aboard the engine deck of a Lee belonging to A Squadron 3rd Carabiniers, fighting in support of the 2nd British Division. The private was shot dead by a burst of machine gun fire from another Lee but not before the officer had killed the tank commander with his sword, then dropped into the top turret as the body collapsed and similarly killed the 37mm gunner. He then set about the 37mm loader who, partially protected by the gun breech, was able to draw his revolver and fire six shots into his opponent. Even this did not stop the man and it was not until the loader grabbed the dead gunner's pistol and fired three more shots that the fight ended. Throughout, the sponson-mounted 75mm gun had remained in action and neither the weapon's gunner and loader, nor the vehicle's radio operator and driver, were aware of the carnage taking place behind them.

While XXXIII Corps was pinning down the Japanese along the Irrawaddy, Messervy's IV Corps was engaged in its 300-mile approach march to Pakokku. This took it through the sparsely populated Chin Hills and along buffalo tracks which the corps engineers made passable with the assistance of elephants and bulldozers. Although every effort was made to maintain secrecy, it was naive to expect that the movement of thousands of men and vehicles would not be reported to the Japanese at some stage. Takuo Isobe, then serving as a captain with the 215th Infantry Regiment, and subsequently the author of several books on the war in Burma, records that on his regiment's sector alone reports of IV Corps' activities were passed to 33rd Division, thence to Fifteenth Army and on to HQ Burma Area Army, not once but on several occasions.

On 15 January the headman of a village in the Gangaw valley reported an estimated 400 tanks and other vehicles moving south; later in the month a spy confirmed the headman's story but placed the numbers at 300 tanks and 3,000 wheeled vehicles; and on 10 February the same force was reported to have concentrated 200 tanks and 2,000 wheeled vehicles west of Pakokku. The only reaction from Burma Area Army was to issue a reprimand direct to 33rd Division for what was considered to be gross exaggeration.

From start to finish, Kimura's HQ refused to recognise that a threat was developing from this direction for the simple reason that, while it was aware that Slim could field two armoured brigades in central Burma, it was absolutely convinced that these were deployed to the north and west of Mandalay, partly because it had been totally deceived by Operation 'Cloak' and partly because of XXXIII Corps' aggressive use of tanks in its bridgeheads. In the eyes of the Burma Area Army's staff, therefore, if British tanks were closing up to Pakokku, logic dictated that they were few in number and therefore engaged in an operation of purely local significance.

The 255th Indian Tank Brigade, commanded by Brigadier Claud Pert, was equipped with Shermans and consisted of 116 Regiment RAC (Gordon Highlanders), 5th King Edward VII's Own Lancers (Probyn's Horse) and 9th Cavalry (Royal Deccan Horse), plus B Squadron 11th Cavalry with Daimler armoured cars. It had been hoped that for much of the long approach march to Pakokku the tanks could be carried on transporters, so saving wear and tear, but in the event the primitive nature of the route, which included hundreds of bends as it wound through the mountainous terrain, and heavy going worsened by occasional downpours, meant that they had done an average of 200 miles on their own tracks. Few arrived without with some essential part of their running gear having been replaced but, thanks to the efforts of the regimental Light Aid Detachments, who frequently worked through the night and received spare part deliveries by air, they arrived in battleworthy condition.

The first phase of Messervy's corps plan involved Major-General G. C. Evans' 7th Indian Division, with 116 Regiment attached, clearing the enemy from the vicinity of the actual crossing site at Nyaungu, south of Pakokku, then securing a bridgehead on the far bank of the river. The crossing took place during the early hours of 14 February and through-out the following week the perimeter was expanded and consolidated while the force detailed for the coup at Meiktila, Major-General D. T. Cowan's 17th Indian Division and the remainder of 255th Indian Tank Brigade, crossed into the bridgehead and completed their preparations for the breakout.

At first the Japanese were unable to understand why a fresh bridgehead had been established on the east bank of the Irrawaddy, so far from the battle which was raging to the north, and they certainly saw no threat in it to Meiktila. Their belief was that it was a diversion intended to distract attention from a major thrust somewhere else along the river, and to encourage this Messervy despatched 28th East African Brigade and one squadron of 116 Regiment down the west bank to Letse, opposite the oil town of Chauk, which seemed a probable objec-tive. To this the Japanese, now believing that they were faced with a kind of Chindit raid, responded at once, pouring troops across the river to contain the threat. Against these the East Africans fought a number of stiff actions then, their task complete, withdrew.

Together, Messervy, Cowan and Evans formed an ideal partner-ship for the task in hand. Messervy had commanded the 7th Armoured Division for a while in North Africa, and had subsequently held the post of senior armoured adviser at GHQ in India; more recently he had led 7th Indian Division to victory in the Arakan and at Kohima. Cowan was the most experienced of Fourteenth Army's divisional commanders, he and his division having fought the Japanese continuously ever since they had invaded Burma. Evans had been responsible for the successful defence of the Admin Box the previous year. When the Japanese finally awoke to the terrible danger in which they stood, which would happen once the coup de main force had been launched at Meiktila, they would spare no effort to eliminate the 7th Division's bridgehead and Evans could again be relied upon to conduct an aggressive defence which would keep them off balance.

On 21 February Cowan's division smashed through the thin shield of Japanese troops covering the bridgehead and headed for Meik-tila along two parallel axes with 63rd Brigade on the right and 48th Brigade on the left, spearheaded respectively by the Shermans of Probyn's and the Deccan Horse. Far ahead and on the flanks the advance was screened by 11th Cavalry's Daimlers and the Humbers of 16th Light Cavalry, the corps armoured car regiment which, despite its low number, was the senior Indian cavalry regiment, yielding precedence only to the Viceroy's (now President's) Bodyguard, and the first to be commanded by an Indian officer, Lieutenant-Colonel J. N. Chaudhuri. Above the leading troops circled a cab rank of Thunderbolt fighter-bombers, handled efficiently by the RAF Forward Air Controller attached to each squadron who, whenever local opposition was encountered, would smother it in a welter of bombs and strafing machine gunfire.

Yet, though the armoured car commanders might believe that they were leading the advance across the arid, sandy terrain, they would often be surprised by the sight of an Auster light aircraft flying straight towards them. The aircraft would bump down beside the cars and out would step Messervy himself to spur on the troop leader with a shout of 'Press on! There's nothing in front of you!'.

At the village of Oyin, however, Probyn's and 63rd Brigade found that the enemy garrison, though administrative troops, were just as capable of selling their lives as dearly as possible. Here, for the first time, tank crews encountered the enemy's anti-tank version of the kamikaze air attack. Suicide squads had been formed from volunteers who, with specially prepared charges, would throw themselves beneath tanks' vulnerable belly plates in a desperate attempt to destroy themselves and the vehicle in the resulting explosion. Of the half-dozen or so attacks made in this way one succeeded in disabling a tank and killing its driver; a second might have achieved a similar result if the quick-witted tank commander had not ordered his driver to reverse immediately; but the remainder of the squad was shot down or blown apart by its own charges. Their efforts evoked admiration tinged with pity, although they were also un-nerving and provided some indication of the form the battle for Meiktila would take.

On 24 February the Royal Deccan Horse and 48th Brigade captured the small town of Taungtha, containing the maintenance depot of the Japanese 33rd Division. At Taungtha Cowan's axes of advance converged and that night Probyn's and 63rd Brigade also arrived. By now British intentions regarding Meiktila should have been crystal clear to Kimura and it had been anticipated that he would reinforce the town's garrison, a contingency for which Messervy and Cowan had made due allowance when planning the operation.

In fact, a signal had already been despatched to HQ Burma Area Army reporting that a column of 2,000 vehicles had broken out of 7th Indian Division's bridgehead and was heading for Meiktila. Until recently it was believed that in transmission the figure was corrupted to

200, so that when the news reached Kimura who, with his chief-of-staff was attending an army commanders' conference in Meiktila, the whole thing was dismissed as a hit-and-run raid of no great significance and no further steps were taken.

A detailed investigation by Takuo Isobe, however, has revealed an altogether different state of affairs regarding the signal itself. The concentration of 17th Indian Division and 255th Tank Brigade at Taungtha was observed by an operations staff officer of 33rd Division and one of Fifteenth Army's intelligence officers from a hill to the north of the town. Both agreed that 200 tanks were present (actually 100, although the numerous armoured cars were probably included in their estimate) plus 2,000 wheeled vehicles, and reported the fact to Fifteenth Army. In turn, Fifteenth Army relayed this information to HQ Burma Area Army in Rangoon with the recommendation that everything should be thrown into the defence of Meiktila. That the coded message arrived in its correct form is now beyond reasonable doubt. However, since the information it contained was completely at variance with the intelligence section's assessment of the British armour's whereabouts, mentioned above, they refused to believe it and even ordered the telegraphists to amend the figure of 2,000 to 200, which the latter declined to do. Nevertheless, it seems that the intelligence section changed the figure on its own initiative and it was in this form that it reached Kimura. The Burma Area Army's reply to Fifteenth Army told it not to overestimate the enemy's strength in the Meiktila area and concentrate instead on the battle in progress around Mandalay; furthermore, when 33rd Division transmitted further messages including the figure 2,000 it was reprimanded sharply for repeated exaggeration.

Curiously, despite the terrible danger inherent in the situation if the report was true, no attempt was made by Burma Area Army to verify the position with its admittedly limited air assets, which would have provided immediate confirmation. This stubborn refusal to accept the evaluation of the troops on the spot, coupled with face-saving adherence to pre-conceived ideas, was to have catastrophic consequences for the Japanese cause in Burma.

On 26 February the Royal Deccan Horse led 48th Brigade in a cross-country advance which secured the undefended airfield at Thabukton, 15 miles north of Meiktila, by mid-afternoon. Engineers promptly put the airstrip into an operational condition and the following day a stream of Dakota transports airlanded the 17th Division's third brigade, the 99th, enabling Cowan to launch his assault on Meiktila at full strength.

Simultaneously, a probe towards Meiktila itself by two troops of 16th Light Cavalry encountered stiffening opposition centred on a chaung bridge at Egyo. It was decided that while one squadron of Probyn's supported a frontal attack on the position, a second squadron would carry out a wide left hook and establish a road block two miles in the enemy's rear. When, under pressure, the defenders attempted to retreat, they were caught between the two and shot down, losing several guns in the process.

Whatever the construction placed by HQ Burma Area Army on British activity to the west, the day's events at Thabukton and Egyo convinced Major-General Kasuya, Meiktila's commandant, that the town was about to be attacked in far greater strength than had been anticipated. Under his command were the base depots of the two Japanese armies to the north and, as the fearful implications inherent in their loss began to dawn, he gave orders that every building was to be turned into a fortress. In total he had approximately 3,500 men available, but of these only about half were professional infantry, including the 168th Regiment, which had been halted as it marched through the town on its way to the Mandalay sector; the remainder consisted of his own administrative troops and the patients of a military hospital. In the very limited time which was left as the British approached he was unable to complete his defences, although he achieved much.

Meiktila lies on a neck of land between its North and South Lakes and approach from the west is hindered by water courses. However, if Kasuya was relying on these natural defences to buy time he was disappointed, for Cowan's intention was to attack from the east across open ground. On the morning of 28 February, led by 11th Cavalry's armoured cars, 255th Tank Brigade drove past the North Lake, then swung south and west to roar across the airfield. The attack seems to have taken the landing ground's defenders by surprise; had it gone in 24 hours later it might well have incurred far heavier loss than was the case, as extensive preparations had been made to mine the area and numerous heavy aerial bombs had been placed beside the pits which had been dug for them. Once the airfield had been secured the tanks and infantry closed in on the town's suburbs where the Japanese offered such determined resistance it was clear that Meiktila would not fall without a struggle.

Three days of ferocious street fighting were needed before Cowan's tank and infantry teams were able to eliminate the last of Kasuya's scratch garrison. The Japanese fought until they were killed or the blazing buildings beneath which they had constructed their bunkers fell in on them. Against the tanks they employed every means of attack possible, including the few anti-tank guns at their disposal, Molotov cocktails, and pole charges. Suicide squads attempted to fling themselves beneath the vehicles or sat concealing themselves in craters in the road, a 250lb bomb between their knees and a stone in one hand ready to strike the primer when a tank passed overhead; most were spotted and killed by the tanks' close escort of infantry before they could do any damage. Here and there tanks were disabled or their commanders were shot dead by snipers, but not in sufficient numbers to affect the outcome. Inexorably, house by house, the defenders were pushed back until the few survivors were confined to the area of the town jutting into the South Lake. There, rather than fall alive into the enemy's hands, they deliberately drowned themselves or were shot down as they waded into the shallows. Their stand evoked the sincere admiration of their opponents and would have earned an honoured place in the history of any Western army; in the Japanese service, however, no other ending was possible.

For Kimura, the sudden and unexpected loss of Meiktila and its priceless supplies was a shattering blow. Unless the town was recaptured immediately, neither Honda's Thirty-Third Army to the north nor Katamura's Fifteenth Army could be maintained in their present position. The problem was: where were the troops to come from? In the Arakan, Sakurai's Twenty-Eighth Army was fully extended in its attempts to contain the landings made by Christison's XV Corps, while closer at hand the Fifteenth Army was locked into its struggle with Stopford's XXXIII Corps around Mandalay. It would be wrong to suggest that Kimura had become reconciled to losing control of the Burma Road since this was one of the major reasons for the Japanese presence, but in the prevailing circumstances there was no prospect whatever that it might be recovered. Northern Burma, therefore, would have to be abandoned and Honda would come south to take overall command of the efforts to recapture Meiktila, for which task he was allocated the 18th and 49th Divisions, elements of 53rd Division and the 14th Tank Regiment.

Because of the universal shortage of motorised transport, these formations reached the Meiktila area piecemeal, so that it was not until 10 March that Cowan's staff were aware that they formed part of the same force. In fact, subsequent interrogation of senior Japanese officers revealed that until 15 March the 18th and 49th Divisions remained under the respective command of Fifteenth and Thirty-Third Armies. Contact between the two was restricted to an unsatisfactory radio link routed through HQ Thirty-Third Army, and one visit by a liaison officer; co-ordinated operations against the British in Meiktila were therefore impossible. Of the 14th Tank Regiment, only seven Type 97s reached the operational area, where they were employed as mobile pill boxes; having unwisely decided to undertake its road march by day, the regiment had been pounced upon by Allied fighter-bombers and two-thirds of its strength lay wrecked and burning along the route. Faced with such difficulties, the best that Honda's troops could do was impose a distant sort of blockade although they did manage to cut direct communication between Meiktila and 7th Indian Division's bridgehead by re-occupying Taungtha. Even this modest success came to naught when, after several days' fighting, the garrison was overwhelmed on 12 March by two squadrons of 116 Regiment and 1/4th Gurkhas, despatched by Evans for the purpose.

Those in Meiktila, though isolated far behind enemy lines, were therefore in no immediate danger and retained the initiative throughout what has become known as the Second Siege. Even as Kasuya's men were dying, 16th Light Cavalry patrols were scouring the roads for many miles in every direction around the town. Once Meiktila had been secured, columns of tanks, armoured cars, artillery and lorried infantry set out daily in aggressive sweeps which intentionally sought contact with the Japanese and destroyed Honda's pretentions of imposing a siege so effectively that the 18th Division was forced to abandon an entire sector of its perimeter.

Officers questioned after the war confirmed that for them the fighting around Meiktila was essentially an anti-tank battle for which they were ill-equipped; they had not expected that the tank crews would be able to operate continuously in the high temperatures prevailing and, having also under-estimated the ability of the regimental and brigade fitters to keep vehicles running without major workshop facilities, they were surprised that there was no apparent reduction in the British tank strength. Throughout this period, in which the columns sometimes stayed out for two or three days at a time, their losses were comparatively light, although the Japanese could never be taken for granted; at Shawbyuggan on 18 March, for example, C Squadron Royal Deccan Horse sustained the loss of five tanks plus four men killed and 11 wounded when the garrison opened the village's irrigation sluices, softening the ground to the extent that, to avoid bogging down, the tanks' approach was restricted to an anti-tank gun killing ground.

Nor did it improve Japanese morale to observe the constant stream of transports arriving at Meiktila airfield with supplies. Worse still, on 17 March the 9th Brigade of 5th Indian Division was flown in to reinforce Cowan, the landing being made under shellfire which caused few casualties but destroyed several aircraft on the ground. By 20 March, however, Honda had scraped together sufficient troops to mount an attack on the airfield, the use of which was denied Cowan until the intruders had been eliminated or pushed back out of range. Even then, the air supply continued by means of para-drop well inside the defences. Then, quite suddenly, the Japanese had gone and 17th Division's administrative troops, followed by the remainder of 5th Division, arrived from the bridgehead by way of Taungtha; the Second Siege of Meiktila was over.

The reason for the disappearance of the enemy was that, as Slim had predicted, Katamura's Fifteenth Army, deprived of ammunition, food and reinforcements, had been unable to contain the increased pressure by XXXIII Corps in the battle around Mandalay and had simply fallen apart. On 3 March, the day Meiktila had been captured, 19th Indian Division had begun advancing south on Mandalay, led by a fast-moving mechanised column, and by 7 March had penetrated the city's suburbs. The battle for Mandalay continued until 20 March when the garrison's survivors, unable to halt the further advance of 2nd British Division from the west, attempted to escape to the south. In this they were unsuccessful as on 19 March a second and more powerful mechanised column, consisting of 3/4th Gurkha Rifles, two squadrons of Stuarts from 7th Light Cavalry, one Lee squadron from 150 Regiment RAC, two 11th Cavalry armoured car squadrons and 18 Field Regiment, Royal Artillery, with Priest 105mm self-propelled howitzers, broke out of 20th Indian Division's bridgehead and headed south-east to capture Wundwin, lying on the main Meiktila-Mandalay highway, on 21 March. As a result of this, the Japanese were compelled to route their withdrawal well to the east and the following day Honda ordered his troops to abandon their positions around Meiktila and retreat to the south, where Kimura had instructed him to establish a new defensive front based on Pyawbwe.

Although Slim had achieved his object of smashing Kimura's army group, there were still tens of thousands of Japanese troops in central Burma and, while for the moment they were fragmented, lacking organisation, direction and supply, they could still become a formidable force once they had been rallied. This he was not prepared to allow and, with the additional knowledge that the monsoon rains would begin at the end of April, rendering the going more difficult and inhibiting air activity of every kind, he decided to make an immediate thrust at Rangoon, some 300 miles to the south, thereby administering the coup de grace to his opponent. There was a high element of risk in the plan, but it was calculated that in by-passing centres of resistance, leaving large bodies of the enemy behind to be mopped up later, and maintaining an average rate of advance on 10-12 miles per day, allowing for demolitions, Rangoon could be reached in time. For this final offensive, which would take place along two parallel axes, it was necessary for the Fourteenth Army to carry out a reorganisation of its corps, based on the positions held by their divisions at the end of the Mandalay-Meiktila battles. Stopford's XXXIII Corps, consisting of the 7th and 20th Indian Divisions and 254th Tank Brigade, was to advance straight down the Irrawaddy while Messervy's IV Corps, now with 5th, 17th and 19th Indian Divisions and 255th Tank Brigade, was to follow the main railway line through Toungoo into the Sittang valley.

The Japanese, still forming their new defence line at Pyawbwe as decimated units straggled in from the north, were in no condition to meet a renewed offensive and were again thrown off balance by the speed with which the Fourteenth Army completed its re-deployment. Under the command of Brigadier Pert, a mechanised column consisting of 6/7th Rajputs, two squadrons each of Probyn's Horse and 16th Light Cavalry, a self-propelled artillery battery and engineers, turned their western flank and cut the main road south of Pyawbwe. It then turned north and destroyed the supply dumps which, with infinite trouble and labour, Honda had only recently managed to accumulate. Subsequently, Honda's Chief-of-Staff, Major-General Sawamoto Rikichiro, described the column's presence as 'most unsettling' at a time when, on 10 April, the Royal Deccan Horse was supporting converging attacks by Cowan's 17th Division against the main position. The defences were overwhelmed next day and IV Corps' tanks, artillery and infantry began streaming southwards through the gap. Honda and his staff, reduced to the level of fugitives, narrowly escaped capture on several times and on one occasion actually prepared themselves for ritual suicide rather than be taken alive.

The XXXIII Corps was also moving down the more difficult Irrawaddy axis and by 2 May had reached Prome. Stopford had less armour at his disposal and tended to use it as divisional advance guards or in pursuit of divisional objectives, where its mobility was sometimes used to turn the enemy's flank. Messervy, on the other hand, employed his armour as IV Corps' spearhead, the shaft of the spear being the infantry divisions which, in rotation, followed behind. Leading the advance, with the primary task of securing bridges before the enemy could destroy them, was one of two composite squadrons formed by merging one squadron each from 7th and 16th Light Cavalry, thereby exploiting respectively the armoured cars' speed and the mobility and firepower of the light tanks; the second composite squadron was often used to protect the flanks of the advance, being despatched to screen villages and other possible centres of resistance on either side of the road. Some distance behind the reconnaissance units, but within striking distance, was the corps advance guard, containing two Sherman squadrons from one of 255th Tank Brigade's three regiments (116 Regiment RAC had rejoined the brigade at Meiktila), a lorried infantry battalion part of which was carried on the tanks, a self-propelled artillery battery and an engineer troop equipped with Valentine scissors-bridgelayers. Behind the corps' advance guard was 255th Tank Brigade HQ, to which a ground-attack air liaison unit was attached, the reserve Sherman squadron, the rest of the self-propelled artillery regiment and an engineer squadron. Then came the leading infantry division's advance guard, the division itself, and the rest of the corps. This order of march ensured rapid deployment and an immediate all-arms response as soon as opposition was encountered.

In this way IV Corps smashed through, brushed aside or by-passed resistance at Yamethin (14 April), Pyinmana (19 April) and Toungoo (22 April). On 27 April a brief check was sustained at Payagale, where the village had been expertly fortified by enemy engineers and the garrison offered resistance comparable to that experienced at Meiktila. In the end all three Deccan squadrons, 6/7th Rajputs and 1/3rd Gurkhas had to be committed to the close-quarter fighting. The infantry suffered severely from mines and booby traps and the tanks, as well as having to duel with cleverly-sited anti-tank guns, became the target of numerous suicide squads armed with pole charges, who often remained concealed until after the attack had rolled past them. The worst hazards for the Sherman crews, however, were buried aerial bombs; one such blew the engine clean out of a tank, which then rolled onto its turret roof, and a second blew out the final drive assembly of another, badly wounding the vehicle's driver and hull gunner. By the time the village was finally cleared at about 1700 the day's advance had been restricted to six miles, well below the required average.

During the evening, however, the composite reconnaissance squadron pressed on to cut the east-west road between Waw and Payagyi and at 2030 ambushed and destroyed a convoy including a staff car containing a major-general of the Indian National Army and two Japanese colonels. This confirmed that the enemy was already evacuating Rangoon and retreating into Lower Burma. Kimura and HQ Burma Area Army had already left for Moulmein some days earlier. So, too, had the traitor Subhas Chandra Bose, expressing profound regret that important political matters demanded his attention elsewhere, but nonetheless leaving his wretched Indian National Army units to fend for themselves.

On 29 and 30 April little opposition was encountered and, contrary to the normal rules governing a protracted offensive, the pace of the advance actually increased despite the fact that the heavy mango showers, precursors of the monsoon proper, had already begun to make going difficult off the metalled road. By now, too, even the efficient air supply system was stretched to its limits and, as fuel and ammunition held priority on the drops, the corps spearhead was placed on half-rations. Pegu was reached late on 30 April and assaulted the following day. That night the Japanese abandoned those parts of the town they still held and withdrew, having blown the road and railway bridges. After a Bailey bridge was put in four miles west of Pegu a composite force under Lieutenant-Colonel Chaudhuri, consisting of 4/12th Frontier Force Rifles, both reconnaissance squadrons, a Sherman squadron from Probyn's, a troop of self-propelled guns and engineers, crossed and set off down the Rangoon road. Progress was slow, largely because both sides of the road were mined with heavy aerial bombs placed at 25-yard intervals and wired ready for remote detonation. It took until last light before the Frontier Force, with the Shermans in support, had cleared the enemy's covering position and the engineers were able to disarm them. Chaudhuri's spearhead force reached Hlegu without further incident on 3 May only to find that the main bridge had been blown, as had every bridge up and down-stream for several miles. Bridging material was in short supply and here, just 32 miles short of Rangoon, the long advance halted, having covered 300 miles in three weeks.

It was an undoubted disappointment for Messervy's troops to be denied the covetted prize at the last minute, although this was lessened by the startling news that Rangoon was actually in British hands. Both Slim and Lord Louis Mountbatten, the Supreme Commander South-East Asia Command, had been worried by the risks inherent in the monsoon's arrival and to reduce these Christison's XV Corps had been ordered to mount an amphibious operation at the mouth of the Rangoon river, thereby catching the Japanese between two fires. This, codenamed 'Dracula', began with a drop by a battalion of 50th Indian Parachute Brigade at Elephant Point on 1 May and was followed next day by the landing of Major-General H. M. Chambers' 26th Indian Division. By then air reconnaissance had confirmed that the Japanese had left the city which was occupied without opposition from the Indian and Burma National Army units left behind. It remained only for Chambers to push out columns which met the advance guard of IV Corps at Hlegu on 6 May and the leading elements of XXXIII Corps near Tharrawaddy, 60 miles from Rangoon, on 15 May.

During the period between 1 January and 15 May 1945, which included XXXIII Corps' holding battles around Mandalay, IV Corps' seizure of Meiktila by coup de main and the rapid advance by both corps on Rangoon, the Burma Area Army had been destroyed, a minimum of 28,700 of its men were known to have been killed, 430 of its guns had been captured and its armour had ceased to exist. The Fourteenth Army's losses amounted to approximately 2,800 killed, 10,000 wounded and some 30 tanks destroyed or disabled.

Complete as the victory was, it took until July to eliminate the last formed Japanese units in Burma. Honda did his best to direct the survivors of the shattered Twenty-Eighth and Thirty-Third Armies across the frontier into Thailand, but the larger elements failed to fight their way through, the smaller groups were hunted down by regular troops and those individuals who penetrated as far as the Karen Hills were slaughtered by tribal guerrillas specially raised and armed for the purpose.

When Japan surrendered in August just 50,000 men, all that were left of the once-formidable Burma Area Army, came in to lay down their arms, and of these the majority were from Lower Burma, which had scarcely been touched by the fighting. After the first shock of their country's capitulation their officers were perfectly frank in their assessment of the recent fighting. The capture of Meiktila, they said, had been the master stroke of the entire Burma campaign; with Meiktila lost to them defeat had been inevitable.

CHAPTER 9

Taken at a Run: The Capture of the Ludendorff Bridge at Remagen, 1945

B y the time February had turned to March in 1945 no doubts remained on either side that the Third Reich had been brought to the verge of collapse. In the east the Red Army had reached the Oder and was building up its strength for the final mighty drive across eastern Germany to Berlin. In the west the last gains made by the German counter-offensive through the Ardennes the previous December had been pinched out and a second, less dramatic, counter-offensive in Alsace and Lorraine in January had merely resulted in heavy losses without any significant return. Field Marshal Gerd von Rundstedt, the German Commander-in-Chief West, recognised that his troops had shot their bolt and now, under pressure from three Allied army groups, he was pulling them back behind the formidable water barrier of the Rhine.

Hitler, diseased in mind and body, refused to accept the idea of defeat and increasingly took refuge in a fantasy world where armies which existed mainly on paper were ordered to perform impossible feats of arms. When they did not, he saw the cause as being treason and treachery among his senior officers, his long-felt contempt for whom had, in his eyes, been fully justified by the attempt made by some of them to assassinate him only eight months earlier. If, because of such men, and a people he no longer felt worthy of him, it became impossible for him to fulfil what he believed to be his historical destiny, he was determined that rather than fall alive into the hands of his many enemies, he would end his days in a Gotterdammerung setting of fire, blood and death. In the event, this proved to be a shabby affair of cyanide pills and a bungled cremation, destitute of Wagnerian grandeur.

The perspective of senior members of the Party, the Allgemeine SS and the Gestapo was somewhat different. They, too, recognised that in the event of a German defeat they would receive short shrift from the victors, but they wanted to cling to power as long as possible, either in the hope that some miracle would occur, or at least until they had prepared a suitable bolt-hole abroad. They had already begun to descend

160

on field headquarters close to the front, not to participate in the defence of their homeland, but to arrest, try, dismiss, demote, imprison or shoot any officer they felt was doing less than his duty. The Army, which already had problems enough on its hands, was subjected to a reign of terror for the remainder of the war, and as the hysteria grew commanders were changed with bewildering frequency, often before they had time to familiarise themselves with their tasks.

Nor, by coincidence, did complete harmony prevail within the camp of the Western Allies at this period, although they were in sight of bringing the war to a satisfactory conclusion. Such dissension as there was, however, was confined to the uppermost command echelons and much of it centred on the relationship between some senior American generals and Field Marshal Sir Bernard Montgomery, whose 21st Army Group contained one British, one Canadian and one American army. During the Battle of the Bulge the Allied Supreme Commander, General Dwight D. Eisenhower, had given Montgomery the task of containing the northern shoulder of the German penetration. This he had performed efficiently, but with an unfortunate degree of condescension and a lack of tact which had been fully exploited by the press in reports which provided an inaccurate portrayal of American troops or their commanders. Many American generals were still smarting from this when Eisenhower announced that the major crossing of the Rhine, which would confer immense prestige on its participants, would be carried out by Montgomery's army group in a huge set-piece operation centred on Wesel, to the north of Cologne. Eisenhower's decision, in fact, was based on the realisation that the North German Plain offered better going for an exploitation of the crossing than the mountainous country surrounding the central and upper reaches of the river. Nevertheless, the United States now had more men in the field than any of the Western Allies, and neither Lieutenant-General Omar Bradley, commanding the all-American 12th Army Group in the centre, nor Lieutenant-General Jacob Devers, commanding the Franco-American 6th Army Group in the south, were particularly pleased to find themselves once more playing a secondary role to Montgomery, although in no sense did this divert them from pursuing an aggressive advance into the Rhineland.

Such, then, was the overall situation as Bradley's army group, with the US Third Army (Lieutenant-General George S. Patton) on the right and the US First Army (Lieutenant-General Courtney Hodges) on the left, closed up to the Rhine during the early days of March 1945. No one under Bradley's command, nor anywhere else for that matter, expected to find any of the bridges still standing, the general belief being that the enemy would long since have blown them as soon his rear-guards had crossed. Indeed, the Allies had themselves given very serious consideration to the idea of destroying the bridges with air attacks while the Germans were still retreating across them, thereby trapping large numbers of enemy troops on the west bank of the river, but Eisenhower's Air Staff had counselled against this, partly because the German anti-aircraft defences were still sufficiently effective to make low level attacks very expensive, partly because seasonal cloud cover provided very few opportunities for high level pin-point bombing, and partly because the only remaining alternative, saturation bombing through the clouds, would require too great a diversion of aircraft and bomb-loads that were needed for use against higher priority targets elsewhere.

Despite this, routine interdiction air attacks had been mounted on the bridges and the result of one of these had far-reaching consequences. As a simple matter of military precaution, the bridges' supporting piers incorporated demolition chambers in their construction. By a remote chance, a bomb aimed at the Cologne-Mulheim bridge had penetrated a demolition chamber and the bridge had been destroyed, thereby depriving German troops on the west bank of one of their major axes of withdrawal. Hitler, forever meddling in battlefield detail, had promptly decreed that charges were not to be emplaced in demolition chambers until enemy troops were within five miles of a bridge and that even then the detonators would not be inserted until the last possible moment. Then, to make life even more difficult for his engineers, he added that anyone who blew a bridge too early would be shot; so, too, would anyone who blew a bridge too late.

Another bridge which had been hit on several occasions by Allied bombs was that at Remagen, which sustained damage and was weakened but remained operational. The bridge carried two railway tracks with a footway on either side and had been constructed during World War 1 as part of a communications improvement programme to facilitate the rapid transfer of troops between the eastern and western fronts. When completed in 1918 it had been named after General Erich Ludendorff, the German Army's First Quartermaster General. With an overall length of 1,069 feet, it consisted of a central bow arch resting on piers, connected to boths banks by box girder sections. At each end of the bridge were two rather ugly octagonal stone towers containing weapon ports. On the eastern bank the bridge ended 100 yards from the towering 600-foot Erpeler Ley, the cliffs of which rose almost from the water's edge, and the railway vanished into a tunnel driven right through the hill. During the first few days of March the space between the railway tracks had been decked over with planking so that wheeled traffic could also use the bridge.

On the morning of 7 March 1945 the engineer officer responsible for the demolition of the bridge was Captain Karl Friesenhahn, who had 120 men under his immediate command. Friesenhahn's task had been complicated by the fact that when the French Army occupied the Rhineland after World War 1 it had filled the piers' demolition chambers with concrete. He had, therefore, resorted to using 60 zinc-lined boxes attached to critical members of the bridge, connected by means of a cable buried beneath the tracks to the control position just within the tunnel. In accordance with Hitler's directive, the charges themselves had not been placed in the boxes and were stored ready for use close by. In the event of the system failing, an emergency charge could be fired by means of primer cord. Friesenhahn had very serious doubts as to whether this would be powerful enough to drop the bridge, as he had only been supplied with low grade industrial explosive for the task and received just half the quantity he had asked for. As an additional precaution, however, he had placed charges to blow a wide crater in the bridge approach on the Remagen side of the river, and as the Fuhrer's restrictions did not extend to this he could feel satisfied that he had taken every possible step to prevent the bridge falling intact into Allied hands.

The officer responsible for the security of the bridge was Captain Wilhelm Bratge. The nature of his command revealed the extent to which the German Army was now scraping the bottom of the barrel, as the bulk of it consisted of elderly members of the Volksturm (Home Guard), boys of the Hitler Youth, and Russian volunteers, on none of whom could much reliance be placed. In theory he could enlist Friesenhahn's engineers and approximately 200 anti-aircraft gunners manning weapons in the town and on the Erpeler Ley, but it was more than likely that when the moment came they would have their hands full. In fact, although something like 750 men had been mobilised for the defence of Remagen and its bridge, the only 'infantry' on whom Bratge could rely were 36 convalescents from the nearby military hospital in Linz who had been handed an assortment of German and captured weapons.

Such was the frenzied atmosphere in which the German Army was attempting to conduct its operations that the Bonn sector of the front, which included Remagen, had been commanded by no less than three different officers in succession since 1 March. The most recent arrival was Lieutenant-General Otto Hitzfeld, who had only been advised of his new responsibilities at 0100 on 7 March. Aware of the deteriorating situation, Hitzfeld immediately despatched his adjutant,

Major Hans Scheller, to Remagen to monitor the situation there. Scheller set off with his own car and a radio truck but sent the latter on ahead while he detoured in search of petrol. The signallers found that American troops were already between themselves and the town and were unable to get through. Scheller, however, reached Remagen from another direction at about 1100. As the senior officer present, he was now automatically responsible for whatever happened there, with tragic consequences for himself.

That same morning Hodges' US First Army was pushing steadily eastwards against slight opposition through pleasant, wooded, rolling country. Leading part of the advance was Major-General John Leonard's 9th Armored Division which, like most American armoured divisions of the time, consisted of three tank battalions, three armoured infantry battalions, three artillery battalions, an engineer battalion, a reconnaissance squadron and divisional services. Operationally, these were allocated as the situation demanded to the division's three Combat Commands, designated A, B and Reserve, each of which equated with a British brigade HQ. Combat Command B, commanded by Brigadier-General William Hoge, had captured the town of Meckenheim the previous evening and its further advance on 7 March was spearheaded by a task force under Colonel Leonard Engeman containing the 14th Tank Battalion and the 27th Armored Infantry Battalion.

At 0600 Engeman sent for Lieutenant Karl Timmermann, who had just assumed command of the 27th's A Company. Timmermann hailed from West Point, Nebraska, and, as he name suggests, he was of German extraction. His grandparents were German and his father had served briefly with the US Army of Occupation in Germany after World War 1, then deserted. He married a German girl and in due course Karl was born in Frankfurt. With Quaker assistance, Timmermann Senior returned with his family to the United States in 1924 but was unable to live down the disgrace and achieved little. Karl, on the other hand, showed an early interest in a military career, and in 1940 enlisted on his 18th birthday. He was commissioned three years later, fought in the Battle of the Bulge and was wounded near St Vith.

Engeman told Timmermann that his company was to spearhead the day's advance, which had Remagen as its objective. The infantry in their half-tracks would have immediate tank support provided by 14th Tank Battalion's A Company. This was good news, as the company's M4 Shermans had been reinforced by one five-tank platoon equipped with the new M26 Pershing heavy tank. Designed as an answer to the German Tiger and Panther, the Pershing was armed with a 90mm gun and protected by 102mm frontal armour. As yet, comparatively few had reached the front, although those that had were producing excellent results. A Company's Pershings, commanded by Lieutenant John Grimball, still had to show their teeth and, to their annoyance, had been forced to trundle along at the rear of the column. The reason for this was that the tank was over 10 tons heavier, and almost three feet wider, than the standard Sherman and it tended to damage the decking of the military bridges it crossed. Grimball had been forced to endure numerous harsh words from the divisional engineers and at the majority of pre-fabricated bridges the column had crossed since the Roer river his platoon had been forced to wait until everyone else was over. Now, the country was intersected by fewer waterways and Grimball's four tanks – one had been damaged by shellfire on 1 March and was still undergoing repair – became A Company's point platoon, travelling just behind Timmermann's infantry.

As the exit from Meckenheim was blocked by debris from the previous day's fighting, a path had to be bulldozed before the column could grind its way over the rubble. Timmermann's infantry became understandably tense as they entered the enemy's country but were well aware that in close terrain and villages, both of which would be encountered along the way, the tanks would be at risk from concealed Panzerfaust teams whereas their own flexibility would enable them to deal with the majority of situations. In fact, such opposition as they encountered

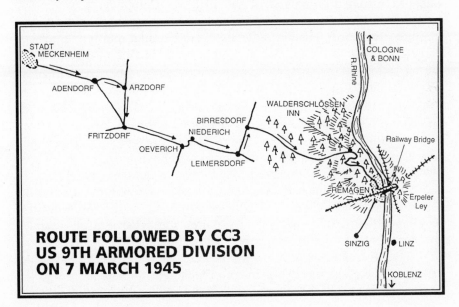

ROUTE FOLLOWED BY CC3
US 9TH ARMORED DIVISION
ON 7 MARCH 1945

appeared to come more from groups of stragglers than any attempt at an organised rearguard.

The first two villages, Adendorf and Arzdorf, had been abandoned by the enemy. Outside Fritzdorf, however, there was a brief exchange of fire when the point platoon came within range of an improvised roadblock, the defenders of which surrendered when Timmermann deployed part of his company to outflank them. As the column approached the next village, Oeverich, a Panzerfaust round flashed past the leading half-track, which quickly reversed into cover. At Timmermann's request Grimball brought his Pershings forward and after a few 90mm rounds had blown holes in the buildings a small group of Germans came out to surrender. The advance continued, passing through a hamlet named Niederich, beyond which a further skirmish took place. Here, as the prisoners were being rounded up, it became necessary to shoot a German officer who went berserk and began firing wildly at the Americans with his pistol.

This, in fact, was the last opposition the column encountered before it reached Remagen. In Leimersdorf, where it turned left, the streets were empty; in Birresdorf they were hung with white sheets. Beyond Birresdorf the vehicles swung right onto a road which led them through increasingly wooded country up onto the range of hills bordering the western bank of the Rhine. This was ideal terrain for an ambush and tension increased, but nothing happened. At about noon Timmermann pulled up his jeep outside the Walderschlossen inn and had just been informed by the innkeeper's wife that there were no German troops in the vicinity when he noticed several of his men shouting and beckoning him from further down the road. They belonged to Lieutenant Jim Burrows' platoon, which had recently taken over the lead and reached the point where the road descended into Remagen through a series of hairpin loops. Timmermann went up to join them and there, spread out below him, was a panorama of the Rhine valley and the town of Remagen. To his amazement, the railway bridge was still standing and German troops were still crossing it from west to east.

Engeman arrived, as did Major Murray Deevers, commander of the 27th Armored Infantry. The Americans' first reaction was that the bridge would make a splendid artillery target, but fortunately Engeman was unable to obtain the necessary authority. When patrols revealed that the town was not held in strength Engeman drafted a plan of attack in which, with tank support, it would be cleared by the 27th, using Lieutenant Jack Liedike's B Company and Lieutenant William McMarter's C Company against, respectively, the south-eastern and north-western suburbs while Timmermann's A Company fought its way through the centre to the bridge. Brigadier-General Hoge, commander of Combat Command B, arrived shortly after 1300 and, somewhat annoyed that the attack had not already begun, ordered it to start at once. It was successful everywhere, very little serious resistance being offered by Bratge's collection of old men, boys and invalides, and by 1500 Timmermann's men were closing in on the bridge approach. During the fighting the German engineers could be seen on the bridge itself, loading charges into demolition boxes which, together with their connecting wires, were plainly visible along the length of the structure.

Across the river Friesenhahn was watching the Americans' advance closely. As Timmermann's leading squads filtered towards the western end of the bridge he blew the charge in the approach ramp, creating a deep crater some 30 feet wide; that, at least, would keep the enemy's tanks off the bridge. Regaining the tunnel entrance, which was now coming under fire from American tanks, he was urged by Bratge to blow the bridge at once. He had already checked the main demolition circuit just before the detonators were inserted and confirmed that it was working, but had been forbidden to proceed further without Major Scheller's express permission. At that moment Scheller was close to the far end of the tunnel, so that Bratge had to push his way through a crowd of civilian refugees before he found him. In the circumstances Scheller could not possibly have been aware of the developing situation at the bridge and, mindful not only of Hitler's directive but also that at least one German artillery battery was still on the west bank, he was reluctant to grant Bratge's request. After some discussion, however, he relented and signed the authorisation, timing it at 1520, then ordered the nearest German artillery units to fire on the bridge as an additional safeguard. Bratge rejoined Friesenhahn who immediately turned the firing key. Nothing happened. He tried twice more, without result. German and American fire was now sweeping the bridge from both ends and obviously the circuit had been severed at one or more points. Friesenhahn's call for a volunteer to light the emergency fuse was answered by Sergeant Faust, who courageously sprinted across 80 yards of open ground and succeeded in doing so.

Meanwhile, the progress of the assault had been watched from the high ground near the Walderschlossen inn by Hoge, Engeman and Deevers. Hoge was on the horns of a dilemma. Because of the difficulties presented by the Erpeler Ley and the close country beyond, the higher command had never considered Remagen to be a suitable crossing site. On the other hand, he was aware of the opinion of Major-General Leonard, his divisional commander, that if the bridge was still standing it should be captured. Against this, an order had been received from HQ III Corps, under whose command 9th Armored was operating, to the effect that Remagen had become a secondary objective and Combat Command B was to drive south, where better crossing sites existed in the area of Koblenz. The problem was that III Corps did not possess a real-time picture of events - any more than did Scheller, deep inside the tunnel below the Erpeler Ley. If Hoge disobeyed the order and attacked the bridge instead he could face disciplinary charges, yet if he did not attempt to capture the bridge intact he would be accused of negligence. Two further aspects of the problem had to be taken into account. His second task force had entered Sinzig, a mile or two south of Remagen, and been told by prisoners that the bridge was to be blown at 1600. This might be – and in fact was – nothing more than hearsay, but sporadic shell bursts had begun to erupt in the water round the bridge, and since they could only be German in origin it seemed to confirm the rumour. If an attack was to be made on the bridge, therefore, it must be mounted at once. Hoge reached his decision and curtly ordered Engemann and Deevers to proceed.

Inside the town they quickly briefed the junior officers involved. Timmermann's company, being closest to the bridge, would make the assault, with direct gunfire support from Grimball's Pershings; in the wake of the attack Lieutenant Mott, a platoon commander in B Company 9th Armored Engineer Battalion, would move onto the bridge with a small team and neutralise the demolition charges. When, at the end of the briefing, the time for questions arrived, Timmermann's was inevitable: 'What if the bridge blows up in my face?' As that was precisely what all those present expected to happen, the only possible answer was a shrug.

Timmermann was briefing his own platoon commanders when the burning primer cord lit by Sergeant Faust reached the emergency demolition charge. There was a huge explosion, the bridge seemed to leap momentarily from its seatings, and flame, smoke and flying timbers mushroomed skywards. When the last of the debris had fallen Timmermann looked up, understandably hoping that the bridge had been destroyed, but it still stood and the only apparent damage was to sections of the decking. His officers and NCOs began rooting out their dirty, tired riflemen. The latter, fully aware of the risks, were less than eager and some, having helped themselves to beer, wine and spirits in the town's inns, were becoming truculent. For some 'Come on!' was enough; for others it had to be 'Get going! Move it – now!' In a mood of sullen anger the squads filed past Deevers towards the bridge approach. The major wanted to encourage them but could come up with nothing better than the promise of a chicken dinner on the far bank; they told him where he could stuff it.

By ones and twos, then squads and finally platoons, they followed Timmermann up onto the bridge approach until the whole company was moving warily into the lattice of steel girders. Suddenly a Spandau in the far right-hand tower ripped into life, joined by fire from a semi-sunken barge 200 yards upstream and positions on the Erpeler Ley. Bullets clanged off girders, screamed as they chipped stone splinters from the near towers and ripped gouges in the timber decking. The forward progress of the riflemen, now conscious of the water far below, became a rapid series of movements as they ran from the temporary shelter of one girder towards the next. Behind them they could hear the sustained rattle of the tanks' co-axial Brownings, punctuated by the ear-splitting bangs of their main armament. The 90mm guns of Grimball's Pershings, extremely accurate and capable of delivering a very powerful punch, first silenced the barge then, one by one, picked off the other sources of enemy fire. Reaching the eastern towers, Staff Sergeant Joseph DeLisio entered that on the right and ran up the spiral staircase to find five Germans huddled beneath the fire slits, their machine gun jammed. Belligerent by nature, DeLisio fired two shots at the wall above and they promptly surrendered, as did two more men on the floor above. The remainder of the company completed the attack with a headlong charge for the far bank, gaining it with remarkably few casualties. A handful of Germans near the tunnel entrance surrendered while others retired deep into its interior. Mott and two of his engineers, following up the assault, cut every wire in sight as they went. The time was now 1600 and the bridge was still standing.

Timmermann's men had not quite finished for the day. The bridge was no use to the Americans unless the Erpeler Ley was captured as well and, together with the 27th's two remaining companies, which Deevers had pushed across the bridge following the successful assault, they began scaling the heights. These were taken without difficulty but a long, lonely night followed for much of which they were the only American troops on the enemy bank of the river.

Inside the tunnel the civilians were clamouring for the troops to surrender. There was no fight left in them and at 1730 Bratge reluctantly did so; by then Scheller had already left by the rear exit to report the loss of the bridge. In the meantime, Mott continued to render the charges harmless and patch up the damaged decking as best he could. Hoge, anxious to get tanks across, authorised the 9th Armored Engineers to demolish the nearest buildings and use the rubble to fill the crater on the bridge approach. At about midnight Mott declared the bridge safe enough for single-lane traffic. Grimball may have had hopes that he would be first across, but the engineers were not prepared to risk his heavy Pershings on the weakened structure and he had to wait for five days before they were rafted to the far bank. Instead, nine Shermans were sent over. They moved slowly at five-yard intervals, skirting white-taped holes in the decking. On the far side they spread out to cover the approaches and brushed briefly with some German infantry. Hoge decided to reinforce them with a platoon from the 656th Tank Destroyer Battalion which, during the evening, had sunk a river craft, an incident ending on an unexpectedly formal note when its commander, a naval officer in dress uniform, had himself rowed ashore to surrender his sword. The tank destroyers were lighter than the Shermans and, because it seemed as though a German counter-attack was imminent, they entered the bridge at a higher speed. This resulted in the driver of the leading vehicle missing a tape and one of its tracks ploughed into a hastily repaired hole. There it remained firmly wedged, blocking the passage of other vehicles until it was heaved free at 0530 the following morning.

Somehow, word that the bridge was blocked reached the 27th Armored Infantry up on the Erpeler Ley. Someone started a rumour that an immediate withdrawal had been ordered and before it could be stopped about one-third of those present had begun making their way back across the bridge. On the footways they met men of 1st/310th Infantry, a regiment of the 78th Division, moving forward to consolidate the perimeter on the east bank, and the panic subsided. It was as well that these reinforcements arrived when they did, for they were able to defeat a determined attempt by a German engineer unit with fresh demolition charges to fight its way through to the bridge, capturing many of the survivors.

With the removal of the obstruction, men and vehicles began to flow in a steady stream across the Ludendorff Bridge. Remagen became the focus of the First Army's activities and within 24 hours of the bridge being captured no less than 8,000 American soldiers were across the Rhine, rendering the success of a German counter-attack against the bridgehead less and less likely. The units responsible for the coup received Presidential Citations and the principal participants appropriately honoured.

The Allied and German reactions to the event, and their respective efforts to defend and destroy the bridge, were as interesting as the coup itself. Hoge's disobedience was supported by Leonard and immediately forgiven by III Corps. At First Army HQ Hodges barely referred to it and promptly telephoned Bradley at 12th Army Group. Bradley's jubilant reaction – a spontaneous shout of 'Hot dog, this will bust him wide open!' – might be taken to refer either to the enemy or to Montgomery. For some reason he waited until the evening before calling Eisenhower, who was equally delighted and authorised him to push the 9th, 78th and 99th Infantry Divisions across the river. For a moment, while the world spotlight was fixed firmly on Remagen, Bradley believed that the leading role in subsequent events would be his.

If, when Eisenhower called Montgomery as a matter of courtesy, he expected the latter to be miffed at not being first across the Rhine, this was far from being the case. Montgomery was supremely indifferent to the personal opinions of his American critics and, as Chester Wilmot commented in his book *The Struggle for Europe*, 'His first inclination always was to pursue what he thought was the right military course without regard for national prestige – British or American.' His reaction to the news that a crossing had been secured at Remagen was, therefore, entirely professional: 'It will be an unpleasant threat to the enemy and will undoubtedly draw enemy strength onto it and away from the business in the north.' That is, the major crossing around Wesel. This was undoubtedly true, and Allied plans were too far advanced for radical alterations to be made at this stage. Having slept on the matter, Eisenhower spoke to Bradley next morning and told him that the bridgehead's expansion was to be limited to 1,000 yards per day and, for the moment, was not be extended beyond the Bonn-Frankfurt autobahn.

Neither of the German field marshals on the Western Front, Gerd von Rundstedt as Commander-in-Chief and Walter Model as commander of Army Group B, had believed that the Americans would attempt a crossing in the Remagen area and for that reason very few troops were available to contain the bridgehead. Hitler regarded the events at Remagen as being symptomatic of the rot which was bringing down his Thousand-Year Reich. In his fury he dismissed von Rundstedt, who was not sorry to go, issued orders that deserters were to be shot on the spot, and promised the troops that reprisals would be taken against their families if they surrendered without being wounded or were unable to provide irrefutable proof that they had fought to the last. Field Marshal Albert Kesselring, summoned hotfoot from the Italian Front, was ordered to restore the situation in the West. His memoirs indicate that he gave immediate priority to the Remagen bridgehead, commenting that: 'The counter-measures against the first enemy forces to cross the Rhine had not been taken with the uncompromising fierceness which might have ensured a swift and relatively easy restoration of the line, and the fate of the whole Rhine front hung on our wiping out or containing the bridgehead. ' This was the reaction Eisenhower and Montgomery had hoped for and Kesselring frankly admitted that by feeding all his available reinforcements and reserves into the Remagen sector he made life difficult for his commanders in other areas of the Western Front. Yet, for all his efforts, including repeated attacks by 9th and 11th Panzer Divisions, the American perimeter around the bridge-head continued to expand slowly throughout the next two weeks.

The Ludendorff Bridge had provided the Americans with a means to an end, but it would have been foolish for them to have relied solely on this one already damaged structure to maintain contact with the troops on the east bank. A pontoon treadway for infantry and light vehicles was put in downstream of the railway bridge and opened to traffic at 0700 on 11 March. Seventeen hours later a heavy pontoon bridge was operational one mile up-river at Linz. Together, these proved adequate and on 13 March the engineers closed the Ludendorff Bridge and began to repair the worst of the damage.

Throughout this period the area of the bridges remained under shellfire and regular air attack. The Luftwaffe, ordered by Kesselring to make a maximum effort, flew up to 400 tactical sorties per day against the bridgehead with Messerschmitt Me 262 and Arado Ar 234 jets, Focke-Wulf Fw 190 fighter bombers and Ju 87 Stuka dive bombers. The Americans, however, had brought forward so many anti-aircraft guns that the area immediately around the bridges possessed the most con-centrated air defence in Europe. The first raid, on 8 March, resulted in the attackers sustaining a loss ratio of 80 per cent; on 15 March they sustained 75 per cent losses; overall, during a nine-day period, of 367 aircraft which attacked the bridges, 106 were shot down.

The railway bridge also came under fire from one of the German Army's monstrous Karl super-heavy semi-self-propelled howitzers. With a calibre of 540mm, these were capable of hurling a two-ton high explo-sive shell a distance of four miles and had been successfully employed against fortifications on the Eastern Front, notably at Sevastopol. No hits were obtained and, as the bridgehead expanded day by day, the weapon was withdrawn until it was no longer within range. Next it was decided to target the bridge with V-2 rockets, but again the results were disappointing. Of 11 missiles launched from Bellendoorn in Holland, one exploded 300 yards from the bridge and the remainder impacted in an extended pattern between Remagen and Cologne.

As the Army and the Luftwaffe had failed in their attempts to destroy the bridge Kesselring now appealed to the Navy. The previous autumn German frogmen with explosive charges had succeeded in wrecking one of the bridges captured by the Allies in Nijmegen and now it was decided to deal likewise with the Ludendorff Bridge. The Americans, however, were well aware of the danger and fully prepared to meet it. At first they had simply exploded depth charges at five minute intervals, then nets had been slung across the river from bank to bank, and finally, with Eisenhower's personal authorisation, one of the war's most secret weapon systems was actively deployed for the first time.

Manned by the US 738th Tank Battalion (Spec), this was the so-called Canal Defence Light (CDL), a British invention codenamed the 'Shop Tractor' in American service. The CDL consisted of an M3 Lee/Grant chassis and hull fitted with a specially designed turret housing a 13 million candlepower carbon arc, the intense light from which was reflected through a narrow slit controlled by the rapid movements of a mechanically driven shutter. The effect of the light was to induce temporary partial blindness, often accompanied by nausea, loss of balance and disorientation; its rapid flickering also prevented the enemy identifying its source, or even whether it was moving or stationary, and in the inky black space between two CDL beams it was possible for troops to advance completely unseen towards their brilliantly illuminated objective. Although trained CDL units had been been formed as early as 1942, obsessive security had prevented their employment until now, a mistake described by Major-General J. F. C. Fuller as the greatest blunder of the war.

At 1915 on the evening of 17 March six frogmen commanded by Lieutenant Schreiber slipped into the Rhine south of Linz. Using oil drums for buoyancy, their intention was to allow the current to carry them downstream to Remagen and there fix charges to the bridge. While still south of Linz they were illuminated by the CDLs. Half blinded, confused and under fire from both banks, they were rounded up and brought ashore. In due course, since the matter could not be concealed from him for very long, Schreiber was told that his journey had not been necessary; the Ludendorff Bridge had collapsed into the river at 1500 that afternoon.

The precise cause of the collapse is uncertain, but many factors contributed to the fatal weakening of the structure, including Friesenhahn's emergency demolition, shells and bombs exploding in the water nearby, many tons of additional timber decking, vibration caused by the engineers' plant, the shock waves set up by the continuous firing of

American medium artillery batteries nearby, and overstressing of the few sound load-bearing members remaining. The collapse had come without warning and claimed the lives of 28 of the 200 engineers working on the structure at the time. Although the two pontoon bridges were already coping satisfactorily with the traffic flow, the contingency of one being damaged had to be allowed for and a third was completed downstream of the treadway within 36 hours.

For a few more days Remagen remained the focus of attention. Then, on 22 March, Patton's Third Army crossed the Rhine against light opposition at Oppenheim and Nierstein. This achievement in turn was eclipsed when, during the next two days, Montgomery's army group secured no less than eight crossings. By the end of the month all three Allied army groups were across and the war in Europe had only weeks to run.

In the meantime, Scheller had been subjected to a drum-head court martial and shot. The efforts of his widow to clear his name were finally rewarded in 1967 when a court ruled that he was innocent of any capital crime under German military law. Bratge and Friesenhahn were tried in their absence, the former being sentenced to death and the latter exonerated; the verdicts were of academic interest only as both were prisoners in American hands. Timmermann had the personal satisfaction of knowing that he had expunged a family disgrace and for a while he enjoyed the status of a national hero. Unable to settle in civilian life, he rejoined the Army in 1948 and fought in the early stages of the Korean War. In 1951 he died of cancer in a military hospital.

CHAPTER 10

Going for the Jugular: The Inchon Landings, September 1950

The Korean Peninsula is approximately 600 miles long from north to south and for much of its length is about 100 miles across, increasing to a width of 200 miles where it broadens to join the main Asian land mass. It is dominated by the high and rugged Taebaek Mountains, running the length of the east coast. The tilt of the country is therefore from east to west with the principal rivers flowing in a south-westerly direction, save in the extreme south, and major north-south road and rail routes follow the gentler terrain to the west, being channelled through the city of Seoul. On the peninsula's eastern coast the mountains drop abruptly into the sea, there are few harbours, and the tidal range is small; the heavily indented western and southern coastlines, however, provide numerous harbours, although the tidal range is high. The country's ancient name of Chosen, The Land of Morning Calm, tends to conceal other aspects of its climate, including baking, humid summers, a monsoon season lasting from June to September, and an arctic winter with winds howling down from the frozen wastelands of inner Siberia. In 1950 the Korean economy was based on agriculture, with rice, barley and soybeans being the principal crops. At that time the peninsula's entire population numbered 30 million, of whom only nine million lived in North Korea, occupying 58 per cent of the country, while 21 million lived in South Korea.

The boundary between the two Koreas was artificially drawn along the 38th Parallel and stemmed from a series of inter-related geographical and historical factors, the most important of which was that the peninsula lies at the meeting point of frequently conflicting Chinese, Russian and Japanese interests. The short Sino-Japanese War of 1894–95 eliminated Chinese political influence in Korea, but also produced rivalries between Russia and Japan which resulted in the humiliating defeat of the former in the Russo-Japanese War of 1904-05. After this Korea became a Japanese colony in 1910 and was absorbed into Japan itself in 1942. When, during the closing days of World War 2, the Soviet Union declared war on Japan and overran Manchuria, it was decided that in the immediate post-war period Korea would be divided into Soviet and American spheres of influence respectively north and south of the 38th Parallel, with a further view to establishing a Korean government by means of nationwide elections. The policy of the communists, however, was to consolidate their power base in whatever territory they occupied, and their intransigence effectively wrecked any prospect of this. By August 1948 North Korea was governed by a communist administration and South Korea by an elected assembly, each claiming authority over the whole country. In December that year the United Nations General Assembly recognised the legality of the South Korean constitution and requested the withdrawal of the Soviet and American occupation forces. The Soviets left at once, followed by the last Americans in July 1949.

From this point onwards the two Koreas embarked on a bitter propaganda campaign against each other, punctuated by border incidents and acts of sabotage. With Chinese and Russian assistance the North Korean People's Army (NKPA) was steadily built up until in June 1950 it consisted of seven first line infantry divisions, three reserve infantry divisions, an armoured brigade, one independent infantry regiment, a motor-cycle regiment and units of the Border Constabulary. This produced a total of 135,000 men, of whom approximately one-third were veterans of the Chinese Civil War.

The NKPA infantry division contained three rifle regiments, each of three battalions, an artillery regiment with 12 122mm howitzers and 24 76mm guns, a self-propelled gun battalion with 12 SU 76s, and an anti-tank battalion with 12 45mm anti-tank guns. Heavy weapons at the disposal of the commanders of infantry regiments included six 120mm mortars, four 76mm howitzers and six 45mm anti-tank guns.

By far the most important formation in the NKPA's order of battle was the 105th Armoured Brigade, which was to be elevated to divisional status, if not size, shortly after the outbreak of hostilities. This consisted of the 107th, 109th and 203rd Armoured Regiments, each with three 13-tank companies, and the 206th Mechanised Infantry Regiment. In addition, an independent armoured regiment with 30 tanks was formed from the personnel of the tank training school in June 1950 and attached to the 7th Infantry Division. The standard equipment of the armoured regiments was the Russian T34/85 medium tank which, in both its earlier and present forms, had created so many problems for the Wehrmacht on the Eastern Front. Possessed of a combination of speed, mobility, well-angled armour and a powerful main armament, the T34 is still regarded as being the starting point of modern tank design and although by 1950 it was beginning to look a little dated it was still a formidable opponent.

The NKPA was, therefore, by Far Eastern standards, an experienced, balanced, well-equipped and thoroughly trained army, although its logistic infrastructure left much to be desired. A small air force, equipped with YAK fighters and fighter-bombers, was available to provide tactical support for its operations.

In sharp contrast, while the American-trained and equipped army of the southern Republic of Korea (ROK) possessed a strength of about 98,000 men, of whom 65,000 were serving in combat units, it had more in common with a gendarmerie than a field force. It consisted of eight infantry divisions, each with two or three regiments and, while adequately supplied with small arms, automatic weapons and medium mortars, was woefully deficient in all other areas. Only five artillery battalions existed, and these were equipped with the short M3 105mm howitzer, the 8,200 yards maximum range of which bore no comparison with the 14,000 yards of the NKPA's 76mm divisional field gun. For defence against tanks the ROK Army relied on some 140 37mm anti-tank guns and approximately 1,900 2.36in bazookas; the former had been regarded as obsolete as long ago as 1940, and the latter was now considered to be so ineffective against modern armour that it was on the point of being replaced in the US Army. Tanks were totally absent from the army's order of battle because its American advisers, believing that the terrain was unsuited to armoured operations, had blocked a request for them, with the result that the only fighting vehicles south of the 38th Parallel were 27 M8 Greyhound light armoured cars performing Presidential Guard duties in Seoul. Stocks of artillery and heavy weapons ammunition would not outlast a few days' serious fighting, no supply of spare parts existed, and while training had been completed to company level it had not progressed far beyond. The striking power of the tiny air force consisted of 10 elderly Mustang fighters, delivered so recently that their pilots had yet to qualify on them. Nevertheless, the American military mission in South Korea was unaware of the extent to which the threat from the north had grown and believed that in the event of a communist invasion the ROK Army would be able to look after itself.

Both the Soviet Union and China regarded South Korea as an undesirable presence in the communist sphere of influence and, believing that the United States was now indifferent to events in the area, agreed that it should be overrun. Anxious not to be seen in the role of aggressors themselves, they were prepared to support a North Korean invasion which would give the world the impression of an internal power struggle in an artificially divided country. The operation would be executed with such weight and speed that the entire peninsula would be occupied before the Americans and their allies could react. The United Nations could hardly be expected to approve but, having been presented with a fait accompli, it was expected that in due course it would move on to other business and the matter would be forgotten. The idea was eagerly accepted by the communist administration in Pyongyang, the North Korean capital.

At 0400 on 25 June 1950 the NKPA, commanded by General Chai Ung Jun, opened a protracted bombardment along the 38th Parallel and then, spearheaded by its tanks, advanced into South Korea along several routes. To the dismay of the South Koreans, neither their anti-tank guns nor their bazookas made any impression on the T34s. More often than not, the communist armour simply smashed through their positions without bothering to deploy, driving on to create panic and rout in the rear areas. Those ROK units which did stand their ground were then assailed by the North Korean infantry which would divide towards the flanks of a position and then launch an assault into its rear. Within hours the four ROK divisions closest to the border had become involved in a disordered and precipitate retreat. When, on 28 June, the NKPA captured Seoul, it had advanced so quickly that it was in danger of out-running its supplies, so while a brief halt was called to allow these to catch up, it took the opportunity to regroup for the next phase of the drive to the south.

Although it was not apparent at the time, this pause, while necessary in terms of orthodox military principles, actually wrecked the communists' grand design, since it not only permitted the ROK Army to rally but also gave the United Nations time to react. The Security Council's condemnation of North Korea on 25 June itself was expected and duly ignored; what had not been anticipated was that two days later the Council would call on all the UN's member states to provide active support for South Korea; nor had the immediate response of President Truman of the United States, who ordered the US Seventh Fleet into Korean waters, gave permission for air strikes to be made into North Korea, and authorised the despatch of ammunition and equipment to the hard-pressed ROK Army.

On 29 June General Douglas MacArthur, the victor of the Pacific War against Japan, flew to Korea to assess the situation for himself. At this period he concurrently held the appointments of Supreme Commander Allied Powers in Japan, Commander-in-Chief US Forces

Far East, and Commanding General US Army Far East. He was, therefore, a man of immense authority and influence upon whose judgement Truman relied. MacArthur's opinion was that without prompt and large scale intervention by American ground forces South Korea would collapse and the President therefore had no hesitation in sanctioning their use.

The nearest American troops were the 7th, 24th and 25th Infantry Divisions which, together with the 1st Cavalry Division (actually an infantry formation despite its name), formed the US Eighth Army and were based in Japan. All were below their established strength, badly armed and equipped, poorly trained and physically softened by their undemanding occupation duties. It was, however, essential that they should be committed to the battle at the earliest possible moment. The 24th Division began arriving in Korea on 1 July and four days later its leading elements were in contact with the enemy near Osan. The 25th Division followed between 10 and 15 July and then the 1st Cavalry Division on 18 July. Under the command of Lieutenant-General Walton H. Walker, who had served as one of Patton's corps commanders during World War 2, the Eighth Army HQ moved to Korea and became responsible for the conduct of UN operations.

The intention of the UN commander was to contain the communist drive until the arrival of substantial reinforcements enabled him to take the offensive. This was more easily said than done, largely because of the piecemeal manner in which the American formations had to be committed to shore-up the crumbling front. The 24th Division had been mauled in the first encounters and sustained heavy losses, including a large number of men captured. The NKPA's tactics of infiltration around the flanks were unsettling, as was its human wave method of assault. For a while the ground troops' only effective weapon against the T34 was the artillery's HEAT round, which was in very short supply. The situation began to improve a little after supplies of the new 3. 5in anti-tank rocket launcher were hurriedly flown in, enabling unit commanders to organise effective tank hunting parties. For the first weeks of the fighting the only armoured support available to the Americans consisted of the few M24 Chaffee light tanks possessed by their understrength divisional tank battalions, which were hopelessly outclassed. More tank battalions, equipped with rebuilt M4A3E8 Shermans, M26 Pershings and M46 Pattons were on their way to Korea but would not arrive before August. Fortunately, the UN possessed complete air superiority and were able to pound the NKPA's spearheads and supply lines at will with bombs, rockets and napalm.

Nevertheless, though delayed at certain points, the communist advance continued. By the beginning of August the American and ROK armies had been pushed back until all they held was an area measuring 80 miles from north to south and 50 miles from east to west, centred on the port of Pusan at the south-eastern tip of the Korean peninsula. Here Walker decided to establish a defensive perimeter, manned by the rallied and re-equipped ROK divisions along its mountainous northern sector, and by his American divisions along the east bank of the Naktong river. Reinforcements continued to arrive, including regiments from Okinawa and Hawaii, the first units of the 2nd Infantry Division direct from the United States, the 1st Provisional Marine Brigade and, from Hong Kong, the British 27th Infantry Brigade, consisting of the 1st Battalions of the Argyll & Sutherland Highlanders and the Middlesex Regiments, joined in September by the 3rd Battalion Royal Australian Regiment. Despite this, the line was thinly held and sustained communist pressure prevented Walker from establishing a sufficiently strong reserve with which to strike a telling counter-blow. Unable now to inflitrate past their opponents' flanks, the NKPA launched frenzied attacks at points all round the perimeter. Most were broken up by concentrated artillery fire and air strikes, but some penetrations were achieved and only contained with difficulty. On the other hand, local counter-attacks by Walker's troops met with very limited success.

In fact, the NKPA had been very badly hurt. In planning the campaign its High Command had estimated that it possessed the resources for two months sustained fighting, but little more. This meant that victory had to be achieved by the end of August and accounts for the intensity of the fighting throughout that month and on into September. Such had been its losses that divisional strengths had fallen to about half or less than those with which the invasion had been launched, despite an infusion of unwilling South Korean conscripts who were driven to attack at pistol point and shot on the spot if they attempted to desert. Equipment losses had been equally heavy and weapon superiority had become a distant memory, for although the Soviet Union attempted to make good the deficiencies, replacement tanks and supply convoys were frequently pounced upon and destroyed by UN aircraft on the long road south.

At the beginning of September, therefore, the NKPA's 70,000 men and 70 tanks deployed around the Pusan Perimeter were outnumbered by the UN forces, which included 85,000 American and British troops, 80,000 South Koreans and 400 medium tanks. For a number of reasons, however, morale within the Perimeter remained low. One

Eighth Army estimate credited the NKPA's strength and potential as being far greater than it was, commenting: 'Currently the enemy is on the offensive and retains this capability in all general sectors of the Perimeter. It is not expected that this capability will decline in the immediate future.' Secondly, while the US element alone was apparently stronger than the communists, the proportion of administrative and support personnel to riflemen in the American divisions was far higher than in the NKPA, and it was upon the rifle companies, some reduced to a quarter of their established strength, that the daily burden of the war was falling. Thirdly, American casualties were already unexpectedly high – 4,599 killed or died of wounds, 12,058 wounded, 2,508 captured or missing – and in the first two weeks of September were actually greater than in any comparable period to date. In the circumstances the prognosis suggested a long and bloody war of attrition, although this was far from being the case.

The war had hardly begun before MacArthur started planning an operation which he believed would result in the destruction of the NKPA. His thoughts centred on Seoul, which, as the hub of communications for the entire peninsula, was as vital to the communists deployed around the Pusan Perimeter as Meiktila had been to the Japanese armies in central and northern Burma. The loss of Seoul would deprive the NKPA of the means to fight and, its line of retreat cut, it would collapse; furthermore, as the capital of the Republic of Korea the city was an important political objective, and its liberation would result in the communists losing face throughout the Far East.

Seoul, MacArthur decided, was to be seized by means of a landing at the port of Inchon, 18 miles to the west, where the immense experience in amphibious warfare acquired by the Americans during the Pacific War could be employed to best advantage. As early as 4 July his staff had begun planning an operation codenamed 'Bluehearts' which would involve the 1st Cavalry Division landing at Inchon just 18 days later. This proved to be wildly optimistic and was overtaken by a deteriorating situation which required the despatch of the division to the Pusan Perimeter.

Far from being discouraged, MacArthur embarked on planning a much larger operation codenamed 'Chromite', scheduled for mid-September. This, like its predecessor, attracted unfavourable comment, notably from the Navy, who were quick to point out that as a site for an amphibious landing Inchon possessed almost every possible disadvantage they could think of. The tidal range of 32 feet was the second highest in the world. Instead of open beaches the falling tide exposed wide, soft mud flats, backed by sea walls 16 feet high. At high tide the infantry landing craft could clear the flats without difficulty, although ladders would have to be used to climb the walls, beyond which there were built-up areas in which costly street-fighting might be expected at once. The LSTs (Landing Ships, Tank), with landing force's artillery and tanks aboard, drew 29 feet of water, but as the highest tides only prevailed for a maximum of three hours twice daily for three or four days each month, the operation would have to be mounted during these. The seaward approach to Inchon was from the south by means of two narrow channels the better of which, Flying Fish Channel, was tortuous and rock-strewn. This meant that the larger vessels would have to approach in daylight and that the main landings timed to coincide with an evening high tide. This, however, was complicated by a further factor. Lying immediately off Inchon, and connected to it by a causeway, was the island of Walmi-do on which the enemy was known to have constructed defences, and as this could not be left unsubdued on the flank of the main landing it would have to be captured by a preliminary landing executed during the early morning high tide, following a hazardous night approach. As suitable tidal conditions coincided with operational timings on 15 September, but not again until 11 October, it was decided to opt for the former date.

Reservations concerning the plan were so strong that in Washington the Joint Chiefs-of-Staff were most reluctant to give their approval. On 23 July a conference was held at MacArthur's HQ in Tokyo, attended by General Lawton J. Collins, US Army Chief-of-Staff, Admiral Forrest P. Sherman, Chief of Naval Operations, and the senior Army, Navy and Marine Corps officers involved in preparing the operation. The objections were fully discussed and for a while it seemed as though the plan might be rejected. In reply, MacArthur pointed out that enemy was equally aware of the objections and, having decided that a UN landing at Inchon was not a practical proposition, had retained very few troops in the area; that, he commented, was the mistake the French had made in 1759 when they failed to guard the Anse au Foulon against Wolfe, with the result that they had lost Quebec and Canada. He was confident that the landing would achieve surprise, would succeed, and would produce immense strategic benefits. Most, but by no means all, of those present were won over. Nevertheless, the doubters were to continue their opposition for several more weeks and suggested several alternative sites for a landing to the south of Inchon. MacArthur, however, had a powerful ally in Secretary of Defense Louis Johnson, who was able to support his arguments in presidential circles. Even so, the

Joint Chiefs did not finally approve the plan until 9 September.

In the meantime, despite the controversy surrounding 'Chromite', preparations for the operation had continued without pause. In overall command of the landing phase was Admiral Arthur Struble, Commander-in-Chief of the US Seventh Fleet. In total, Struble assembled over 230 vessels for the landing, including contingents from the Royal Navy, the Royal Australian, Canadian and New Zealand Navies, and the French Navy. The major problem had been mustering the 57 LSTs required, as the US Navy had only 17 available in Far Eastern waters. Fortunately, a large number of surplus LSTs had been handed over to Japanese owners after World War 2 for use as inter-island ferries and 40 of these were commandeered, complete with crews.

The landing force itself was designated X Corps and commanded by Major-General Edward Almond, a veteran of both World Wars and until recently MacArthur's Chief-of-Staff. The Corps contained the 1st Marine and 7th Infantry Divisions, both of which had only been assembled with difficulty. The 1st Marine Division, which included a number of recalled reservists, was drawn from the United States itself, from the Fleet Marine Force Atlantic and from the Mediterranean; one of its regiments, the 5th Marines, formed the major element of the 1st Provisional Marine Brigade and had to be pulled out of the line in the Pusan Perimeter, despite strenuous objections from General Walker. The 7th Infantry Division was the last of the four divisions which had formed the original garrison of Japan and its strength had been seriously eroded by the need to provide drafts for the other three when they embarked for Korea. It was decided, therefore, that the division would receive the lion's share of the reinforcements reaching Japan from the United States, but as not even this could make good the shortfall resort was made to the extreme measure of filling the ranks with South Korean recruits, for whom American squad members were made responsible under a scheme known as 'The Buddy System'.

Intelligence sources estimated that the NKPA had approximately 6,500 men in the Seoul-Inchon area, of whom 2,500 were probably manning the port defences at Inchon. To obtain the latest information on conditions in and around the harbour, on 31 August a small party under Lieutenant Eugene F. Clark, US Navy, was put ashore by a British destroyer on the island of Yonghung-do, lying at the mouth of Flying Fish Channel, 15 miles from Inchon. The island's fishermen were friendly and agreed to obtain the details he required while selling their catches in the port; some even penetrated the town and its hinterland and returned with additional information on the enemy's strength and dispositions. All of these reports were passed by radio to warships lying below the horizon, then relayed to Tokyo and Admiral Struble's task force. Inevitably, Clark's transmissions were eventually picked up by the enemy's intercept operators, who were also able to identify their source as Yonghung-do, but before the NKPA was able to do anything about it the party had moved to another island, Palmi-do, on which was the flashing electric beacon marking the entrance to Flying Fish Channel. This, disused since the war began, was restored to working order during the evening of 14 September, D-1.

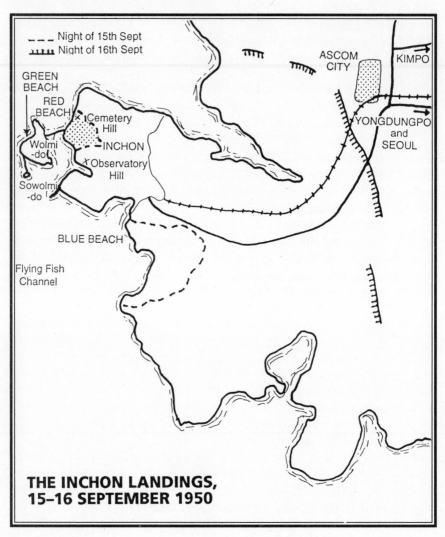

**THE INCHON LANDINGS,
15–16 SEPTEMBER 1950**

By then, the task force was already closing in and the preliminary phases of the operation had begun. Wolmi-do and Inchon were hit by air attacks on 10 September. On 13 September the task force's Gunfire Support Group, consisting of two American heavy cruisers, two British light cruisers and five American destroyers, closed in to batter Wolmi-do under cover of more air strikes. The destroyers, engaging point-blank at less than a mile, opened fire at 1230 and during the next hour eliminated most of the island's five heavily protected 76mm coast defence guns. At 1352, as the destroyers withdrew down the channel, it was the turn of the cruisers, lying 8–10 miles offshore. For 90 minutes Wolmi-do was blanketted in bursting 6in and 8in shells. The island was then subjected to another heavy air strike, after which the cruisers renewed their punishing bombardment for a further 30 minutes before withdrawing.

It was difficult for the North Koreans to read too much into this, as the deception plan for 'Chromite' included air activity, bombardments and diversionary landings at other points along the coast. When, the following day, carrier aircraft and the Gunfire Support Group returned to Inchon, the latter extending their bombardment to mainland targets after they had left the Wolmi-do batteries wrecked and silent, some might have suspected the truth; if they did, the time for counter-measures had long passed.

At 0200 on 15 September the bombardment force, supplemented by rocket ships, led the Advance Attack Group up Flying Fish Channel. Once again the surface of Wolmi-do erupted under the impact of air strikes, naval gunfire and salvo after salvo of rockets. At 0530 the battalion detailed to assault the island, Lieutenant-Colonel Robert Taplett's 3rd/5th Marines, began scrambling aboard their landing craft. After an unopposed run-in the first wave, consisting of G and H Companies, touched down on Wolmi-do's western shore, designated Green Beach, and began moving inland. The second wave, consisting of 1st Company and nine Pershings, three of which were fitted with dozer blades and three with flamethrowers, came in shortly afterwards. The few enemy soldiers who emerged to open fire or fling grenades were quickly dealt with; those of the survivors who refused to surrender were walled up in their bunkers by the tank dozers.

By 0750 Wolmi-do had been cleared and Taplett was able to turn his attention to the islet of Sowolmi-do, south of and connected to the main island by a causeway. Attacked by three tanks and an infantry squad, some of the enemy platoon holding the islet were killed, some surrendered and some attempted to swim to Inchon harbour breakwater. The capture of Wolmi-do had cost 3rd/5th Marines just 17 men wounded; North Korean casualties amounted to 108 killed, 136 captured and about 100 sealed in their positions.

For the rest of the day, as the tide ebbed and began to flood again, Taplett's isolated battalion had a grandstand view of events. While aircraft flew interdiction sorties up to 25 miles inland, the shipping involved in the main landing emerged from the channel and took up position. At 1430 the Gunfire Support Group began pounding the Inchon beaches. Disembarkation commenced an hour later and at 1645 the lines of landing craft began heading for the shore, those aboard being heartened by the spectacular sight of the rocket ships blasting their objectives with 2,000 fiery projectiles. During the final minutes of the run-in, strafing aircraft roared so close overhead that the assault troops were showered with expended ammunition cases.

The 1st Marine Regiment reached Blue Beach, just to the south of the town, at 1732. Negligible opposition enabled the sea wall to be surmounted without difficulty, but smoke and the gathering darkness resulted in units being landed in the wrong place. At length the confusion was sorted out and by 0130 the following morning the regiment had secured a mile-deep beach-head and reached the Inchon-Seoul highway, the last of its objectives for the day.

Covered by the fire of their comrades on Wolmi-do, 1st and 2nd/5th Marines landed simultaneously on Red Beach, at the northern end of the town. Here the bombardment had breached the sea wall in places, enabling coxswains to nose their craft into the gaps, although elsewhere ladders had to be used. The degree of resistance encountered varied considerably. On the extreme left an enemy position just beyond the wall put up a stiff fight which cost A Company's 3rd Platoon eight killed and 28 wounded before it was subdued. Nearby, on Cemetery Hill, the North Koreans tamely surrendered to the same company's 2nd Platoon. By midnight other elements of 1st/5th had fought their way to the top of Observatory Hill. On the right, 2nd/5th met scattered opposition which inflicted a number of casualties but was unable to prevent the battalion reaching its objectives.

As soon as the assault wave had cleared Red Beach, eight LSTs closed up bows-on to the sea wall and began discharging their tanks, heavy weapons and supplies. This work continued apace throughout the night so that the ships' places could be taken by a further eight LSTs on the morning tide. It attracted enemy mortar and machine gun fire to which the crews, uncertain of the precise situation ashore, replied wildly with their heavy automatic weapons, killing one man and wounding 23 more in 2nd/5th Marines before they could be brought under control. Despite this unfortunate accident, the total casualties incurred by the 1st Marine Division in the seizure of Inchon amounted to 20 killed, 174 wounded and one missing.

By 0730 on 16 September the two Marine regiments had established a continuous perimeter around Inchon and, leaving a ROK Marine unit to mop up the town, they began to advance into the hinterland. Three miles down the Seoul road, a prowling flight of eight Corsairs from the carrier USS *Sicily* pounced on the enemy's first identifiable response to the landing, a column of six T34s accompanied by infantry, moving in the direction of the port. Swooping in with napalm and 500lb bombs, the aircraft scattered the column and claimed to have damaged three of the tanks, but lost one of their number to return fire. A second flight renewed the attack and reported all the tanks destroyed. However, as was often the case in air-to-ground strikes, the pilots over-estimated the damage they had done, for as the 1st Marines' point platoon and its accompanying armour approached the still smouldering site three of the T34s began moving into fire positions; all were promptly engaged and destroyed by the Marines' Pershings. By evening the high ground east of Lichon was in American hands and the perimeter had been pushed forward six miles, thereby placing the landing area beyond the range of the enemy's field artillery. The divisional commander, Major-General Oliver P. Smith, landed with his staff and formally assumed command of operations ashore.

Before dawn on the 17th, the North Koreans repeated the probe which had come to grief the previous day. At 0545 an outpost of D Company 2nd/5th Marines gave warning that six T34s and a large body of infantry were moving along the Seoul highway in the direction of the battalion's main position. As the tanks ground past the outpost the Marines noted that some of the infantry were riding on them. By 0600 the enemy had reached the still-silent American lines. Suddenly, at a range of 75 yards, a bazooka team slammed its bomb into the flank of the leading T34. It burst into flames, illuminating the column. Within five minutes the combined fire of Pershings, recoilless rifles and bazookas had finished off the enemy's armour and what was left of his infantry, flayed by machine guns, had fled into the darkness, leaving the bodies of 200 of their comrades behind.

Later that morning the ambush site was examined with satisfaction by MacArthur, Struble, Almond and other senior officers. The 2nd/5th had already moved on and by evening had taken half of Kimpo Airfield. After beating off several company-sized counter-attacks during the night the battalion secured the rest of the airfield on the morning of 18 September. As the first aircraft began landing that afternoon the 5th Marines resumed their advance and by the evening of the 19th had reached the south bank of the Han river, which they prepared to cross the following day.

Meanwhile, on the right, the 1st Marines were moving more slowly, partly because of more difficult terrain and partly because the opposition was becoming progressively stiffer. By the evening of 16 September the North Korean commander in Seoul had recognised that, with one terrible and totally unexpected stroke, MacArthur had sealed the fate of the NKPA unless the advance on the city could be halted. The newly raised 18th Division, on the point of leaving for the Pusan Perimeter, was committed to the defence of the northern and western approaches, while other units were ordered to converge on Seoul from north and south. Some of the latter, travelling by rail, took four days to complete the journey as their trains were forced to hide in tunnels during daylight hours to avoid prowling UN aircraft. On 19 September X Corps intelligence estimated that the NKPA had up to 20,000 troops in the Seoul area and predicted that while these might offer a stubborn defence it would not be protracted.

Thus, when 5th Marines crossed the Han in LVTs on 20 September and swung right down the railway line to approach Seoul from the north-west, they were halted by determined resistance at a line of low hills on the city's outskirts and unable to make further progress. Likewise, the previous day the advance of 1st Marines had been brought to a standstill west of Yongdungpo, an industrial township on the south bank of the Han opposite Seoul. Fortunately, Major-General David G. Barr's 7th Infantry Division had now landed and one of its regiments, the 32nd Infantry, took over some of 1st Marines' positions, enabling the latter to concentrate on the developing battle, while another, the 31st Infantry, held the southern flank of beach-head and prevented the intervention of NKPA reinforcements arriving from the Pusan Perimeter.

The battle for Yongdungpo lasted for three days during which the enemy's counter-attacks, often mounted with armoured support, were defeated with heavy loss, while an attack by 1st Marines on 21 September was fought to a standstill, save on one vital sector. Due to a remarkable oversight on the enemy's part this had been left undefended and, quite by chance, the gap was penetrated by Captain Robert Barrow's A Company. With fierce fighting raging on either side of them, Barrow's men slipped through the town unchallenged and, after ambushing an enemy party hurrying towards the front, they dug in at a point where a high dike joined the Seoul-Inchon highway. Their presence, lying as it did on the enemy's line of retreat, seriously unsettled the North Koreans. At dusk the company beat off an attack by five tanks, destroying one and damaging two with its bazookas. A pause followed, after which it was assailed by yelling infantry no less than five times between 2100 and midnight. Dawn revealed no less than 275 enemy dead sprawled around the position. By degrees it became apparent that the North Koreans, some of whose units had sustained 80 per cent casualties in their defence of Yongdungpo, had abandoned the town during the night.

On 24 September the 1st Marines were ferried across the Han and took up position on the right of the 5th Marines, still locked in a bitter struggle with the defenders of western Seoul. The 1st Marine Division's third regiment, 7th Marines, was now ashore and, having moved into the line on the left of 5th Marines, it began to advance eastwards past the northern suburbs of the city, thereby turning the North Korean flank. Almond, however, was becoming concerned that it was taking so long to break the enemy's resistance and he shifted the emphasis of the battle to 7th Infantry Division's sector. At dawn on 25 September the 32nd Infantry, followed by the 17th ROK Infantry, crossed the river in LVTs and secured the most important features in eastern Seoul, notably South Mountain. This, together with the final collapse of their defence line to the west, signalled the end for the North Koreans, who were now in serious danger of being encircled. At dusk their columns were seen streaming north out of the city in the direction of Uijongbu and the border. Nevertheless, a strong rearguard was left behind and heavy street fighting continued for the next three days, when the last pockets of resistance were eliminated.

Simultaneously, Almond had been extending X Corps' beach-head to the south in anticipation of the expected junction with Walker's Eighth Army, which had already broken out of the Pusan Perimeter. After an overnight advance in very confused conditions, reconnaissance troops and an armoured task force secured the airfield at Suwon, 21 miles south of Seoul, on the morning of 22 September. They were relieved the same day by Colonel Richard Overshine's 31st Infantry Regiment. Prisoners taken during the early part of this operation claimed that a regiment of the 105th Armoured Division was on its way north to help the Seoul garrison. Shortly before midnight on 24 September enemy armour did indeed attack the 2nd/31st, holding an advance position on a hill to the south, but was beaten off with the assistance of artillery fire and lost four of its T34s.

Although there was to be further fighting on this sector, the southern boundary of X Corps' beach-head had been established and all that remained was to await the arrival of the Eighth Army's spearheads. Altogether, the Inchon landings and the capture of Seoul cost the United Nations forces about 3,500 casualties, of which the heaviest proportion fell on the 1st Marine Division, with 364 killed, 53 who died of wounds, 1,961 wounded and five missing; 7th Infantry Division sustained 106 killed, 409 wounded and 57 missing. It was estimated that

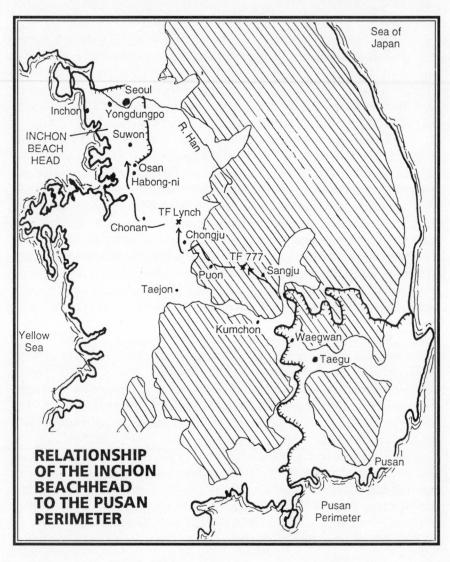

RELATIONSHIP OF THE INCHON BEACHHEAD TO THE PUSAN PERIMETER

14,000 North Koreans had been killed and 7,000 were captured. Most of the enemy's heavy weapons had been destroyed or captured, including some 50 tanks.

The Eighth and ROK Armies had commenced their breakout operations from the Pusan Perimeter on 16 September, one day after the landing at Inchon, the main effort being directed along the axis Taegu-Kumchon-Taejon-Suwon with the object of effecting a junction with X Corps. However, as the US Army's official historian of the campaign comments: 'The general attack set for 0900 did not swing into motion everywhere around the Perimeter at the appointed hour for the simple reason that at many places the North Koreans were attacking and the United Nations troops defending. In most sectors an observer would have found the morning of 16 September little different from that of the 15th or the 14th or the 13th. The battle for the hills had merely gone on another day. Only in a few places were significant gains made on the first day of the offensive.'

Those who had expected the enemy's morale to be adversely affected by the Inchon landing were disappointed, for the very good reason that the NKPA's leaders deliberately concealed it from their troops for several days. Nevertheless, by 19 September even the most dedicated communist was forced to concede that there were insufficient resources to contain the UN's sustained pressure, and on that date the NKPA began to withdraw its troops from the southern end of the Perimeter; on 22 September the retreat had become general. At first it was conducted in good order, with rearguards holding blocking positions in suitable terrain, but it quickly became a rout as the NKPA, savaged by pursuing armoured spearheads and harried constantly from the air, began to fall apart. Near Waegwan the advance of 1st/7th Cavalry traversed a road which 'presented a picture of devastation – dead oxen, disabled T34 tanks, wrecked artillery pieces, piles of abandoned ammunition and other military equipment and supplies littered its course'. Elsewhere, there were grimmer discoveries; hastily dug and incompletely covered mass graves containing the bodies of South Korean politicians, local government officials and American prisoners of war, vindictively murdered by the communists before they fled.

Responsibility for effecting the junction with X Corps was given to Major-General Hobart R. Gay's 1st Cavalry Division, the advance guard of which, commanded by Lieutenant-Colonel William A. Harris, was known as Task Force 777 since it consisted of the 7th Cavalry, 77th Field Artillery Battalion and 70th Tank Battalion. Task Force 777's own advance guard, commanded by Lieutenant-Colonel James H. Lynch, consisted of 3rd/7th Cavalry, B Company 8th Combat Engineer Battalion, two Sherman tank platoons from C Company 70th Tank Battalion, two batteries of 77th Field Artillery, the 7th Cavalry's own jeep-mounted Intelligence and Reconnaissance (I&R) Platoon, one of the regiment's heavy mortar platoons, and an air control party; the whole being known collectively as Task Force Lynch.

Gay briefed his senior officers in a schoolhouse at Sangju during the morning of 26 September; the division would move off at noon and not halt again until it had reached X Corps' perimeter at Suwon. Harris passed on these orders to Lynch and at 1130 the latter's task force moved out of its harbour areas at Puon, led by the I&R Platoon and a platoon of six Shermans commanded by Lieutenant Robert W. Baker, who had been told to drive at maximum speed and only fire if fired upon.

Baker's force quickly out-distanced the rest of Task Force Lynch, driving mile after mile along roads which were deserted save for the inhabitants of villages who turned out to cheer them. The town of Chongju was found to be empty save for a few civilians. At 1800, having covered 64 miles, Baker halted at Ipchang-ni to replenish the Shermans' empty petrol tanks. For some reason the fuel lorry which should have accompanied the column was absent, but by collecting every jerrican in the column it was possible to refill three of the tanks. At this point the remarkable luck which was to accompany Baker throughout his mission began to manifest itself. In the gathering dusk three North Korean lorries drove up and, suddenly finding themselves under the guns of the American force, their drivers abandoned them. The lorries carried sufficient petrol for the column to complete refuelling by 2000.

As contact with the enemy could be expected soon, Baker led the column with three of his tanks and ordered the rest to bring up the rear. He spoke to Lynch on the radio and was given permission to open fire if the situation demanded it; he was also given permission, at his discretion, to use headlights, and his decision to do so almost certainly saved his own life and those of his men. At 2030 the column reached the main highway running south from Seoul and turned right towards Chonan. The town was crowded with enemy troops, none of whom paid them much attention. At a road junction Baker halted, uncertain which way to proceed.

'Osan?' he shouted at a North Korean soldier. The man indicated the Osan road and took to his heels. No alarm was raised and the rest of Task Force Lynch also negotiated the town without incident.

Beyond Chonan, Baker increased speed again. Soon his three tanks were several miles ahead of the task force and had lost radio contact with Lynch. Intermingled with the enemy's own traffic, they drove on across guarded bridges and on one occasion they used their machine guns to shoot up an enemy infantry company marching north. Unknown to any of them, they ran unmolested through the harbour areas of part of the 105th Armoured Division, the occupants of which mistook the tanks for some of their own. Roaring through Osan, Baker halted briefly just beyond and noted the presence of T34 tracks in the road. Three miles further on he ran through the North Korean front line, attracting scattered fire as he did so. More tank tracks were revealed by the head-lights, but they were unmistakably those of Pershings. Suddenly the Shermans became the focus of small arms and 75mm recoilless rifle fire which sliced off the third tank's anti-aircraft machine gun and killed the loader. Baker's platoon had run into 31st Infantry's perimeter and, now firmly in the gunsights of 73rd Tank Battalion's supporting Pershings, were a split second away from death.

What saved them was their apparently reckless speed, their blazing headlights and the sound of their engines, all of which caused the Pershing crews to doubt that they belonged to the enemy. Even so, one tank commander, having let the first Sherman pass, was on the point of destroying the second when its white recognition star was illuminated by a bursting phosphorus grenade. Baker's platoon, having covered 106 miles during the day, had established the first direct contact between the Eighth Army and X Corps at 2226 on 26 September.

It may well have been this burst of gunfire which caused Lynch, still some miles south of Osan, to order his task force to extinguish its headlights. At about midnight the column became involved in a savage close-quarter brawl with a 12-strong T34 battalion near the village of Habong-ni. During this Task Force Lynch lost two killed and 28 wounded, two of its three Shermans and 15 wheeled vehicles. Of the three T34s which escaped, one was knocked out by bazooka fire and two were found abandoned when the advance was resumed the following morning. Contact with 31st Infantry, engaged in an operation to capture two hills covering the road and railway between Osan and Suwon, was established at 0826.

The 1st Cavalry Division's drive had cut a swathe across the peninsula, isolating many North Korean units in the south. For all practical purposes the NKPA had been destroyed, its divisions reduced to mere skeletons of their former selves. One regimental commander, finding his retreat blocked, dropped in at a police station to surrender the remnants of his command, amounting to 167 men. Of all those who had invaded South Korea only 25,000 to 30,000 straggled back across the

38th Parallel in small groups or as individuals, leaving behind all their heavy weapons and equipment. A subsequent survey counted 239 destroyed or abandoned T34s and 72 SU-76 self-propelled guns, accounting for almost all of the NKPA'S armour; significantly, one quarter of these vehicles were captured without visible signs of damage.

President Truman's message of congratulation to MacArthur summed up the general feeling: 'Few operations in military history can match either the delaying action where you traded space for time in which to build up your forces, or the brilliant maneuver which has now resulted in the liberation of Seoul.' The Joint Chiefs-of-Staff, one of whom had been opposed to the Inchon landing from the start, were also generous in their praise: 'Your transition from defensive to offensive operations was magnificently planned, timed and executed. We remain completely confident that the great task entrusted to you by the United Nations will be carried to a successful conclusion.'

MacArthur was authorised to cross the 38th Parallel and complete the enemy's destruction. The NKPA, though rallied somewhat and augmented by up to 50,000 conscripts in various stages of training, remained a beaten, under-equipped and out-numbered army incapable of imposing anything more than temporary delays. However, on 17 October two incidents took place which hinted at the shape of things to come.

The 27th Commonwealth Brigade had been placed under the operational command of 1st Cavalry Division and was advancing on the town of Sariwon, some 30 miles south of Pyongyang, the North Korean capital. The Argylls were in the lead, accompanied by Shermans of the 89th Tank Battalion. Four miles short of the town the column was fired on from an orchard, some 200 yards distant on a hillside. As the tanks began blasting the trees and many of the enemy fled over the crest. Two platoons of the Argylls' A Company then attacked with the bayonet from a flank and cleared the orchard, killing about 40 and capturing others. No further opposition was encountered and, while the Argylls took possession of Sariwon, the 3rd Royal Australian Regiment passed through to establish a roadblock five miles to the north.

The overall situation remained fluid, with both armies moving northwards, somewhat intermingled. At dusk large numbers of North Korean infantry marched unconcernedly into Sariwon from the south. So friendly were they that at first the Argylls thought they were a ROK unit or perhaps South Koreans attached to the 24th Division, which was also known to be converging on Sariwon. For their part the North Koreans, unfamiliar with the British battledress and knitted cap comforter, were convinced that the Scots were Russians. Some of them clapped the Argylls on the back, called them Comrade and offered them cigarettes; the offer of red star cap badges, however, settled the question of identities once and for all.

'They're... Gooks!' yelled someone, and close-quarter fighting broke out at once. 'During this scrambled night at Sariwon,' wrote the American official historian, 'about 150 North Koreans were killed; strangely, the British lost only one soldier.' Most of the North Koreans by-passed the fighting and headed north, only to run into the Australians, who bluffed them into surrendering and took 1,982 prisoners.

The second incident had already taken place that afternoon. Colonel Peter D. Clainos' 7th Cavalry, moving along secondary roads from the east, had cut the Sariwon-Pyongyang highway at Hwangju, some miles beyond the Australian roadblock. A message from the divisional commander advised Clainos that the enemy were pulling out of Sariwon and that he should direct one battalion southwards towards 27th Brigade in order to trap them. 1st/7th conformed to these instructions but was fired on from a ridge which lay between them and the Australians. After a brief skirmish, the battalion's South Korean interpreter approached the nearest enemy platoon, shouting that it should stop firing on its Russian comrades. Intrigued, the platoon emerged to greet the new arrivals and was promptly disarmed. Believing that they were witnessing a general surrender, over 1,700 enemy soldiers descended the ridge to lay down their weapons.

The possibility of intervention by the Soviet Union or China was, therefore, already in the minds of both sides, for the communist powers had sustained a humiliating defeat at MacArthur's hands and it seemed highly unlikely that they would be prepared to let the matter rest. When, in November, intervention became a fact, it was funded and supplied by the USSR while China provided the troops. Offensives were followed by counter-offensives, Seoul was lost again and recaptured, and gradually the war became one of static positions. By then fundamental differences between Truman and MacArthur had resulted in the latter being recalled to the United States, where he received a hero's welcome. His successors fought a different kind of war, using their superior firepower to write down the enemy's vast manpower resources. When an armistice was finally concluded in 1953 South Korea had secured a defensible frontier, the Soviet economy was seriously dislocated and the Chinese People's Liberation Army had been bled white.

CHAPTER 11

Earthquake on Chu Pong: The Ia Drang Valley Campaign, Vietnam, 1965

In the years between the ending of the Korean War and the disastrous Soviet invasion of Afghanistan in 1979, the major communist powers pursued their expansionist aims by surrogate means, usually with guerrilla forces posing as 'national liberation fronts', and generally in difficult terrain which prevented their opponents employing firepower to the best advantage. The strategy was long term and the tactics were those of the raid and ambush. Generally an engagement began with a raid on an isolated post, but the capture of the post was not necessarily the object of the operation, for even heavier casualties could be inflicted on government troops by ambushing the road-bound column sent to its relief. After the action, the guerrillas would simply melt back into their jungles. By these means, together with a campaign of murder and intimidation which cowed the civil population, the will of the government army would be eroded and large areas of the countryside would pass under communist control. In due course, the war would be extended to the cities and finally, according to the master plan, the government would be swept from power by a nationwide rising.

This form of 'revolutionary' warfare failed against the British in Malaya but it succeeded against the French in Vietnam, forcing the latter to abandon their empire in Indo-China. In 1954 Vietnam was artificially divided into a communist North, ruled by Ho Chi Minh, and a pro-Western South. After a brief pause in which he crushed surviving political opponents at home, Ho commenced operations to bring South Vietnam into the communist fold. At first, despite the presence of American advisers, the South Vietnamese Army (ARVN) performed poorly, but improved to the point that Ho's commander-in-chief, General Vo Nguyen Giap, was forced to commit substantial elements of the regular North Vietnamese Army (NVA) to support the local guerrilla forces, the Viet Cong. Nevertheless, the South's position continued to deteriorate and in 1965 American ground troops were formally committed to a war that was being fought without established lines and in which physical possession of territory counted for little.

There had, however, been a notable change in battlefield conditions since the communists formulated their philosophy of guerrilla warfare. Formerly, the guerrillas had retained the initiative because they possessed a mobility in difficult country which their opponents could not match. Now, in the helicopter, the Americans had the means to respond to or pre-empt a threat very quickly, regardless of the terrain below; once a guerrilla group had been located, and its position fixed by artillery and air strikes, it had become possible to lift infantry into the area and eliminate it. In theory, paratroops had always provided this facility, and indeed had been so employed by the French, but helicopter troops offered much faster response times and precision landings in tactical units which had rarely been possible with other forms of airborne assault.

The concept of airmobility had evolved in a very short space of time. Helicopters had already been employed by the UN forces in Korea, by the French in Vietnam and by the British in Malaya, but their poor power-to-weight ratio had seriously limited the loads that could be carried and, in the main, their use was restricted to such roles as casualty evacuation, reconnaissance and liaison. Then, in 1955, the problem was solved by the introduction of the turboshaft engine and it became possible to purpose-build helicopters to perform many other functions, including ground-attack gunships, troop transports, cargo carriers and flying cranes capable of transporting artillery weapons.

The US Army recognised the implications for the land battle and formed an experimental formation known as the 11th Air Assault Division (Test), supplemented by units from the 2nd Infantry Division, to carry out trials under Brigadier-General Harry Kinnard, a paratrooper with previous active service experience in Normandy, Holland and Bastogne. The concept was proved to be viable and on 1 July 1965 the force was re-designated the 1st Cavalry Division (Airmobile) and granted the privilege of carrying the colours of the old 1st Cavalry Division which, at that time, was still serving in a static infantry role in Korea. This apparent departure from airborne lineage arose largely from the wishes of former cavalrymen now holding important positions in the Pentagon to restore the mobility which was in keeping with the traditions of their arm.

Internally, the division possessed a flexible organisation which consisted of three brigade HQs, eight infantry battalions, an aviation group, an artillery group which included three 105mm howitzer battalions and helicopter gunship units, signals and engineer battalions and divisional services. This enabled the divisional commander to allocate the appropriate number of infantry battalions and supporting arms to individual brigade HQs as required by the missions in hand, after which they reverted to divisional control. The division had a strength of 16,000 men and possessed 428 helicopters, including the Bell UK-1 Iroquois series, better known as the Huey, which performed numerous tasks but was most frequently employed as an armed troop transport with an eight-man infantry section aboard; the Bell AH-1 Cobra gunship, which served as an escort and fire support craft and was armed with a variety of weapon systems, including one or two six-barrel miniguns capable of tearing a target to shreds with their high output, one or two 40mm grenade launchers or pods containing 76 2. 75in rockets, each as powerful as a medium artillery shell; the twin-rotor Boeing-Vertol CH-47 Chinook transport, capable of carrying 33 troops or their equivalent weight in cargo, plus a field gun or stores slung from a ventral hook; the Sikorsky CH-64 Tarhe flying crane, which could lift medium artillery weapons and other awkward loads as well as recover crashed aircraft; and the Bell OH-58A Kiowa and Hughes OH-6 Cayuse light observation and reconnaissance helicopters.

In addition to its pre-planned operations the division, in common with other airmobile units in Vietnam, maintained a rapid response capability with its Eagle Flights, which remained on permanent alert. These might consist of one command craft, seven troop-carrying Hueys, five Cobras for escort and fire-support and one casualty evacuation Huey, and were employed to bring guerrilla groups to battle once they had been located, or pin them down if they were trying to withdraw, pending the arrival of reinforcement flights.

Commanded by Kinnard, now promoted to major-general, the 1st Cavalry Division (Airmobile), reached Vietnam in September 1965 and began settling into its base at An Khe in the Central Highlands, a mountainous, heavily forested and almost trackless area stretching from the Cambodian border to the South China Sea, justifiably regarded at the time as containing the most serious enemy threat to the country's stability. In fact, the strategy of General Chu Huy Man, commander of the NVA's Western Highlands Field Front, involved nothing less than a sustained advance from the Chu Pong Massif, straddling the frontier, straight through the Central Highlands, thereby cutting South Vietnam in two. So important was the operation considered that, for the first time since it had been committed to the fighting in the south, the NVA would be employing a division-sized force consisting of its 32nd, 33rd and 66th

Regiments, reinforced by local Viet Cong battalions, under the direction of Chu's Chief-of-Staff, Senior Colonel Ha Vi Tung.

Ha began with something of a problem. The indigenous tribes of the Central Highlands, collectively named Montagnards by the French, bitterly resented the communists' campaign of intimidation. Taking advantage of the situation, American Special Forces teams, more commonly known as Green Berets, organised them into Civilian Irregular Defence Groups (CIDGs) which operated from fortified camps. Armed and trained, the CIDGs ambushed the communists and preyed on their supply lines to such effect that, as a preliminary step, Ha decided to eliminate the most troublesome of their camps, starting with Plei Mei, some 20 miles east of Chu Pong and 30 miles south of the town of Pleiku. As usual, his plan contained several elements. First, the 33rd Regiment was to surround Plei Mei and maintain sufficient pressure against the camp for the ARVN to despatch a relief column to its assistance; secondly, the 32nd Regiment was to ambush and destroy the relief column; and finally, both regiments would combine to swamp the remaining defences with a human wave assault.

The garrison of Plei Mei consisted of 10 American advisers and approximately 300 Jarai tribesmen, one third of whom were absent on patrol when the attack commenced at 2300 on 19 October. Behind a barrage of mortar, recoilless rifle and rocket fire, the North Vietnamese

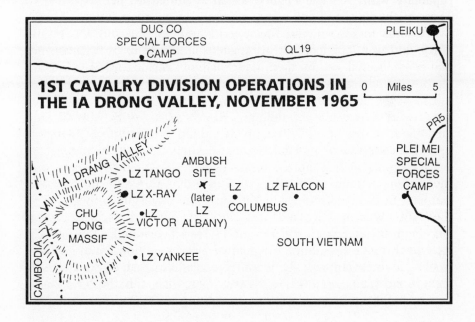

199

attacked with suicidal courage, piling up casualties in and around the perimeter wire. The defences began to crumble and at midnight the garrison commander, Captain Harold M. Moore, asked for air support. By 0200 a flare ship was overhead, flooding the landscape in brilliant white light that starkly illuminated the attackers. The first air strikes followed at 0400, smashing up a co-ordinated assault, then built up to a crescendo that was to last for several days as the US and South Vietnamese air forces, joined by carrier aircraft from offshore, were vectored to the area. So continuous was the pounding with napalm, bombs, rockets and machine gun fire that traffic control stacking had to introduced above the target. Ha had expected air intervention and for that reason had deployed a battalion of heavy anti-aircraft machine guns along its probable routes; what he had not anticipated was its scale nor its extended use through the hours of darkness, so that while his anti-aircraft gunners scored several kills they amounted to no more than a tiny fraction of the strength deployed against them. Pinned down and semi-stunned as they were, his men could only watch as the garrison's third company, returning from its patrol during the evening of the 20th, suddenly appeared and, pursued by sporadic fire, dashed across open ground to enter the camp through its main gate. For the moment, there was little more that the North Vietnamese could do save sit and absorb punishment while, as one day followed another, they waited in vain for news that 32nd Regiment had successfully ambushed the ARVN relief column.

The reasons for the delay rested partly with the ARVN and partly with the Viet Cong. The American advisers to the ARVN commander in Pleiku had insisted that he should include a larger infantry element in the column than he intended, but he had argued that this meant stripping the town of its garrison and declined to move until replacements arrived. The column, spearheaded by six M41 Walker Bulldog light tanks, an APC company equipped with M113s, two guns and an engineer section, followed at a distance by a convoy of wheeled vehicles carrying fuel, ammunition and supplies, set off along a secondary road leading south from Pleiku on the morning of 21 October, but had not proceeded far when it was halted by a blown bridge. The demolition was the work of a local Viet Cong unit and, had the communists' intention been simply to storm Plei Mei it would undoubtedly have been the correct thing to do; however, the plan was more complex than that, and the time taken to effect repairs also delayed the arrival of the relief column at 32nd Regiment's ambush site, thereby prolonging the ordeal of the battered 33rd Regiment around Plei Mei. Clearly, liaison between the NVA and Viet Cong was not all that it might have been.

It was not until the morning of the 23rd that the relief column began moving again, travelling slowly behind pre-planned air strikes against possible ambush sites. The North Vietnamese remained hidden some distance behind these but at about 1750 they ran forward to occupy their fighting positions and opened fire. Contrary to their expectations, the ARVN crews did not panic but swung their tanks and APCs left and right in a herringbone pattern to lace the jungle with canister and heavy machine gun fire. Against the wheeled element of the column the communists did somewhat better, destroying six vehicles, including two M8 armoured cars, and damaging a further eight, but failed to inflict many casualties on the ARVN infantry, which once again unexpectedly stood its ground, supported by air strikes. Fighting continued for much of the night but by dawn the 32nd Regiment had broken contact, having incurred heavy casualties. Despite this the ARVN column commander's inclinations were to return to Pleiku and, when pressed to resume the advance by his American advisers he emphatically refused to do so unless he received artillery support the whole way. This led to the 1st Cavalry Division deploying several of its batteries, behind the fire of which the column inched forward. It finally reached Plei Mei at dusk on 25 October, having taken five days to cover the 30 miles from Pleiku, an uninspired performance crowned by a bloodily-bungled sweep around the camp the following morning.

By then Ha had accepted defeat and begun to withdraw his troops towards Chu Pong. Both regiments had sustained severe casualties and the loss of equipment, especially mortars and anti-aircraft machine guns, had been particularly heavy. In the past, once the North Vietnamese had broken contact they had been able to conduct their retreat through broken, trackless terrain without fear of being molested. On this occasion, however, they were harried without mercy. Somehow, the nature of the battle had changed without their being able to understand why.

During the evening of 27 October General Westmoreland visited the HQ of the 1st Cavalry Division at An Khe and instructed Kinnard to interdict the enemy's withdrawal. Operations commenced the following day, with infantry companies and artillery batteries being set down operationally in jungle clearings then moved on a day or so later before the local NVA commander could react. Once detected, an enemy unit became the focus of helicopter gunships, artillery fire and air strikes until it broke up. In this way battalions fragmented into companies and companies into platoons until control no longer existed. On 1 November the 33rd Regiment's field dressing station was captured and held against a determined counter-attack. This engagement cost the NVA 78 killed, perhaps twice that number wounded, and 57 men, half of them patients in the hospital, taken prisoner; American casualties amounted to five killed and 17 wounded. The dressing station also yielded arms and ammunition, foodstuffs, tons of medical supplies and a large quantity of documents which were immediately passed to the intelligence staff. Two days later, on the northern slopes of Chu Pong, a company from the 1st Squadron 9th Cavalry mounted an ambush with Claymore mines that wiped out a North Vietnamese column within seconds. The company then withdrew to its landing zone, where it was attacked by the equivalent of an NVA battalion. A second company was flown in to relieve the pressure and, after gunships had silenced the opposition with salvos of rockets, both companies were lifted out.

On 10 November the last North Vietnamese units straggled across the border into the safety of Cambodia. That evening Ha conferred with his regimental commanders and it became clear that during the Plei Mei operation and the retreat the 32nd Regiment had been seriously hurt while the 33rd Regiment had lost half its strength and most of its equipment. This in itself worried Ha less than the loss of face involved in so public a defeat. The irony was that had the 33rd Regiment exerted its whole strength instead of mounting a series of holding attacks designed to provoke the despatch of the relief column, the little camp could have been overrun at any time. It was decided, therefore, that the offensive would be renewed and this time Plei Mei would be erased from the map altogether. The strength of the Field Front, he was able to point out, was now actually stronger than at any time since operations in the Central Highlands had commenced – replacements were emerging from the Ho Chi Minh Trail to fill the depleted ranks, the 66th Regiment had arrived and, following close behind, were a battalion each of twin 14. 5mm anti-aircraft machine guns and 120mm heavy mortars. The attack would commence on 16 November.

In planning their renewed offensive Ha and his commanders rashly mistook an operational pause during which Kinnard relieved his most advanced formation, the 1st Brigade, with Colonel Thomas W. Brown's 3rd Brigade, as an indication that the Americans had abandoned their aggressive tactics. In fact, the mission given by Kinnard to Brown was search the heavily wooded area lying south of the Ia Drang river and the eastern slopes of the Chu Pong Massif, the epicentre of NVA Field Front's activities in the Central Highlands, situated directly on Ha's projected thrust line against Plei Mei.

The battalion detailed for the task was Lieutenant-Colonel Harold G. Moore's 1st/7th Cavalry, which was to secure its landing zone with an airmobile assault on 14 November and carry out search-and-destroy patrols for the next two days; in support would be A and C Batteries 1st/21st Artillery, firing from Landing Zone 'Falcon', eight miles west of Plei Mei.

Moore had the choice of three landing zones, codenamed 'Tango', 'X-Ray' and 'Yankee'. He selected 'X-Ray', the most central of the three, consisting of a clearing measuring 100 yards by 200 yards at the foot of the mountain. The surrounding area was flat but covered with trees up to 100 feet high and elephant grass dotted here and there with tall conical ant hills; as the ground rose to the west the vegetation became denser.

At 1017 on 14 July the artillery and the battalion's escorting gunships began firing on all three landing zones to confuse the enemy. At 1030, B Company touched down and its platoons began to advance up the lower slopes of Chu Pong. They quickly became involved in a heavy fire fight and one platoon was cut off. A Company came in and moved up in support but was soon pinned down. By the time C and D Companies arrived the landing zone was under such heavy mortar and machine gun fire that Moore waved off the last eight helicopters, ordering them by radio not to attempt a landing.

It was clear that the enemy, consisting of the 33rd and 66th Regiments, was present in overwhelming strength and that they were determined to overrun the landing ground. By evening it was apparent to Moore that his battalion was fighting for its life and, having already informed Brown of the situation, he reluctantly abandoned attempts to break through to the isolated platoon and pulled back A and B Companies to complete a defensive perimeter around 'X-Ray'. The enemy fire slackened to the extent that Brown's only available reserve, B Company 2nd/7th, was flown in at 1800. With it came a pathfinder team which set up landing lights under fire, enabling a re-supply of ammunition, food, water and medical stores to take place as well as a partial casualty evacuation.

Throughout the night the North Vietnamese, now joined by H-15 Viet Cong Battalion, constantly probed the perimeter. They were kept at bay by the sweating gunners at Fire Base 'Falcon', who fired 4,000 shells in support of 'X-Ray', and by air strikes delivered by the light of flares. Meanwhile, Brown had been doing everything in his power to assist Moore's embattled troopers, despatching the remainder of 2nd/7th Cavalry to Landing Zone Macon and 2nd/5th Cavalry to

Landing Zone 'Victor', respectively six miles north and two miles south-east of 'X-Ray', with orders to reinforce 1st/7th the following day. He also discussed the situation with Kinnard, who made an additional battalion, 1st/5th Cavalry, available and in turn made such representations up the chain of command that Moore was promised some very powerful assistance indeed.

At first light on the 15th the communists launched a succession of determined attacks, closing in on the perimeter despite their losses from the Americans' artillery, gunships and fighter bombers. In places there was savage hand-to-hand fighting but a breakthrough was averted by Moore forming one reserve after another and committing them to the threatened sectors. At 0755 he ordered his riflemen to throw coloured smoke grenades to mark the perimeter and called in the artillery and air support as close to it as possible. As a result, two napalm tanks cartwheeled over the smoke line and fireballed in the clearing itself, fortunately without causing casualties; likewise, shards of red-hot metal from exploding shells and gunship rockets ripped across the cavalrymen's trenches and these, together with a heavy volume of hostile fire, made any movement above ground extremely hazardous. With professional interest, Moore noted that white phosphorus shells were particularly effective in breaking up the enemy's assaults, especially those of the aggressive but inexperienced 66th Regiment, which had not witnessed their horrific results before.

For a while it seemed as though 'X-Ray' would be overrun. The 7th, however, set great store on the traditions of the Little Big Horn where, in 1876, under the command of Lieutenant-Colonel George Armstrong Custer, five of its troops had fought to the last man while the rest of the regiment, though badly mauled, beat off repeated attacks by Sioux and Cheyenne Indians. So deeply implanted were these traditions that Moore, a fair man, was nicknamed Yellow Hair by his troopers, the name by which Custer had been known to the Indians. 'It certainly entered my mind that we were the 7th Cavalry,' he recalled later, 'and, by God, we couldn't let happen what happened to Custer. ' As an option, surrender was not even considered; the life expectancy of those who fell alive into the communists' hands was said to be short and indeed was proved to be so very shortly.

The critical attack was held and pressure eased sufficiently for A Company 2nd/7th to be lifted in and take some of the strain off the exhausted defenders. Simultaneously, Lieutenant-Colonel Robert Tully's 2nd/5th Cavalry were fighting their way forward from Landing Zone 'Victor' and by noon had entered the perimeter. Brown had also established a new firebase, codenamed 'Columbus', halfway between 'X-Ray' and 'Falcon', using B Battery 1st/21st Artillery and C Battery 2nd/17th Artillery. The crisis at 'X-Ray', now held by twice the number of infantry with twice the artillery support, had passed.

Shortly after noon the moment had come for the Americans to employ another terrible weapon from their armoury. To the west of 'X-Ray' the North Vietnamese and Viet Cong were attempting to regroup out of artillery range on the Chu Pong Massif. Suddenly and without any warning whatever the earth began to erupt in a series of huge explosions that unrolled at tremendous speed across the mountain's slopes like a gigantic carpet. Shock waves transmitted through the heaving ground caved in trenches, bunkers and command posts. Those caught in the path of the storm were simply obliterated by what seemed to be elemental forces. Far above, flying so high as to be invisible and beyond the reach of the human ear, the USAF's B-52 strategic heavy bombers, now deployed for the first time in tactical support for a land battle, continued to disgorge their 30-ton payloads. In the deep silence that followed their departure the badly shaken enemy emerged to salvage what they could from the pitted landscape.

During the afternoon the cavalrymen broke through to the platoon that had been cut off the previous day. Only seven of its men remained alive and unhurt. They owed their survival to one of the squad leaders, Sergeant Clyde Savage, who had taken over when the platoon commander, his sergeant and the senior squad leaders were killed, expertly controlling the artillery's supporting fire and that of his own men to such effect that three major assaults had been thrown back during the hours of darkness.

Ha's troops probed the defences of 'X-Ray' again that night but met even stiffer resistance; by first light on the 16th they had apparently faded away. Company patrols pushed out to a distance of 500 yards met no opposition, counted 634 bodies and returned with six prisoners. American casualties incurred during the defence of 'X-Ray' amounted to 79 killed and 121 wounded. The remainder of 2nd/7th Cavalry arrived and Moore's weary battalion was lifted out. As 'X-Ray' itself now possessed no value, Kinnard gave orders that the 2nd/5th and 2nd/7th Cavalry should march overland by separate routes to 'Columbus', and in so doing unwittingly triggered the last major engagement of the battle.

Ha's planned advance had been stopped dead in its tracks and, once again, his regiments had taken horrendous casualties to no purpose. Nor had he shone in his conduct of the battle, for the entire 32nd Regiment and one battalion of the 66th Regiment were within striking distance of the battlefield yet had not been committed. Badly needing a success to justify his loss he decided that he would eliminate one of the firebases from which the American infantry had drawn so much of their killing power. His choice rested on 'Columbus', against which he directed the 66th Regiment's reserve battalion on the morning of 16 November.

The North Vietnamese were moving about 20 minutes ahead of the Americans and had just halted for the noon meal when their outposts spotted the approaching column of the 2nd/7th Cavalry. An ambush was hastily set in a clearing later known as Landing Zone 'Albany'. When it was sprung the fighting took the form of a brutal hip-shoot in which M16 was opposed to AK47 at close quarters amid the long elephant grass. Because the combatants were so intermingled, calls for air and artillery support could not be answered until early evening, by which time the Americans had been able to rally into two perimeters which were marked with smoke grenades. When, at dusk, a company of 1st/5th Cavalry arrived from 'Columbus', the worst of the fighting was over. The ensuing night was one of horror, punctuated by the screams of American wounded known to be lying among the enemy, followed by pistol shots as they were murdered in cold blood. Next morning, the North Vietnamese had gone, leaving behind 403 bodies, 212 assault rifles, 39 light and three heavy machine guns, six 82mm mortars and eight rocket launchers, a clear indication that the NVA battalion had been shattered by the encounter. American losses amounted to 151 killed, 121 wounded and four missing, two-thirds of 1st Cavalry Division's total casualties in the Ia Drang fighting.

During the next 10 days further fighting took place as the stricken Field Front dragged itself across the border into Cambodia. Had Kinnard been permitted to pursue it would almost certainly have been destroyed, but the US Army, unlike the NVA, was emasculated by political considerations. Senior Colonel Ha and his immediate superior, Major-General Chu Huy Man, put the best possible face on their defeat by claiming a stunning victory in which 1,000 Americans had been killed and 100 helicopters shot down. General Giap, whose stated version of reality was sometimes equally vague, commented that Kinnard's division had 'never been able to achieve surprise or to destroy a single section of the Liberation Armed Forces. Troops of the Air Cavalry Division are even weaker than ordinary US infantry troops because they lack the mechanised support of artillery units. Units of the Air Cavalry Division have been battered by the Liberation Armed Forces in Plei Mei, Binh Dinh and elsewhere. ' Obviously, the truth was far too painful to be spoken aloud. The communist strategy in the Central Highlands had been wrecked, and never again would the NVA willingly close with the 1st Cavalry Division, as it had done at 'X-Ray' and 'Albany'.

In one respect, however, Giap and Ho Chi Minh were scrupulously honest. Neither was unduly concerned by the appalling casualties inflicted on their troops in one battle after another, and both stated that they were willing to continue the sacrifice, year after year, until the Americans grew weary of the war and sought disengagement at the conference table.

Postscript:
The Coup Comes of Age

By the late 1960s it was apparent that the coup de main, once regarded as a rare event, had become an almost commonplace means by which commanders sought to win their battles. Naturally, some armies had an instinctive feel for the game, and the Israeli Defence Force in particular was remarkably adept at turning a situation to its own advantage in this way.

Once the IDF had broken the Egyptian defensive front in Sinai during the Six Day War of June 1967, for example, a small battlegroup from Major General Yoffe's armoured division was detailed to drive through the retreating enemy, much as the Japanese armour had driven through the British in Malaya, and establish itself at the Mitla Pass, thereby blocking one to the Egyptians' major axes of withdrawal to the Suez Canal. Spearheading the drive were a dozen Centurion tanks which soon caught up with and ploughed through the retreating columns, guns blazing, causing them to scatter across the sand. By the time the tanks had overcome local opposition and established themselves at the eastern end of the pass, breakdowns and fuel shortages had reduced their number to nine, two of which were on tow. Shortly after, two mechanised infantry platoons and three 120mm mortar half-tracks arrived, enabling the position to be consolidated. This handful beat off repeated attacks during the night and at dawn the Israeli Air Force pounced on the three-mile traffic jam that now trailed back along the road. Despite this, heavy fighting continued for the next 24 hours so that by the time the rest off Yoffe's division broke through the blocking force's four remaining Centurions were down to their last few rounds. Nevertheless, its epic stand had ensured that the remnants of several Egyptian divisions were destroyed.

Again, in the Yom Kippur War of 1973, it was the IDF's use of the unexpected which produced decisive results. Amid fierce fighting on the central sector of the Suez Canal front, it secured a bridgehead on the west bank during the early hours of 16 October, breaking out two days later to swing south and isolate the Egyptian Third Army. The latter, marooned and waterless on the east bank, would have been forced to surrender had not pressure from the United States and the Soviet Union brought an end to the fighting.

By now all first class armies had developed rapid deployment forces, including airborne, airmobile and mechanised elements, appropriate to their needs. The Soviet Union maintained a huge airborne force of seven divisions, lavishly equipped with helicopters and air-portable armoured vehicles, the uses to which this might have been put in a war with the West being demonstrated during the 1977 Ogaden War between Ethiopia and Somalia. So seriously did the Kremlin regard this that the task of ejecting the Somalis from the Ogaden was given to General Vasili Petrov, then First Deputy Commander of Soviet Ground Forces. Petrov, unwilling to trust the local troops, was allocated 11,000 Cuban surrogates, including a parachute regiment, with which to spearhead his counter-offensive, and these were quickly trained in the use of Soviet air-portable vehicles.

After the northern end of the Somali line had been unhinged by a series of parachute and air-landing operations involving twenty Mil-8 and ten Mil-6 helicopters flown by Soviet pilots, Petrov decided to break the back of the enemy's resistance by capturing the stronghold of Jigjiga, using the same means. On 5 March a landing zone was secured at Genasene, 17 miles north of Jigjiga, and into this were lifted seventy ASU-57 assault guns. These were then driven south and attacked the Somali defences from the rear while they were simultaneously under pressure from a frontal assault. Resistance collapsed quickly with heavy loss of life and three days later Somalia agreed to withdraw from the region.

The Soviet Army also attached great importance to the coup in planning its possible ground offensives into Western Europe, and intended using two types of force which could be formed quickly from local resources. The first of these was the Forward Detachment, employed by divisional commanders and consisting of a reinforced tank or motor rifle battalion group with its own reconnaissance, artillery, engineer and NBC troops, its mission being to penetrate the enemy hinterland to a depth of 20-30 miles then seize and hold important bridges or other features until relieved. The second was the Operational Manoeuvre Group, the purpose of which was to destabilise the enemy's command and control apparatus at a critical moment by creating a serious threat in his rear just when his attention was fully occupied by the threat developing to his front. Ideally, the OMG was to break through a lightly defended sector of the front during the first hours of an offensive and co-operate with simultaneous airborne or airmobile operations. It would then achieve its object by attacking command or logistic areas, engaging reserves as they moved forward to join in the battle, or establishing blocking positions behind troops already fully engaged. Like Forward Detachments, OMGs were organised on an all-arms basis, with the formations involved only being detailed for the task at the last moment. In theory, no limit was set on the size of an OMG. Thus, a division might employ the major part of its second echelon, an army might employ a division, and a front an even larger force. Just how effective these might have been when due allowances have been made for the reduced flexibility of the Soviet system, the NATO response and the increasingly built-up nature of the western European landscape, remains a matter for speculation.

The Falklands War of 1982 provided few opportunities in which a coup could be mounted as the infantry-dominated land battle was fought in harsh terrain and the helicopter assets of both sides were stretched to the limit. When, however, Major General Mario Menendez, the Argentine commander, stripped Mount Kent of its defenders during the battle for Goose Green, the fact was immediately noted by SAS patrols and British troops were promptly lifted onto the mountain. Thus, at no cost to his opponents, Menendez forfeited the highest feature in the outermost and potentially most formidable of the lines of concentric defence with which he hoped to defend Port Stanley. Even if his troops had possessed the marching abilities of the British, it would have been almost impossible for them to have retrieved the situation.

It was in the Gulf War of 1990/91 that many of the strands forming the narrative of this book were drawn together. When Saddam Hussein, the dictator of Iraq, occupied the tiny Gulf state of Kuwait in August 1990, he miscalculated international reaction to a situation which would leave him in control of so great a portion of the world's oil supplies. Soon, with the backing of the UN, a Coalition of nations assembled an army in north-eastern Saudi Arabia with the objects of, first, preventing further aggression in the Gulf region, and second, liberating Kuwait by force if Iraq did not withdraw.

Much thought was given to the problems of the latter, some of it provoked by the groundless overestimation of the Iraqi Army's potential. It was indeed the fourth largest army in the world, equipped and trained by the recently collapsed Soviet Union, and it had just emerged from a protracted and bloody conflict with its Iranian neighbours. Some analysts therefore took the view that its size and experience were automati-

211

cally reflected in its efficiency, although the truth was that it had not done very well at all against the Iranians whose own post-revolutionary army had degenerated into a militia that harnessed fervent religious beliefs and employed them in brutally unscientific human wave assaults. There was, too, a failure to penetrate the psyche of Saddam Hussein, and there existed a widespread belief that since he had not hesitated to use chemical weapons against his own people, he would also use them against the forces of the Coalition, to whom he promised 'the mother of battles' if they attempted to interfere with his presence in Kuwait. He preyed upon the American fears of heavy casualties, a legacy of the Vietnam War, to the extent that many believed that his troops were capable of inflicting them. Yet, though he might posture as the successor of the Great Kings who had once ruled his land, and indulge in such huge gestures as flooding the Gulf with crude oil and blackening the sky with the smoke of burning oilfields, he remained at heart the simple political gangster, lacking strategic or tactical ability, who, with the assistance of his henchmen, ruled his army with terror. In the end he could think of nothing more imaginative than stuffing divisions into Kuwait, leaving the territory to the west largely undefended, and constructing a Kursk-style defence in depth backed by his Republican Guard, the function of which was to counter-attack and eliminate any Coalition force that succeeded in breaking through.

As time passed and it became clearer that Saddam, worried by the prospect of retaliation, was not inclined to use chemical weapons. Nor, curiously, did he seem interested in offensive operations, for which his armoured and mechanised divisions had been designed and which alone could have inflicted the casualties he hoped would affect American public opinion. On the night of 16/17 January 1991 waves of Coalition aircraft commenced a prolonged offensive intended to obtain air superiority, then wreck the Iraqi Army's command, control and logistic infrastructure, and finally destroy its ability and will to fight by sustained battering with means which varied from laser-guided precision bombing to explosive carpets laid by B-52 strategic bombers. By 22 January those Iraqi pilots whose aircraft had not been destroyed on the ground had fled to Iran, leaving the ground troops to endure the full fury of the onslaught, day after day.

While the air offensive was in progress the Coalition's Commander-in-Chief General H. Norman Schwarzkopf, US Army, was making his final dispositions for the ground assault. His plan was aimed at nothing less than the complete destruction of the Iraqi forces in Kuwait, although the critical stroke would be delivered into Iraq itself, and his dispositions, like those of Hannibal at Cannae, reflected the equipment, temperament and abilities of the many diverse nationalities that constituted his army. The major deception element of the plan was provided by a 17,000-strong US Marine amphibious force lying offshore in the Gulf, which Saddam was encouraged to believe would mount an Inchon-style landing behind his defences, with the result that several divisions were deployed to meet the threat. Along the southern border of Kuwait, where the Iraqis believed the Coalition's major blow would fall, armoured and mechanised formations from Syria, Egypt, Saudi Arabia, Kuwait, Oman, Qatar and the United Arab Emirates, together with two US Marine Divisions and a brigade from the US 2nd Armored Division, were to mount a holding attack which was to be exploited in the direction of Kuwait City when a breakthrough was obtained. Further west, beyond the point where the border swung north, the US VII Corps, consisting of the British 1st Armoured Division, the US 1st and 3rd Armored Divisions, the 1st Armored Cavalry Division (which had again changed its role since Vietnam), the 1st Infantry Division (Mechanised) and the 2nd Armored Cavalry Regiment, were to advance north into Iraqi territory, then swing east across the Wadi Batin into Kuwait and engage the enemy's armoured reserve before it could intervene in the fighting to the south. During the ensuing tank battle it was envisaged that the British with their reputation for dogged, sustained fighting, would form the anvil against which the Iraqis would be crushed by the hammer of the American armour. Further west still the US XVIII Airborne Corps, consisting of the French 6th Light Armoured Division, the US 82nd Airborne Division, the 101st Airborne Division (Air Assault), the 24th Infantry Division (Mechanised) and the 3rd Armored Cavalry Regiment, was to employ its ground and air mobility to the maximum, driving hard through lightly defended Iraqi territory to establish a blocking position in the Euphrates valley, much as O'Connor had done at Beda Fomm fifty years earlier, effectively isolating Saddam's forces in Kuwait within a strategic pocket.

The ground offensive commenced on 24 February and went entirely to plan, destroying the Iraqi army in 100 hours of fighting. Most Iraqi soldiers had already had the fight knocked out of them and 80,000 prisoners were taken; the lowest estimate of enemy killed was 25,000. Iraq had begun the war with 5500 tanks and 6000 APCs, the greater number of which were present in Kuwait; of these, perhaps 700 tanks and 1400 APCs escaped the debacle. Some 42 Iraqi divisions had been destroyed, leaving only 20,000 men still present with fighting formations in Kuwait when the ceasefire came into effect. Saddam's Republican

Guard, previously spoken of with awe by some commentators, proved to be very ordinary soldiers rather than an élite. The same sources had gloomily predicted that the Coalition forces would sustain between 10,000 and 50,000 casualties in a ground war expected to last up to a month, these estimates being based on an acceptance of Iraqi propaganda at face value. In fact, some 120 Coalition soldiers lost their lives during the ground offensive, including an unexpectedly high proportion killed as a result of 'friendly fire' battlefield accidents.

The Coalition army had fought a fast-moving three-dimensional battle using technology appropriate to the 21st century. The Iraqi army, handicapped by the total lack of air cover, had attempted to fight, at best, in the manner of World War 2, and its doom had been sealed by XVIII Airborne Corps' dash to the Euphrates. Here, in this most ancient of lands, the coup-de-main had come of age.

Bibliography

Alexandrescu, Colonel Dr Vasile, *Romania in World War I* (Military Publishing House, Bucharest, 1985)

Anon, *Destruction of an Army – The First Campaign in Libya Sept 1940–Feb 1941* (HMSO, 1941)

Appleman, Roy E., *South to the Naktong, North to the Yalu* (Center of Military History, US Army, Washington DC, 1992)

Barclay, Captain C., *With the Rifle Brigade in the Western Desert 1940–1941*, entry in *The Rifle Brigade Chronicle, 1941*

Buchan, John, *A History of the Great War* (Vols III and IV, Nelson, 1922)

Burton, Lieutenant Colonel R. S., *Beyond Benghazi and Back to Tobruk – The Action Near Beda Fomm*, entry in *The Royal Artillery Commemoration Book 1939–1945* (Bell, 1950)

Carhart, J. D., *Pleiku – The Dawn of Helicopter Warfare in Vietnam* (St Martin's Press, New York, 1988)

Ellis, Major L. F., et al, *Victory in the West*, Vols I and II (HMSO, 1962 and 1968)

Forty, George, *The Royal Tank Regiment* (Guild, 1989)

Hinterhoff, Captain Eugenjusz, *The Raid by the Late Major Bochanek* and *Motor Raid on Zytomierz Carried Out by Infantry*, articles in *The Tank* magazine (1931 and 1932)

Kutz, C. R., *War on Wheels* (The Scientific Book Club, 1942)

Liddell Hart, Captain B. H., *The Tanks – The History of the Royal Tank Regiment*, Vol II (Cassell, 1959)

McKee, Alexander, *The Race for the Rhine Bridges* (Souvenir Press, 1964)

Macksey, Kenneth, *Beda Fomm* (Pan/Ballantine, 1972)

Mrazek, Colonel James E., *The Fall of Eben Emael* (Presidio Press, Novato, California, 1991)

Orde, Roden, *History of the Second Household Cavalry Regiment* (Gale & Polden, 1953)

Perrett, Bryan, *Desert Warfare* (Patrick Stephens, 1988)

Canopy of War (Patrick Stephens, 1990)

Tank Tracks to Rangoon (Robert Hale, 1992)

Pimlott, John and Badsey, Stephen, Ed, *The Gulf War Assessed* (Arms & Armour Press, 1992)

Ponath, Gustav, *Die Geschichte des 5. Westpreussen Infanterie Regiments Nr 148* (Kommissionsverlag der Buchdrukerei, Breslau, 1933)

Ramsey, Winston G., Ed, *After the Battle No 5 Eben Emael* and *No 16 Crossing the Rhine* (Battle of Britain Prints, respectively 1974 and 1977)

Rees, David, Ed, *The Korean War – History and Tactics* (Orbis, 1984)

Roberts, Major-General G. P. B., *From the Desert to the Baltic* (William Kimber, 1987)

Rommel, Erwin, *Infantry Attacks* (Greenhill Books, 1990)

Ste Croix, Philip de, Ed, *Airborne Operations* (Salamander, 1978)

Scales, Robert H., Jr., *Firepower in Limited War* (National Defense University Press, Washington DC, 1990)

Stewart, Adrian, *The Underrated Enemy: Britain's War With Japan December 1941–May 1942* (William Kimber, 1987)

Swinson, Arthur, *Defeat In Malaya* (Macdonald, 1969)

Tolson, Lieutenant-General John J., *Airmobility 1961–1971* (Department of the Army, Washington DC, 1973)

Verney, Major-General G. L., *The Desert Rats* (Hutchinson)

Whiting, Charles, *Bounce the Rhine* (Leo Cooper, 1985)

Hunters From the Sky (Leo Cooper, 1975)

Wurz, Oberstleutnant A. D. Hans, *Das Ulanen Regiment Kaiser Alexander II von Russland (1 Brandenburg) Nr 3 in Romanischen Feldzeug 1916/17* (Mittler & Sohn, Berlin, 1929)

Index